23 99

Damag Control

DAMAGE CONTROL

A MEMOIR OF OUTLANDISH PRIVILEGE, LOSS AND REDEMPTION

BY

SERGEI BOISSIER

Print ISBN: 978-0-7867-5584-4
ebook ISBN: 978-0-7867-5585-1

Distributed by Argo Navis Author Services

Distributed by
Argo Navis Author Services
www.argonavisdigital.com

3 1703 00608 1568

For my daughter, Yasmina Charlotte,
and in memory of my mother, Dolores,
and my grandmother, Jasmine.

CONTENTS

Prologue   Driving South!   3

PART ONE: GOING CONTINENTAL

One   A Baptism and a Funeral   11

Two   Emerging from the Fog   23

Three   Le Bal Des Fleurs   27

Four   Black Bean Soup   39

Five   Fairy Tale   45

Six   Paso Doble   53

Seven   Miss Dolores   61

Eight   Chalet Albosco   67

Nine   Living or Leaving   73

Ten   Africa and Enriqueta   85

PART TWO: THOSE LITTLE TOWN BLUES

Eleven   Blackout   93

Twelve   You'll Get Your Pony When You
Lose Ten Pounds   107

Thirteen   A Serial Killer and a Mexican   125

Fourteen   Be a Man   131

Fifteen   Off to the Butcher   149

Sixteen   Cali Days   159

Seventeen   Post-Op   169

Eighteen   City of Illusions   177

Nineteen   Chelsea Nights   189

Twenty   Conceiving at the Costes & a Visit to the
Adoption Agency   193

Twenty-One   Farewell Manhattan   201

PART THREE: IN THE LAND OF MYTHS

Twenty-Two   Mrs. Dalloway's Last Party   213

Twenty-Three   Absent Almost Always   225

Twenty-Four   Gstaad, My Love   233

Twenty-Five   Grand Exit   241

Twenty-Six   Going Home   253

PART FOUR: POSTSCRIPT—ONE YEAR LATER

Twenty-Seven   Answered Prayers   267

Epilogue   Look, Daddy! I Can See the World!   277

"I know how men in exile feed on dreams."
—AESCHYLUS

"After all, high station in life is earned by the gallantry with which appalling experiences are survived with grace."
—TENNESSEE WILLIAMS, MEMOIRS

"That was the strange thing, that one did not know where one was going, or what one wanted, and followed blindly, suffering so much in secret, always unprepared and amazed and knowing nothing; but one thing led to another and by degrees something had formed itself out of nothing, and so one reached at last this calm, this quiet, this certainty, and it was this process that people called living."
—VIRGINIA WOOLF, MRS. DALLOWAY

Damage Control

DRIVING SOUTH!

I landed at Newark and hopped in a cab to the West Village, where I had just moved into a carriage house on Perry Street. It was my third apartment in two years, my eighteenth since college. Eighteen moves in twenty-one years, which just about matched my track record with relationships. Dollsie had been the same way: a lot of hoping and searching and wishing and "falling in love" and decorating, forever setting up house and then pulling up roots again. In perpetual motion, like a drone missile seeking its elusive target.

I had moved back to New York to care for Dollsie—my mother, my nemesis—and to await the adoption. Birth and death playing itself out in a city which had always felt like the loneliest place on earth. But now, the baby—the baby!—was on its way. I could hardly believe it.

The following morning, groggy with jet lag and sleeplessness yet wide awake in a way that I hadn't been for as long as I could remember, I hit the road. It felt as if I had been on the road for two years, and that finally, the end of the journey was in sight. The drive down south would take about five hours, with the summer heat wave already under way. The rental car was loaded up with clothes and books and magazines and the baby stuff that I had been amassing for the past ten months, wanting to be ready when the time came. I drove across New Jersey, through Baltimore and Washington, D.C., my college town, then Virginia and my final destination, another college town where my life would begin anew, yet again.

I felt rather relaxed for someone who would be meeting the mother of his child for the first time, the next day. Relaxed, and profoundly grateful. I, who had screwed up so much of my life, who had squandered so much privilege and promise, was now being given the chance to begin over and experience the love and balance and security that had somehow eluded me thus far. At the age of forty, I was being given the gift of life. I spent much of the drive in tears; all the tears that I had not shed for Raphael, for Dollsie, for Walt, for myself. Tears that had accumulated over the past decade, as loss followed loss. Tears of joy and gratitude and relief. I had made it this far, and my reward was in sight. Someone had decided that this child should come to me. I didn't know whether it was God, or the agency, or the expectant mother, or the child itself, or the mysterious energies of the universe, but someone had clearly made that call, and I marveled at the wonder of it.

I had reserved a two-bedroom suite at the Marriott Residence Inn, the second room being for the Jamaican nanny who would come down from New York once the baby was born and who would stay with us until we were allowed to leave the state a few weeks later. The motel was near a mall, and about a mile from the hospital where the birth would take place.

The next morning, I walked around the town and campus, killing time until the meeting at noon with Gail from the adoption agency and the birth mother. The summer session at UVA had just begun, and I watched the students as they greeted each other and headed to class, young and gorgeous and blond and athletic and so American, so pure and free and unrestrained, so goddamned happy and confident and sure of themselves, that it hurt just to look at them.

I headed to the coffee shop in the other Marriott, the one right off campus, where we had agreed to meet. I arrived early, as usual. Swiss training. Now I was nervous. Worried that the birth mother might not like me, but also worried that I might not like her. Dr. Berger, the director of the agency, had reiterated the rules to me on the phone: the birth mother could change her mind about giving me the child after meeting me, but I had no choice in the matter. It was take it or leave it: take the child that they had found for me, or lose my place on the two-year waiting list and start all over again. I stared anxiously out the window at every woman that walked by, praying to all the saints that the three-hundred-pound woman smoking a cigarette outside the coffee shop was not her. It felt like waiting for a blind date, but with tremendous consequences.

Gail, the social worker, arrived first. She had never met the mother either. Everything had been arranged by phone. After warning me not to share any "personal information" (like what, I wondered? What would be considered too "personal" under these circumstances?), she again went over the details of the adoption with me: the ethnic background of the parents, health history, family situation, etc. I did not hear much of what she said. I was in a daze, which only deepened as the noon hour approached. It felt surreal.

A few minutes later, she walked through the door, and like the kid in *Animal House* who watches a naked bombshell come crashing through his roof on to his bed, all I could think to myself was: *Thank you, God.* I just sat there, staring at her, too stunned to say anything. Gail introduced us and attempted to make small talk as we both remained silent for a moment, looking at each other.

And then, interrupting Gail in mid-sentence, Daniele handed me an envelope and said: "Do you want to see pictures of your daughter?"

I opened the envelope and inside were the images from the latest ultra-sound. My daughter. Up until that moment, I had not known whether it would be a boy or a girl. Dollsie had been right.

We ordered lunch. I watched Daniele and she watched me. I tried to imagine what her daughter—my daughter—would look like. With her big round eyes and brown skin ("high yellow," as she would later correct me) she resembled a beautiful *mulata* from the islands. Exotic, yet deeply familiar. She was sassy, refined, and sensual, with an air of belligerence about her. She could have been Cuban, like Dollsie. She reminded me more than a little of my mother—and the fact that the call from the agency had come on the eve of the anniversary of her death made me wonder whether she was *still* running the show, from beyond.

I said little throughout the meal, and ate even less. While Gail tried to steer the conversation toward the safety of practicality and facts, Daniele quickly got personal, telling me about her family and the circumstances surrounding her pregnancy.

She had been through a lot in her twenty-four years. She hid her vulnerability behind a veil of fierceness and resolve, as if she needed me to know that she had made her own informed decision, that she was not your typical helpless, minority mom that had become an archetype in America. She did not want me to question her resolve in putting the child up for adoption.

As the days passed, we would come to find that despite our widely divergent backgrounds and upbringing, we had much in common: we were both rebels—the black sheep of our families—a mantle we carried with more than a little pride. Fiercely independent, we had spent our emotional lives warring against our overbearing mothers and chasing "inappropriate" men. We did not take orders kindly, feeling that we were smarter than most, despite a history of stupid mistakes when it came to relationships and other "life choices", and we had a deep, intense aversion to anyone who might try to direct, restrict, or judge us. When it came to values and what we wanted for our children, it basically came down to what we wished we had gotten from our parents: integrity, love, acceptance and compassion.

"Any questions?" Gail asked, as she attempted to wind down the lunch, no doubt feeling that way too much information had already been shared. I had many, but decided not to push the boundaries by prying further. Daniele would let me know what she needed me to know. She was not there to satisfy my curiosity.

"Why me?" I asked, meaning, why me instead of some nice, normal straight couple from Ohio.

"Because I like the fact that you grew up in Europe, that you speak several languages, and that you can offer my daughter a safe environment while also giving her the opportunity to see the world."

Her answer impressed and humbled me; I had not thought of myself in those terms in a long time, and I wondered if it was accurate, if she had made the right call in choosing me, or if she would choose differently were she to peer at me closer.

"But most of all," she added matter-of-factly, "I like the fact that you are single and gay."

"Why's that?" I asked, somewhat taken aback but glad that she had put it right out there. I had wondered if it would come up during this first meeting.

"Because even if I never see my daughter again, I'll always be the only mother she ever has."

I asked if she had any questions for me.

"Just one: do you smoke?"

"No," I said, not adding that I had quit only a few days earlier, after the agency told me that she had requested a non-smoker.

Of all the things that she could have possibly wondered and worried about in terms of my suitability to become a parent to her child, it floored me that she had picked this one issue. None of the questions I had anticipated—and feared—about my health, relationship history, drug use, sex life, dysfunctional family. Nothing about my stability or lack thereof. No questions about how I would raise the child, or with whom, or where. She evidently already had a vision of how her daughter would grow up with me, and she was fine with it.

"Do you want to know more about how it happened? How I got pregnant?"

"No," I answered. Like her, I did not believe in asking more than I needed to know. "I consider that too private. And maybe too painful for you to talk about. I don't think it is information I need, and I don't want to have to hide anything from your daughter later in life."

"'*Your* daughter,' she corrected me.

Wow. There it was again. *My* daughter.

"Our daughter," I said. "But I do wonder why you decided to carry the child to term instead of taking the easy way out. I admire you so much for that."

"Just because I'm not in a position to care for this child, that's not a reason to interrupt the potential for this baby to have a wonderful life, or the privilege of giving you this gift. From my pain to your joy."

I smiled at her through my tears, speechless.

Gail was by now close to exasperation with both the length and intimate nature of what was supposed to have been a brief, casual meeting, centered on facts, free of potential boundary violations. She had kept her social worker composure throughout lunch—cheerful yet neutral—but I could tell that she was more than a little nervous about what had transpired between Daniele and me. It felt, after only knowing each other for a few minutes, that we had been destined to meet, and that the adoption was already a *fait accompli*. Gail felt compelled to caution us that the birth father would have to be found and that he would have to sign off on the adoption. Daniele was worried about this. She had not told her husband, who was in jail, that she was pregnant. She was terrified that if he found out, he would kill her, accuse her of lying about who the father was and of shaming the family. And since he had been behind bars for ten months, with no conjugal visits, there was no chance that the child was his, so she decided that there was no need to inform him about the impending birth.

Nor had she told her mother or other members of her family. In fact, she had managed to keep the pregnancy hidden from everyone she knew, blaming the size of her belly on the bloating caused by the medicine she was taking for her painful hernia.

Gail picked up the tab, explaining that I was not allowed to pay for Daniele's meal directly nor give her any gifts that could be interpreted as "buying the child," but that she would cover it with agency funds and I would in turn be billed by the agency. Daniele and I smiled with complicity at the absurd rules.

As we left the coffee shop, she asked me if I had time to accompany her to the doctor, and to tour the hospital where the delivery would take place.

"I'm not going anywhere; I'm here for the duration."

We had known each other for less than an hour, but already I felt transformed: I was no longer a potential father in waiting mode, as I had been for the past two years; I was now a father-to-be. From that moment on, there was never a doubt in my mind about her resolve to give me her child, and the gratitude and pride and joy that I experienced overcame any lingering doubts about my capacity or readiness to become a parent.

Still, part of me couldn't believe this was happening. Something was finally going my way for the first time, in a very, very long time.

PART ONE

GOING CONTINENTAL

ONE

A BAPTISM AND A FUNERAL

On our way home from the *Marais,* where we had dined with friends at the latest happening *bistro,* Giovanni dropped me off at the *bar a tabac* while he went to park. It was just past midnight, and *Pigalle* was in full eruption. I stepped out of the car into a steamy throng of gorgeous young Parisian revelers and gawking tourists, who stared with fascination at the procession of exotic Brazilian transexual prostitutes parading down the boulevard, along with the legions of North African boys from the *banlieue,* menacing and seductive. To my right rose *Montmartre,* its narrow, winding streets ascending the majestic *butte,* and the *Sacre Coeur,* which at night, brilliantly illuminated, looked like a giant wedding cake perched atop Paris. Both sides of the boulevard were lined with adult cinemas, sex emporiums, massage parlors, and other purveyors of sleaze. At the end, presiding over this mayhem stood the *Moulin Rouge* with its famous windmill: the eternal symbol of Paris's once glorious red light district.

After leaving the *tabac* I walked down the small street south of the *Place,* passing the seedy bars and dodging the *hotesses* who posed wearily in the entrances, wearing almost nothing, leering at potential customers with blank, drugged smiles and looks of barely suppressed despair. As I approached the casino at the end of the block, I came upon Francine, an elegant, respectable *fille de joie,* as she still insisted on being called. She was old school, and she stood guard at the corner—*her* corner—faithful to her post, come rain or shine, even though she and her aging colleagues had long ago lost most of their business to the washed out Eastern European girls—young enough to be their granddaughters—who had been abducted as minors in their native countries and brought to France—the land of *liberté, égalité,* and *fraternité*—as virtual sex slaves.

Francine knew her place, and that was at the intersection of *Rue Pigalle* and the *Avenue Frochot*, a private enclave of *hotels particuliers* and gardens, walled off from *Pigalle* itself by a massive, imperial black wrought iron gate with tall gilded spikes, protecting its illustrious residents from the messy humanity outside its portals.

"*Bonsoir, Francine!*" I exclaimed.

"*Bonsoir, Monsieur!*" she replied, with a combination of friendliness and deference classic to the women of her generation who still walked the streets of Paris.

Over the years, she and I had become friends. On my way home from a late night, I would occasionally offer her a nightcap at the corner bar, and she would fill me in on the latest gossip about my neighbors. She knew more about the residents of *Frochot* than anyone, having been there longer than most of them, and she was considered the unofficial historian of the avenue. She would then launch into a recap of her day. I savored her stories about her odd collection of clients and their strange fetishes—my favorite was the prominent CEO of a large company who would come to her apartment weekly, and pay Francine a small fortune to dress him up in a maid's uniform and make him clean the apartment for hours.

Over time, the pity that I had initially felt for her had morphed into genuine respect. I admired her dignity and resilience. She and I were worlds apart, yet kindred spirits.

During Dollsie's last visit to Paris, on our way home from the opera one night, I had introduced her to Francine, and the two had instantly bonded. Francine had stared at her with unabashed fascination, methodically taking in every aspect of Dollsie's appearance from head to toe, savoring every detail as if she were tasting something exquisite: the perfectly coiffed hair with the luscious blond highlights, which Dollsie had copied from Catherine Deneuve in an attempt to cultivate a resemblance; the flawless make-up, which approached a level of mastery that few women could match; the tight, risqué couture dress, which might have looked ridiculous on other women her age but as always, Dollsie managed to pull it off; the sparkling costume jewelry; the expensive *fuck-me* pumps with the red soles; and lastly, the exquisite beaded evening purse, so small that there was only room for her compact case, her lipstick, her cigarettes and lighter, and a hanky, along with her Amex and a few euros. After regaining her composure, Francine had fallen into a curtsy, as if she were in the presence of royalty. And Dollsie, soaking up Francine's admiration, had returned the favor by making Francine feel, well, important.

"*Madame*," she said to Francine, laying it on thick like she always did when she found herself in the presence of someone she obviously considered to be her social inferior, "would you do me the honor of taking me on a *tour du quartier*?" Francine, genuinely thrilled by the request, eagerly accepted, and the two had set off arm in arm, like two old pals off on a daring adventure.

Upon their return, Dollsie, giggling like a school girl, had proudly exclaimed: "Sergei, you won't believe what happened! I got propositioned! Several times! Astonishing! Can you imagine? Who on earth would pay to sleep with a woman my age? They must be crazy!"

It had been the highlight of her trip, and the tale had since become part of Dollsie's dinner party repertoire: the time she had taken a stroll through *Pigalle* with an aging hooker and been propositioned.

As for Francine, the encounter had clearly marked her in a profound way which I couldn't quite grasp. From then on, every time I saw her, she would repeat the same phrase: "And how is your *chère mère? Quelle femme extraordinaire!*"

I punched in the code to gain access to the Avenue. As I headed up the elegant path paved with eighteenth century bricks, the heavy gate slammed shut behind me, separating me from Francine and all the sleaze and decadence, protecting me from my dark side by enveloping me in a cocoon of rarified privilege. Ever since it had been walled off from the rest of the neighborhood by some enterprising property owner at the end of the nineteenth century, *Frochot* had been populated by illustrious musicians and actors like Django Reinhard and Jean Renais. Nowadays, it was still home to celebrities and other members of the city's cultural intelligentsia, including my upstairs neighbor, Regine Crespin, the imperious and legendary diva of the French Opera and, eclipsing all of them, the clothing designer Jean-Paul Gaultier, the gay Madonna of the Paris fashion world. Period pieces were often filmed on this street, and every time I crossed the gate, I still felt as if I were stepping into another century. During my decade in Paris, I had invariably sought out neighborhoods like this where I could feel like I was "slumming it" by being close to the action, while still maintaining a sense of separateness, an aura of aloof respectability. This was my fourth apartment since I had moved to the City of Lights—and by far the most grand.

It was time to pack for another trip. As I was contemplating what I would need for a baptism and a funeral, the phone rang. Given the late hour, I knew better than to pick up, so I let the machine answer. Sure enough, it was Dollsie again. She was staying at *Chalet Albosco,* her summer home in Gstaad. She had been calling for days.

"Sergei, darling," she said, in her strident, dramatic voice with the unmistakable Cuban accent that she had stubbornly cultivated throughout her life, despite the fact that she was half-American and had only moved to Cuba when she was seven. "It's your mother, and I've been trying to reach you. Nothing serious, but I *would* appreciate a call back."

I had been avoiding her calls for twenty years, pretty much since college, especially the ones that came late at night, after she came home from a dinner party or a night out, intoxicated and in the mood for an endless "chat". It would invariably conclude with one of her cutting, bitchy remarks, leaving me in a state of rage that would last for days. The sound of the ring followed by her loud, shrill, wasted voice, never failed to set into motion a Pavlovian sequence of vivid flashbacks, overwhelming me with anxiety and hurtling me into the toxic past. To this day, even though she's been gone for several years, my heart skips a beat every time the phone rings. Oh no, it's *her.* I never pick up.

Mina—my American grandmother who had spent most of her life in Switzerland—had phoned me earlier that day to calmly inform me that Rolf—her second husband—had died. The funeral would be a quiet affair: "Just the immediate family; no reason to make a fuss." As I was due to spend the weekend in Carcassonne for my goddaughter's baptism, I called the few clients who were still in Paris at this time of year to cancel their appointments for the following week, and made plans to continue on from there to Switzerland.

An historic heat wave had just hit, and all across Europe, especially in France, old people were dropping like flies. The news was filled with images of the thousands of vacationers stranded on the side of the road as their cars conked out in the heat. The wisdom of leaving for destinations at the other end of the country in cars with no air-conditioning, at the height of the summer season, in the middle of the worst heat wave that Europe had experienced in forty years, was not up for debate. It was August, and August meant what it meant: *les grandes vacances.*

As for me, I had never liked the month of August. It always seemed to bring bad tidings.

I set off for Carcassonne the next morning with Walt—my fat old chocolate lab, my Sancho Panza, always faithfully by my side—along for the ride. I would be back in a few days, and then my boyfriend Giovanni and I would figure out what to do for the rest of the month. I had tired of my summer pad in Ibiza, which I had bought on a whim the year after Raphael died, in an attempt to rewind the clock; to preserve something of the exuberant and unbridled life we had led before everything had changed. But when he died, the party died with him. After several summers on the island, I found myself—as I had so often throughout my life—lonely and out of my element. "N.O.C.D.," as my great grandmother Mooma would proclaim in her Southern drawl whenever she found herself in unfamiliar surroundings. "Not our crowd, dear."

Giovanni, a sexy French/Sicilian kid who had moved in two weeks after we had met online, had pushed me to organize something "fun" to take the place of Ibiza, but for once I had resisted. I had been to all of the trendy destinations frequented by hip Parisians—the gays and the *bobos* (bohemian bourgeois)— and recently, I had come to the realization that I was indeed *done* with all of it: the constant effort to be fabulous (epitomized by my shallow relationship with Giovanni, a trophy boyfriend, like most of the ones who had preceded him); the boring, endless, pretentious dinner parties; the gay clubs and restaurants and A-list events which had seemed so vital when I had first arrived; even my practice, and Paris itself.

After a decade of living life on the edge, I was running on empty, burnt out and overcome with a pervasive sense of ennui that overshadowed everything that had captivated me during my first few years in Paris. Those years had been exhilarating; I indulged in hedonism without reserve and experienced a freedom I had never known and only vaguely fathomed. But then Raphael died, and six months later, everything changed. Not in a dramatic way, but slowly, imperceptibly, like the dense fog that often descends over Paris. Little by little, without noticing, I began to withdraw from the busy world I had created for myself, finding scant interest in much of anything. In many ways, my life had been on standby ever since.

But recently, I had made one momentous decision that I knew would alter the gentle drift of my life in ways I could not even begin to fathom. After years of working with kids and their dysfunctional families, I had decided it was time to adopt one of my own. I had always wanted to be a father—it was partly what had driven me to become a therapist—and now that my life had settled into some semblance of domesticity with Giovanni, it felt as if the time was right.

After going through the motions of consulting with Giovanni, I went online and put together a list of ten adoption agencies in the United States (I knew that my chances were far greater there than in France, where adoption itself was a rarity, not to mention adoption by a single parent who happened to be gay and male). I wrote them regarding my intention to adopt and whether that was feasible, given the fact that I was gay and living abroad. A few days later, one of the agencies, located in Pennsylvania, had responded favorably, but at this early stage, the chances of that happening—of me actually becoming a father—seemed quite remote. I sensed a big shift being set in motion, and I remained in suspense, waiting, anxious.

A baptism and a funeral. That at least was something different. A break in the routine. And a chance to get away from Giovanni, who as usual was waiting on me to plan his day and organize his life, making more demands on my patience and on my bank account than on my heart or intellect.

The drive down to Carcassonne was pleasant, with none of the summer vacation traffic inferno I had been dreading. After a refreshing swim followed by a long suffocating meal of steaming clams (just about the last thing I wanted to eat in this climate) and lukewarm rosé provided by our British hosts, I stumbled up to bed. Just as I had anticipated, the quaint farmhouse had no air-conditioning, and the oppressive heat kept me awake for hours, with Walt by my side, panting miserably.

At long last, after an endless night filled with tortured dreams, morning came. The service was held in a dilapidated village church, conducted by a frazzled, hot priest. Fortunately, he had six more baptisms to perform that day in neighboring villages, so the ceremony was mercifully brief. As he rushed through it, I held my tiny goddaughter Tjasa in my arms and gazed into her beautiful eyes, overcome with emotion. How long would it be before I would hold my own child? And when the moment came, would I be ready? I felt as if I had been preparing myself for this all my life, but had taken several long strange detours along the way, and I prayed that I would rise to the occasion.

The picnic lunch that followed, on the other hand, was endless. I always marveled at the capacity of the French to sit around a table for hours. Finally, I mumbled profuse apologies for having to make a hasty exit to be by my grieving grandmother's side, shoved Walt into the passenger's side, and sped off, hoping that I hadn't appeared too eager to leave.

I arrived in Geneva late that night, and checked into *La Reserve*, a luxurious hotel on the lake that I had first discovered as a child. During the last year before the divorce, we had lived nearby, in a cul-de-sac known as *le Creux-de-Genthod*, a beautiful property on the banks of Lake Geneva, and I had spent many summer afternoons lounging by the hotel's pool with Dollsie and my sister Nan, enjoying the luxury and its glamorous, exotic guests. It was still a happening place, as happening as Geneva ever gets, recently renovated to resemble a chic safari camp with Warhol butterflies on the wall, and catering mostly to an Arab and African clientele.

At the reception, I was given a message that Dollsie had called, and that I was to phone her back "immediately." As usual, when it came to her messages, I took this one with a huge grain of salt; it was just Dollsie being Dollsie: impatient and demanding. She couldn't help herself; life had always revolved around Dollsie. Even as a young girl in Cuba, as the eldest of all her siblings and cousins, she had commanded the full attention of everyone around her, from her wealthy and powerful grandparents on down to the workers at the sugar mill and the cattle ranches. She had been incredibly spoiled, all of her whims indulged, and she had managed to maintain this dynamic throughout her life. Through a combination of beauty, fear, and awe, she had mastered the ability to fascinate others and hold them in her thrall.

I seemed to be the only one who, from the age of ten on, had made it a point not to be impressed by her, and since then I had never had a problem standing up to her, feeling like I could see right through her. I had been, in her words, an "obstinate child." I would not take orders from her—or anyone else for that matter—and that stubbornness had only grown with time. I decided not to call her back until the next morning. No one was better at ruining my day, or even my week, with a single five minute phone conversation.

Dollsie had been at the chalet since June. Gstaad—a bucolic village in the Swiss Alps populated by the international jet-set and the local peasants who shared a mutual love of money and tranquility—was where we had spent our winters after moving to Switzerland, where we had experienced our happiest times as a family, before the divorce. And although we had only spent a few glorious seasons in that chalet, it was the place that still, after all these years, felt the most like home.

Ten years later, after her second marriage also ended in divorce, Dollsie had somehow managed to lease the chalet again, and she had spent her summers there ever since, in a futile attempt to recapture a time long since gone when the family had been whole, before she had left Switzerland and taken us back to New York, causing a continental fracture which would never quite heal. But no matter how hard Dollsie tried, it wasn't the same. How could it be? To this day, I can't think of Gstaad without feeling a wave of bittersweet nostalgia. I have been looking for my own personal Gstaad ever since.

I would see Dollsie at Rolf's funeral. I would not let her come between us, like she always managed to do with her own toxic brew of Latin charm, martyrdom, intimidation, and manipulation. She had always been jealous of the close bond which Mina and I shared. From the day we moved to Switzerland, Mina had become the most important person in my world—my best friend, my anchor, my soul mate—and had remained so throughout my life, providing me with the only unconditional love I had ever known.

Dollsie loved to flaunt her close friendship with Mina, her ex-mother-in-law who, after years of feeling deeply betrayed by Dollsie's departure and maintaining a bitter silence toward her, had decided to forgive her and initiate a rapprochement. This had happened soon after Dad's remarriage to "the Chilean woman"—as Mina referred to her—who had come out of nowhere and whom Mina considered to be a most unfortunate choice, what with her polyester prints, her fake, cloying affection, and her total lack of grace and elegance and wit. Such a letdown after Dollsie. "How *could* he," she would always say, whenever she embarked on the subject.

After a bath and room service from the hotel's delicious and outrageously expensive Chinese restaurant, where Mina and I had often lunched when she was still mobile, I felt revived enough to head into town and check out the scene. It was Saturday night, and the *quais* would be bustling. Out of habit, my thoughts turned to getting high and getting laid—in that order. Who knows tomorrow, I told myself. It might be my last carefree night for a while. *Carpe noctem.*

I parked in the lot of *La Perle du Lac,* an elegant restaurant overlooking the lake whose grounds turned into a busy cruising spot late at night. It had been one of the first gay places that I discovered as soon as I could drive; places where, from the get-go, sexual discovery and pleasure and an exhilarating feeling of liberation were inexorably linked with darkness and secrecy and anonymity, along with the shaming stares of my Calvinist ancestors never far away, hovering over our furtive embraces.

It was still early, so there wasn't much action in the gardens yet. When I arrived at the *quais* I found myself immersed in a rowdy and raucous multicultural, multi-ethnic summer festival, an enchanting explosion of color and sound that took me by surprise. I felt energized and renewed by the festive vibe. I walked along the crowded *quais,* from one scene to another, marveling at the transformation of the staid and stuffy city of my youth. When had all this happened? Where had these people come from? I tried to be inconspicuous, wanting to project an air of carefree nonchalance that would mask my shyness and reserve. Along with my hunger and longing. I didn't want anyone to think that I was coming on to them, but at the same time I wanted them to know—in case they noticed me—that I was open to whatever might happen, that I was available. Most of all, I wanted not to feel like an outsider. I wanted to belong, if only just for a moment, in this city I had once called home.

For along with the culture and refinement and manners, the love of art and travel and clothes and beautiful homes, the decorating and staff, Dollsie had also passed on a pervasive sense of isolation and alienation, despite her frenetic socializing. We had been raised with a strong sense of pedigree, and taught to maintain a facade of superiority and imperviousness and polite aloofness at all times—Dollsie's version of *noblesse oblige*—no doubt to mask the insecurities which ran as deep in our veins as our blue blood.

As Dollsie had often told us, "In life, it's not what you do that matters; it's how you do it." Appearance was everything. As long as one behaved in a correct, appropriate manner in public, whatever happened behind closed doors was okay. Just as long as one didn't talk about it. Some would call it hypocrisy, but Dollsie preferred to think of it as the essence of good breeding.

After walking the length of the pier and back, vaguely looking for opportunities to score as I immersed myself in the music and observed the sexy couples gyrating to the rhythms, I spotted a young guy sitting on the low wall that bordered the lake. He was alone and looked approachable, so I summoned my courage, and sat beside him, a few feet away. After exchanging smiles and a "*bonsoir*", I asked him if he knew where I could find some *herbe*. He introduced himself, something I had neglected to do—names having long since lost their relevance in these situations—and produced a joint from his pocket, which he proceeded to light. We smoked and conversed for a while, with him doing most of the talking, telling me about his hard life. I listened through the fog of the high, trying to remember if I had told him that I was a psychotherapist and wondering if that was what had led him to share his life story, as people so often did when they found out.

As the high from the joint set in, I found myself wanting him badly, imagining his thin, smooth, wiry French-boy body sprawled naked across the sensual satin sheets of my hotel bed, his beautiful ass eager and inviting, his penis, surprisingly large and assured... But I knew that the desire I felt for him was more about his ambiguity than his physique: not knowing whether he was into men or women, or both, as so many French kids seemed to be nowadays, far more open-minded and willing to explore than my generation had been. I tried to set aside the thrilling prospect of seducing a "straight" guy so that I could enjoy the moment, the connection. I lived for moments like these: the thrill of meeting a sexy stranger on a sultry summer night, pregnant with possibilities; the momentary banishment of loneliness, the promise of untold pleasures. If the encounter didn't lead to sex this time, so much the better. Hook-ups only lasted as long as they lasted, and once they were over, once one or both partners had come— "*la petite morte*"—the emptiness and loneliness came right back, and with it, the need for another conquest.

After a while, his cell phone rang, and the sexy stranger—whose name I had already forgotten—told me that his friend was on his way and that it was time to conclude our encounter. He proceeded to roll another joint for me—*une pour la route*. I was grateful, for the smokes and for his company, for the connection with someone who had shared himself with me without wanting anything in return. Over the past few years, interacting with other men had become such a complicated affair. I had devoted so much of my life to the pursuit—in parks and bars and clubs and department stores and other random places—and inevitably, I had ended up spending more and more time alone, the frustrated hunter in perennial search of the tracks that would lead to his prey. I had burnt many bridges along the way, and the ones that remained seemed distant. I seemed to prefer being alone or in the company of strangers than with those who knew me. Affection came with its baggage. It was safer and easier to veer toward the anonymous, less complicated than dealing with love and intimacy.

Dollsie had always lamented the fact that despite her best efforts, I had remained stubbornly anti-social, 'like your father." Even as a child, when she would throw huge, lavish birthday parties for me, with tents and rides and monkeys and clowns and loads of children and nannies in attendance, she would invariably find me sitting on the sidelines, apart, with a book or one of the presents I had just received, observing the others as they enjoyed the spectacle. Watching others live their lives. Always one step removed, on the outside looking in, sensing, even at the age of five or six, that I was not like the others—that I was different—and that no matter how hard Dollsie tried to change me, to make me more socially acceptable and gregarious—more *normal*—I would always be this way, whatever *this* meant.

Joint in hand, I left the festivities. For once, I did not feel the pressing need to embark on my usual Saturday night sex marathon, so I didn't linger in the *jardins*. Tonight, I didn't need a fix.

Back at *La Reserve,* as I tried to unwind and let the exhaustion sink in, I thought of the long drive, and the boy on the *quais*. I had left Paris only yesterday, and after driving across France, I now found myself in a hotel bed a few kilometers away from one of our childhood homes, the last place we had lived as a united family. Little did I know that this road trip, which was only supposed to last for a few days, would take me on a long and distant journey, a grand tour of the geographic and emotional landscapes of my childhood, and that after a decade of relative stability in Paris—the longest I had ever stayed put anywhere—I would find myself once again, like Dollsie ever since she had left Cuba, in search of a place to land, a place I could call home.

TWO

EMERGING FROM THE FOG

I wake up late the next day in my usual morning haze—particularly acute on Sundays. Scattered across the bed and floor: an empty juice bottle from the mini-bar, a bag of potato chips, and a pack of M&M's, unwelcome evidence of my nocturnal binging—the middle of the night munchies brought on by the joint, unleashing insatiable cravings. The phone is buzzing, and I lie there in bed listening to it, feeling the familiar loneliness of waking up in a big empty bed in a plush hotel room. CNN is on, as it has been all night, reporting the news in an endless perpetual cycle which has surely permeated my dreams.

I know that it is Dollsie calling again. There are her late night drunken phone calls and her perky calls is in the morning, when she is at her most revved up and most likely to catch me off guard, emerging from the fog, with my defenses down.

"Hello?" I say, trying to remain calm while I collect my thoughts.

"Sergei, it's your mother!" she exclaims triumphantly. "You can run but you can't hide!"

She proceeds to launch into a monologue, her preferred form of discourse, and although I do not try to follow every word—I never do—looking for the remote control and the breakfast room service menu as she goes on and on—I catch the gist of it: there is something wrong with Dollsie.

"They think that it's a gallstone that is blocking something, and they wanted to have it removed yesterday, but I refused. As you may know, my big gala event at the *Palace* took place last night, and I just couldn't miss it, not after all the work I have put in and not after having poor Frédéric—that divine jeweler that I'm launching here—fly in from Paris for the party. I told them that I would go to the clinic today for the procedure, but I became so sick yesterday—positively yellow!—that I had no choice but to miss my event and be taken by ambulance to this dreadful clinic here in Zweisimmen. They say it's the closest village with a decent facility. I refused to be dumped in the Saanen clinic; you remember what happened to poor Ernst Von G. Croaked in a matter of hours for no reason at all. So here I am, waiting to be transferred to the hospital in Bern to have the gallstone removed tomorrow, and I realize that it's a *huge* imposition, what with Rolf's funeral and all—but I was hoping you could come up today and take me to the clinic tomorrow, and you can be back with Mina for the funeral on Thursday. I *know* how much Mina means to you and how much you want to be there for her—and I have already spoken to her to make sure she wouldn't mind sparing you for a day or two."

Before she's even done, I'm already thinking to myself, "*No fucking way.*" My usual reaction to any request of hers. I can't help myself. It's always been that way. And knowing what a drama queen she is—*une actrice manquée*—this time is no different. It doesn't sound all that serious to me, especially if you take into account her tendency to greatly exaggerate everything, and even more so when she's trying to get you to do something. I am furious that she has already brought Mina into it—one of Dollsie's classic strategic maneuvers—to make sure that she has her on her side, knowing full well that Mina is just about the only person on the planet who can get me to do something that I don't want to do. Dollsie and I both know that Mina will insist that I go to her at once. Dollsie wins again.

I finally manage to get off the phone, mumbling something or other about checking with Mina, and ten minutes later, as breakfast arrives, Mina calls, and sure enough, I receive my marching orders:

"How are you, darling?" she says in her deep smoker's voice. "Be an angel and come have lunch with me, then you can continue on to Gstaad. I really don't need you here, dear, and your mother does, so you must go *do your duty* and be by her side. You'll be back in plenty of time to accompany me to the service, and if you're not, it doesn't matter. Rolf wouldn't have wanted a big fuss."

I assent in silence.

It is already past eleven, and I have one hour to shower, pack, check out, and get to the *résidence* in time for lunch. Mina has always been impatient—a family trait—getting furious at the slightest delays, but it has gotten worse with age, her impatience morphing into panic if someone doesn't show up at exactly the right time. Perhaps it is just the feeling that time is running out, and she cannot abide wasting a minute of it.

I pay the bill—trying not to think about how much I have wasted on yet another restless, lonely night of frustrated longing—and wait for the porter to pull up in my freshly washed, gleaming silver *Spyder Cambiocorsa*. Walt heaves himself into the passenger seat. It is now 12:03. If I go 150 kilometers per hour, I can make it in twenty-five minutes, but I will probably be a few minutes late. On the way, I prepare myself for her state of mind. We know one another as well as we know ourselves. She will be anxious about all the arrangements that need to be made, shaken up by the disruption to her routine, and miffed that I am late. But she won't be grieving or making any effort to do so; that much I know. She is not the type to "perform for the peanut gallery," as she often says. And despite her many years as a diplomat's wife, she lacks Dollsie's acting skills and can't be bothered to pretend that she will miss Rolf.

"After all," she says, "what's there to miss?"

THREE

LE BAL DES FLEURS

On the way to La Gottaz, I look up from the autoroute and catch a glimpse of the Château de Vincy, where we had first lived after leaving New York and landing in Geneva, thirty-three years ago.

As a send-off, Town & Country had run a feature on us—"Living in Style with the Boissiers"—which included several striking pictures, including one of Dollsie in a red geometric-patterned dress that matches the wallpaper behind her, and on the next page, an eerie family portrait of the five of us sitting on a sofa beneath a large painting of falling strawberries by Ben Shonzeit, a popular New York artist in the seventies. Dollsie and Dad are impossibly beautiful, regal, untouchable, and the children—all three of us—look like mannequins. My legs are crossed and my head is tilted, as if I were trying to assume Dollsie's pose. There is no question that the boy in the picture is gay, or will be. Anton looks like a happy bully, comfortably occupying his space. Nan seems sad, almost ghostly, like the sculpture of the girl in the standing coffin that is reproduced in the article as evidence of my parents' sophisticated, edgy art collection. One of the few things that Dad and Dollsie had in common was a taste for twisted art. The more gruesome and bloody the images, the better. As a child they terrified me, especially when I would wake up in the middle of the night and go looking for Tata, our nanny. But I learned to ignore them, keeping my eyes on the floor.

Dollsie was leaving New York with a bang, hot pants and all. One of her claims to fame was that she had launched the fad in New York, after seeing

Twiggy wearing a pair in London. I have no idea if the story is true. To Dollsie, the truth was beside the point; it was just one of the many little legends that she created for herself, and for us.

I had been excited about the move for months. I would miss the people who had cared for us: J.C., our gay black butler who talked like he'd just walked off the set of Porgy and Bess, and Maria Jesus, Justa, and Lillian; our cook and maids. But Tata was coming with us, and that was all that mattered. I secretly pretended she was my real mother and suffered terribly when Dollsie sent her away periodically, after one of their raging fights. They both had huge, explosive tempers which sent us running for cover.

Most of all I would miss Mina's mother, Mooma, whom I adored, with her raspy tobacco voice—exactly like Mina's but with a North Carolina twang—and her old-world Southern elegance. The daughter of a tobacco tycoon from North Carolina, she had been born in a small town and then attended Miss Chapin's in New York City, where she would befriend a Cuban girl called Dolores, my other great grandmother. Soon after graduating from finishing school, she had married my great grandfather, Paul—descended from German immigrants—and moved to Buffalo. Like Dollsie and her mother and grandmother, Mooma was inordinately proud of her aristocratic lineage, especially her ancestor John Penn, one of the signers of the Declaration of Independence.

As a merry widow with a fondness for whiskey and bridge, living out her remaining years on Park Avenue, Mooma would routinely get thrown out of taxis by irate black cab drivers after referring to them as "boy". One of my earliest memories was of being in a cab with her and Dollsie, on our way back from tea at the Plaza. As the taxi was taking off, Mooma leaned forward and commanded, "Boy, take me to 64th and Park". With that, the driver screeched to a halt and told us to get out. As Mooma was struggling to exit the car, she turned to Dollsie, and in her loud yet refined southern drawl, said:

"Dollsie, I simply don't understand why these nigros have gotten so uppity these days." No doubt fearing for our lives, Dollsie gave the old woman a big final push that practically sent her flying onto the pavement, and we flew right out after her.

The big day came, and on the way to the airport, Dollsie told us again of the wonders that awaited us in Switzerland: the château with its vineyards, orchards and farm, its formal French gardens and fountains, and its large staff; the chalet in the Alps, where we would spend our winters, living Dollsie's glamorous version of the Heidi life; Dad's very important new job as partner of a bank in Geneva; and the sweet little village school I would attend, and the wonderful friends I would make.

We were in the plane for several hours before it took off, our beloved Tata keeping us calm as Dollsie went from storytelling mode to impatience, bordering on hysteria. To keep everyone calm— her favorite euphemism—she crushed a valium and mixed it into our glasses of milk and then took one herself, much to Dad's relief. By the time we woke up, the plane had landed and we disembarked in a drugged haze, whose effects would only wear off four years later, when we would fly back over the Atlantic in the opposite direction, the family no longer intact, the fairy tale over.

I was six years old, and was Dollsie's most captive audience. For months leading up to the move I would listen to her magical tales without knowing what lay behind them. I did not know that she was attempting to create a fairy tale for us in a foreign land—in a last attempt to save her marriage and preserve the family.

I did not know that three or four years earlier, around the time of my sister's birth, Dollsie had taken up with a Russian man named Jacques, who had been pursuing her for years. And although my earliest memories of Dad were defined by his absences—wandering into his study and wondering where he was—I was too young to grasp that he and Dollsie had decided to separate for a year and that he had moved to Buffalo to work with the family business, returning to the city on weekends to see us. At the end of the year, they reconciled and soon after, they decided to move to Switzerland, ostensibly for Dad's career, but really to get away from Jacques and start over. The stakes were high.

Mina and Rolf were waiting for us as we came through customs. After collecting our suitcases, they drove us to the home they had found for us, known as the Château de Vincy; an eighteenth century "castle" located half way between Geneva and Lausanne, and close to their property, Mimorey, as well as to Le Rosey, a boarding school on the banks of Lake Geneva that catered to the children of the international elite and which Anton would attend, like Dad and his father before him.

The château belonged to a German count who had been obliged to leave the country after a tragic scandal involving the fourteen-year-old-son of the local butcher, who had hung himself after a tawdry afternoon spent with the count. It overlooked the small village that bore its name, and most of its residents either worked in the vineyards or plowed the fields or tended to the orchards and livestock.

Dollsie embraced her new role with gusto, shifting easily from the racy New York glamour girl in hot pants to a Geneva banker's wife and feudal lady of the manor. She had finally arrived. Mina—who had been through her own learning curve as an outsider marrying into this closed, uptight world—impressed upon Dollsie the historic importance of the family name in Geneva, and warned that her new position would require a certain amount of restraint and conformity—qualities for which Dollsie was not known—especially since she was the first Catholic spouse of a banker as well as the first Latin, both of which would create quite a stir in Calvinist Geneva. But Dollsie had no doubt that she would pull it off without a hitch, and she relished the idea of being one of a kind and slightly scandalous. She would keep her long mane, despite Mina's repeated advice that she cut it off and adopt a more conservative look. This was her moment, what she had been waiting for, a chance to recapture some of what she had lost in Cuba and had dreamed about during her thirteen restless years of marriage: a position, property, permanence.

Dad left for work early in the morning and returned in the evening, usually just in time to change for some social engagement that they were either hosting or invited to. He hated to socialize but Dollsie lived for it, and after endless arguments during their years in New York, she had convinced him that it was essential for his new position of prominence.

Given how different they were, in retrospect it seems amazing how long they lasted together. They had met when Dollsie was eighteen and living in Havana, wondering what to do with her life, feeling frustrated by the constraints of her family and the rarefied circles in which she traveled. Dad was twenty-three, and fresh out of the Swiss Army.

As an only child, he had moved around a lot, spending his first six years in Paris and in Bern. When the first stirrings of the war and Hitler's menace began to spread across Europe, he had sailed to New York with his mother, and then had boarded a train for Buffalo, where he was left in the care of Mina's parents for the duration of the war, while she returned to Paris to be by her diplomat husband's side. Two years later, when Mina arrived from Paris to fetch him, he had failed to recognize her at the train station, and although he would remain a devoted and attentive son throughout his life, the divide between mother and son would never be bridged.

After attending Le Rosey and graduating from Williams College, he looked forward to a quiet life, dedicating himself to writing and teaching in a New England prep school with Frannie, the girl he had decided to marry. But Mina had different notions. Sensing that an engagement to Frannie was imminent—a sweet girl, but very "middle class" and utterly incapable of cutting a millefeuille, as Mina had noticed with consternation when Dad had made the introductions over tea at the Plaza—she had conspired with her childhood friend Gladys to send Dad to Cuba for a holiday to meet Gladys' daughter, Dolores. Dollsie had also been frequenting suitors that her parents and grandparents considered to be most unsuitable, handsome Cuban playboys in search of an easy life, and since her parents had not allowed her to attend to college (fearing the worst if she was left to her own devices in a foreign city) it was decided that a suitable marriage might be just what was needed. The sooner, the better.

The plan had worked. Dollsie greeted him at the airport in all her spoiled splendor, and Dad struck a dashing figure with his Swiss army haircut and his gentlemanly ways. They were both instantly smitten. After those weeks together in Cuba, touring Dollsie's grandfather's sugar mill and cattle ranches and living the high life in Havana—frequenting the Tropicana and other glamorous venues—followed by an eighteen-month courtship, Dad proposed. Having known each other for three generations, both families were overjoyed by the union. They married the following April, at the Belen Jesuit Academy in Havana, followed by a lavish reception for six hundred.

After their wedding and a three-month honeymoon motoring through France, Spain, and Italy in a chauffeur-driven Rolls Royce given to them by Dollsie's grandparents, they settled in Grez-sur-Loin, a small village near Fontainebleau where Mina owned a weekend house. The plan was for them to live there and for Dad to write, but Dollsie was miserable from the start. She did her best to adapt, taking cooking courses and gardening and practicing French with the locals. But one night, awaking to an empty bed and not finding Dollsie anywhere in the house, Dad set out to look for her, only to find her swimming in the village fountain in her nightgown with a bottle of champagne, singing and splashing away.

Following extensive consultations with various family members, it was decided that Dollsie might be better off back in Cuba where her "nervous problems" could be managed more effectively. So the newlyweds departed for Havana, to begin their conjugal life anew. Dad set about learning the language by spending his afternoons accompanying cab drivers on their rounds. He often said that if Fidel Castro hadn't come along, he would have been happy to live out his days as a gentleman farmer in Cuba, growing coffee, raising cattle, and perhaps joining in the family's sugar business.

My brother Anton was born the following year, in 1959. Within a year, he and Dollsie and Dad, along with the rest of the family and every last guest at their wedding, would all be gone from Cuba, sent into "temporary" exile. They were allowed only one suitcase per person, leaving behind most of their fortune, including their lands, homes, art collections and fine china. They left with their maids in tow, all wearing three layers of clothes so that they could smuggle through as much of the family silverware and jewelry as they could carry.

Most of the Cuban ex-pats had settled in Miami, ninety miles away, believing that Fidel Castro and his Communist henchmen would soon be overthrown, but many, like my parents, had sought out more sophisticated destinations like New York and Madrid, where they could finally be free; unencumbered by their conventional elders and the archaic rules and restrictions of their Catholic upbringings.

In New York, at the urging of Dollsie and Mina and her brother Paul—the patriarch of the family—Dad had joined an investment firm on Wall Street named Wood Struthers. Being an investment banker was not a career he had ever envisioned, but he found he was surprisingly good at it, and within a few years, he had made partner at a very young age.

In Switzerland, his banking hours were long, and the heady promotion to partner in a private Swiss bank—again at a record young age—weighed heavily on Dad. We didn't see much of him except on weekends when he would sometimes take us camping in the nearby woods, the servants arriving ahead of time to set up the tents and prepare the sleeping bags and set the picnic table, laying out a dinner of salads and meats and cheeses. The next morning, they would come to clean it all up after we were done. That was Dad's version of camping. Dollsie never joined.

At the château, we had many animals, including a chien des Pyrénées named Boris, and Dollsie's miniature Italian greyhound, Borzoi. Dollsie had a thing for

Imperial Russia and Russian literature (as well as Russian men, as I would discover later), and she had named all of us—including the pets—after characters in War and Peace and Anna Karenina.

After taking a few months to settle into the château—oh, how she loved having a staff of ten, plus the two gardeners—it reminded her of the good old days in Cuba—she persuaded Dad to let her throw a big ball to properly mark their arrival. She decided to give it a flower theme: Le Bal des Fleurs. The preparations went on for months: caterers were interviewed, hors d'oeuvres and pastries and cakes sampled, flowers chosen, dresses tried, invitations sent. I followed Dollsie around from appointment to appointment, enchanted and intoxicated by the world she was creating, living the fantasy with her every step of the way.

The day of the ball, it poured and poured and poured. Tents had been erected in the gardens to hold the five hundred guests that had been invited from all over Europe and the States, and the large rectangular fountain had been covered and turned into a dance floor. Dollsie was frantic, convinced that the tents would collapse from the sheer weight of the water. A dozen workers held disaster at bay all day, coming in once in a while to dry off. Dollsie would greet them with a beer in one hand and a towel and one of Dad's folded shirts in the other, pleading with them to persevere, as if her very life depended on the success of the party.

It was still pouring as the guests arrived. As they entered the foyer, someone would assist them to remove their rain-soaked garb, and then they would be given their table assignments. I tried my best to not let it show, to be sophisticated and to rise to the occasion, but I was deeply impressed by the procession of titles and celebrities, the ball gowns and magnificent jewelry. Alexandre had flown in from Paris to comb Dollsie's hair, along with some of her notable guests, including Debbie Sukarno, the Japanese jet-setting wife of the former President of Indonesia. I had never seen anything like it. Dollsie had indeed arrived, and I was very proud to be her son.

The guests danced all night and when I woke up the next morning, there were still a dozen guests drinking champagne and eating crepe suzettes, exchanging gossip about the VIP's who had attended—including Jackie Stewart, the race car driver, and a smattering of minor European royals—and the scandals of the soirée: who had left with whom, which new couples had formed, and which had broken up or were on the verge. The party had been a grand success, far exceeding Dollsie's expectations, and the rain, far from ruining it, had actually been a blessing; it had kept the guests inside the tent, thus preventing any dissipation of the crowds, which had only enhanced the atmosphere and kept the energy at peak level all night. Until the end of her days, Dollsie would regard that night of le Bal des Fleurs as her greatest moment; the apogee of her existence.

The château was fertile ground for a lonely kid with a vivid imagination. I had few friends at first, but I quickly learned to buy affection by stealing coins from my parents to buy candy for the village children. I invited them to the château for tours of the subterranean passages and caves, where I made up elaborate stories of Germans who had been imprisoned during the war and of ghosts who had wandered the attic and the halls for centuries and still did, late at night when we were all asleep. Then I would take them out to the gardens and the maze, which they had never seen before. I would tell them more stories about the nobles and ladies who used to chase each other to steal a kiss while their husbands and wives looked for them in vain. The kids often looked at me in bewilderment, wondering who this strange boy was, and whether they could really believe my outlandish tales.

As Dad would write me years later, "It was definitely the stuff of which fairy tales are made, in the sense that it was bedtime story land and totally unreal. We were like animated characters in a Walt Disney production, but our private lives had little to do with the movie."

Across from us lived three funny-looking men. One was English, one Swiss, and the other American. Dollsie told me that they were homosexuals, which, as she explained, meant that they preferred men to women. I wasn't to spend time with them alone, even though they were perfectly harmless. I had no idea what she meant, but it sparked my curiosity, and I would sneak over to see them often.

The first day of school was a disaster, and pretty much set the tone for the next nine years. Dollsie had dropped me off, and without any explanation or preparation, I found myself being escorted to a classroom filled with boys and girls who spoke a language that I did not understand. Paralyzed with fear, I was dying to pee but I did not know how to ask, so I made my way to my seat. Determined to make it to recess, I held out as long as I could, squirming and squeezing my penis between my legs, but eventually I could no longer hold it, and I slowly let go right in my chair. As the puddle accumulated and then spilled onto the floor beneath me, drop by drop, I felt—much to my horror—the attention of the entire class shift in my direction. Finally, the teacher noticed, and with a look of disgust and disbelief, unceremoniously escorted me from the classroom out to the front entrance of the school, where I waited on the sidewalk for what seemed like an eternity for someone to come get me. Dad showed up in his new yellow Peugeot convertible, with a bunch of towels carefully placed on the seat to protect the new leather. He said little on the way home. These matters were best left to Dollsie.

The next day I was taken to another school, to repeat kindergarten, and within three months I was speaking fluent French. Dollsie was a big believer in the trial-by-fire-toss-them-in-the-pool school of learning.

One of the best things about my new life was that Anton was away at boarding school during the week, which meant that he wasn't around to terrorize and torture me by doing things like trying to stick Coke bottles up my butt. Or aiming at me with his bb gun and narrowly missing. On weekends he would bring his new friends home. I would watch them play soccer in the fields beyond the gardens, fascinated by their beauty; their maleness, their strong, dark legs, sweaty and glistening. Dollsie, who loved dropping names, would always point out who was who—the son of the Maharajah of Jaipur, the nephew of the Aga Khan, and so on—and although I had no idea who she was talking about, I was as excited as she was to have them there. I envied Anton.

The rest of the time I felt like Little Lord Fauntleroy, pretending that the staff were my subjects, along with my younger sister Nan. She would do whatever I said, at least most of the time. Every day, I would inspect her dolls to see if they needed a haircut. I loved playing hairdresser. Nan would protest violently, but to appease her, I would let her play with my soldiers and trucks and guns. The arrangement suited us just fine, but it was one we carried out with the utmost secrecy, because Dollsie, for whatever reason we could not fathom, would throw a fit every time she came into the playroom and saw us playing with the other's toys. "IT'S NOT LIKE THAT!" she would yell, berating Tata as she stormed out for allowing this to happen. After several attempts to correct the situation, she hired an English governess, Carol; the first of several, to teach us how to be proper young men and little ladies. I refused to speak to Carol for a long time, in protest and out of allegiance to Tata, who had been transferred to the kitchen, which in her eyes was a definite demotion and most unjust.

In the evenings Dollsie and Dad would often head out to a dinner party in town. They were considered to be the perfect couple: young, rich, glamorous, and stunning, a breath of fresh air in the staid banking world of Geneva. They were very much sought after: Dollsie, tall and statuesque and almost regal, with her long Cuban mane and her exotic ways, and Dad, even taller, with his Hollywood movie star looks—a cross between Cary Grant and Gregory Peck—and illustrious family name and old world manners.

I would assist Dollsie in her preparations; an elaborate ritual of transformation which I never tired of observing. First, she would do her make-up, which she undertook with an intensity and concentration that fascinated me. She started with her cheeks and then moved to the eyes, applying the eye shadow and the black stick she ran between her eyelids—which was, according to her, a very rare and expensive coal from Egypt used by Pharaonic princesses in ancient times—and lastly, the lipstick. When she was done she would smile at herself in the mirror several times, and if she was in a good mood she would mug for me and make me laugh. Then she would move on to her hair, first throwing her neck forward so that the long dark blond tresses fell over her face, brushing vigorously, then throwing her head backward and continuing to brush until her hair fell about her in luscious abundance.

"Mummy, I love your hair so much. I want to be a hairdresser when I grow up," I told her one day as I watched her.

"Don't ever say that in front of your father. He will have a heart attack. That's not a proper profession for boys," she answered sternly.

"Okay, Mummy, I won't ever say it again," I responded, somewhat puzzled.

"There," she would say, enormously pleased with herself when she was done with the hair, "now come help Mummy choose her dress." I would follow her to the closet, where I would gaze in awe at her extensive collection of couture dresses.

"Oh, Sergei, Mummy can't wear that old thing again," she would often say after I had made my selection, "People will think that Daddy's bank is going under. You can pick from these four. Those are the ones from the latest Paris collections."

So I would pick one of those, and much to my delight, she would usually agree with my choice. Then I would pick the shoes, no easy task since she had so many, but by now I knew what matched with what. Then Dollsie would have me select her evening purse and fill it with the essentials: her compact case, lipstick, hanky, cigarettes and lighter. She would give me a franc by way of reward.

"Thank you, Mummy," I would say, kissing her carefully so as not to ruin her make-up.

After they went out, I would sneak back up to her room and re-enact the ritual, putting on one of her dresses and carefully applying her make-up as I had observed her do, and then, after choosing a pair of her high heeled shoes and one of her tiny bejeweled evening purses, I would proceed to prance around the château pretending that I was Dollsie on my way to some glamorous party with handsome Dad in his black tie. Often, when they got home, they would find me fast asleep in their bed, fully decked out.

Dollsie volunteered at the local sanitarium every day, where she took care of severely mentally disturbed children. This harrowing work gave her balance; a sense of meaning to justify all the frivolity. On weekends, she would sometimes take me along with her to visit patients. I would walk through the ward clutching her hand in utter terror, watching the boys and girls—many of them my own age—tied down to their beds, shrieking, talking nonsense and staring at me and laughing, crazy as loons.

Her favorite patient was called Astrid. She was seventeen, and on Sundays Dollsie would sometimes bring her back to the house. She could not talk, and I could tell that she was very, very disturbed: patches of her hair were missing and she had scars along her arms and on her face. Dollsie explained that she had pulled out her own hair and made the scars by tearing at her flesh. She did all this to punish herself, believing herself to be very bad, because her mother had been so mean to her, according to Dollsie. Once, I had seen the mother at the sanitarium. I could not take my eyes off of her, searching for evidence of the monstrous nature that had created such a child.

These crazy patients were, ironically, the only dose of reality in our otherwise idyllic existence. Like them, Dollsie could often be quite volatile and scary when she lost her temper and yelled and slapped us. But she could also be magical and majestic, the Queen of the Castle, entertaining local high society and her less sophisticated friends from America—many of whom had never been served finger bowls at dinner and who, nonplussed, would often proceed to either drink the contents or drop their deserts in them, which never failed to send us all into hysterics.

FOUR

BLACK BEAN SOUP

Although Nan was an obedient subject, usually doing whatever I told her to, the one thing I could not control was her health. She was sick all the time: mumps, measles, chicken pox, high fevers. I was told that it was because she had been born premature and had spent the first two months of her life in an incubator. Tata explained that it was like putting a pot roast back in the oven when it hasn't been cooked enough. The image elicited a certain amount of pity on my part, but after months and years of having her always be the center of attention, with presents and visitors on a regular basis, I began to deeply resent her very existence. What wouldn't I do to be able to miss school for weeks on end and sit in bed all day, receiving gifts and holding court!

I began to suspect that she was doing it on purpose, faking illness after illness to gain the upper hand and usurp my position. And I figured out that her main strategy involved not eating. Three times a day, Tata would bring her trays of food, and Nan would always say the same thing, "I'm not hungry and this tastes like caca."

So one day, while I was in the bathroom, I came up with a plan. I removed a piece of my own shit from the toilet and wrapped it in tissue paper, then I snuck down to the kitchen, hiding my treasure in my pocket, and when no one was looking, I dumped it into the black bean soup that Tata had just prepared for Nan and placed on her tray. The soup was very hot, and I burned myself as I pushed the piece of shit to the bottom of the bowl so that it wouldn't show.

I followed Tata up to Nan's room, experiencing a thrill of excitement and triumph, and slight terror.

"Miton" she said, using her affectionate nickname for me, "why are you following me? Don't bother your sister anymore. She has to eat and today I've fixed her favorite soup. I don't want you teasing her."

"Please let me come! I'll be good! I promise!" I said, eager to witness the crime that was about to occur.

Nan was in bed as usual, playing with all the latest toys she had gotten as a result of whatever ailed her this time. She loved making me jealous by showing them to me over and over again, flaunting them. But this time I would show her.

"Nanita, look, I've brought you your favorite soup! Black bean soup!"

"I hate black bean soup and I'm not hungry and I won't eat!" exclaimed Nan, with her usual spoiled brat voice.

"You love black bean soup. Come on, just one bite, for me, please." Tata's practiced pleading and look of hurt always succeeded in getting Nan to try at least one bite. She held the spoon out to her, and Nan swallowed it reluctantly.

"It tastes like caca!" Nan proclaimed.

"Nanita, your mother does not approve of that language. Little señoritas don't talk like that. Now try one more."

"NO!"

"One for your grandmother. She's coming this afternoon to visit you, and what will she think when I tell her you didn't eat your lunch, *querida*?"

This had a profound effect on Nan. She loved Mina as much as I did, and did not want to risk her displeasure, so she took another bite.

"Yucky Yucky Yucky!! CACA!!!"

"Stop saying that," cried Tata. "Sergei will take a bite, too, to show you how good it tastes."

I hadn't anticipated this. "But Tata, if I eat from her spoon then I'll get her germs and get sick too!"

Tata reproached herself for not having thought of this. She told Nan that she would take a spoonful herself. She dipped the spoon into the bowl and brought it slowly to her mouth, pretending to savor it and watching Nan's expression to gage her success.

"Caca!" shrieked Nan triumphantly, spotting the piece on the spoon. Her delight and surprise at having been right all along was quickly replaced by disgust. She began spitting to get rid of whatever was left in her mouth.

Tata stared down at the spoon in disbelief. "It's not caca," she said, as persuasively as possible.

"Yes it is! It is! It is! Smell it!"

To prove that there wasn't any caca in the soup, Tata plunged the spoon back into the bowl with determination, and as she lifted it to her mouth, she saw, much to her horror, the offending morsel mixed in with the black beans. She burst into tears and ran out of the room with the tray. I felt badly. I hadn't intended to hurt Tata, whom I loved more than life itself.

I went out to play with my pet rabbits, two brothers—a white one and a grey one—that I had talked Arthur, the retarded gardener, into giving me. I loved Arthur. He was always happy, always laughing, and he spent hours caring for his beloved rabbits.

Tata came out to find me. She was still crying but she was also angrier than I had ever seen her. Poisoning the food that she prepared with so much love and pride with feces was as close to sacrilege as you could get in her book. "How could you do such a thing?" she yelled.

"What did I do?" I protested.

"You know perfectly well what you did, and wait until your mother gets home."

At the mention of Dollsie I was overcome with terror. "You won't tell her," I said pleading.

"I most certainly will. Just you wait."

"Please, Tati, please don't tell her!" I said, sobbing. "She will whip me. I know she will."

"And you deserve it!"

I hugged her and began kissing her all over, crying my heart out. This usually worked with Tata whenever I was in trouble.

"Please, I'll do anything, anything in the world."

"Anything?" she said, her face lighting up. "Then give me one of your conejos." For months, she had been trying to convince me to give her one of my rabbits to cook. It was a delicacy in her native region, Galicia, and she hadn't had the opportunity to cook one since Cuba. She could not grasp the idea of having rabbits as pets.

"Not my rabbits! Please Tati, Please! Te quiero!"

"Well in that case, I'll have to tell your mother," she said, with finality.

I was horrified at the choice that faced me. It was either give up one of my rabbits or risk being whipped to death by Dollsie. I looked ruefully at the rabbits for a long time. "You can have that one," I finally said, my voice barely audible, pointing at the grey one with the long ears.

Tata seized the long awaited opportunity. She opened the cage, and grabbed the rabbit by the ears. She then carried him to the other courtyard, where, to my utter horror, she grabbed him by the hind legs and smashed his head against the wall several times. She then laid the rabbit on the ground. I could see that it was still breathing, and its eyes were wide open.

"Kill it, kill it!" I screamed at Tata. "I hate you! I hope you die!"

At that moment, Dollsie's car pulled into the driveway. She parked and jumped out, her miniature greyhounds in tow.

"What is going on here?" she asked, seeing me upset.

"Nothing," I said. Tata and I were both standing in front of the rabbit, trying to conceal it.

"What are you two up to? What are you hiding?"

"Nada, señora," she answered, looking even more guilty than I did.

"What on earth is going on?" Dollsie demanded, her voice rising. At which point the dogs ran over to the rabbit, and she followed.

"Maria, if you don't tell me immediately what is going on, you will be on the next flight back to Spain," she said, when she saw the almost dead creature.

Tata was as terrified of la señora as everyone else, so she told Dollsie the whole story: about the shit in the soup and the rabbit I had given her in exchange for not telling Dollsie what I had done.

When Dollsie got mad, you could see it coming, like a volcano about to erupt. Her face would grow red, her nostrils would begin to flare, and she would start shaking. She slapped me in the face three times in rapid succession. She then grabbed my arm and dragged me back into the house, her long, pink nails digging into the flesh, twisting, twisting, like a corkscrew, her signature pinch. She held me like this all the way up the grand staircase to her bedroom on the second floor, shrieking "Just wait until your father gets home!" She then went to her large closet and selected one of her belts, and told me to pull down my pants and lean over the bed. She proceeded to whip me twenty times, using the buckle end, murmuring between lashes—like a mantra—"This hurts me more than it hurts you." After it was over, I was sent to my room and she went to deal with Tata.

"MARIA!" she shrieked, as she headed to the servants' quarters.

I cried and cried until I fell asleep. I dreamt of giant rabbit-monsters clawing their way out of the cage and coming after me, with their huge fangs and crazed expressions, a recurring nightmare that would haunt me for years.

I was awakened by the voices of Dad and Dollsie outside my door, arguing.

"Of course, I had to be the one to discipline him, as usual. You are too weak. You just can't handle it," she told him. "Now talk to him, J.J., for God's sake, be firm."

Dad came in the room and with all the passion he could muster, told me that had he been there when it happened, he would have made sure that I ate every last bite. Then he left the room.

Tata came in a little later, bringing me dinner on a tray. I cried in her arms and told her how sorry I was and how much I loved her. I couldn't believe that she had killed my rabbit. I felt so betrayed and disillusioned. I had always turned to Tata for solace and comfort when Dollsie went into one of her rages. How could she have done that to her miton? She smiled through her tears and held me tight against her abundant chest.

By morning she was gone, sent away once again to work elsewhere, only to return a few months later when Dollsie realized that she couldn't manage without her.

The next day, I was taken to see a shrink—the first of many throughout my life. That was how Dollsie rolled: first punishment, then seek professional help. After chatting with me and testing me, the psychiatrist reported back to my parents. Years later I would come across the report: I was a "normal" child with an exceptionally high IQ—and also highly sensitive. But as far as Dollsie was concerned—and by extension, Dad—the incident had confirmed that something was wrong with me. From that day on, I was the fucked up middle child, needing more attention than the others and acting out to get it. The problem child.

FIVE

FAIRY TALE

In the summers, we would fly back to the States to visit relatives. When we went to Buffalo, we would stay with Uncle Paul and Aunt Jane at their country spread in Lewiston. Paul was Mina's brother and the family patriarch, and like most people in his orbit, I was slightly terrified of him. But I adored Jane, a wacky and wonderful woman of Irish descent who, like Dollsie, loved nothing more in life than entertaining and running a household full of servants. There was always a multitude of decrepit Irish and black maids stumbling around the place whom Jane treated as if they were her unruly brood of children, including a senile kleptomaniac called Hattie who over the years had amassed quite a collection of stolen valuables from guests. Her nicknames was Sticky Fingers, and Jane refused to part with her, so when Mina and Dollsie came to visit, they always traveled light.

Lewiston was a great place to spend the holidays, mainly because of Aunt Jane, who had a knack for making her guests feel like they were having a ball, all the time. Every morning I would get up early and sneak out of the house to go see my cousins David and Annie, who lived down the street. David was fifteen and gorgeous, and at the age of five or six, I fell madly in love. I adored Annie and we would spend most of the day together, but I was always on the lookout for David.

In the summer we would also travel to different European destinations, usually by car, starting with Munich for the Olympics, where we found ourselves caught up in the panic following the infamous Munich massacre, during which eleven members of the Israeli Olympic team had been taken hostage and eventually killed by Palestinian terrorists.

The following year we went to Port Grimaud, near Saint Tropez, to stay at Tante Odette's house. Odette was Dad's paternal aunt and one of my favorite relatives. Imperious and haughty and impossibly elegant, she had served at her husband's side as Ambassadress to the Court of Saint James during the war, and she had never quite been able to descend from that lofty perch and return to reality. She lived with her cocker spaniel, her parrot, and her African *"majeur d'homme"*, whose duties clearly included more than keeping house. They fought constantly, with the parrot shrieking in the background, mimicking their rows. Later, I would visit her often in Paris, and she would tell me hilarious stories of her drama-filled days, including the time she had found her beloved dog sniffing a used kleenex in the Bois de Boulogne, and had rushed him to the vet to find out if he could catch AIDS that way.

Dad had hauled his boat from Geneva, and we spent our days going for long rides along the Cote D'Azur, visiting friends in their fantastic villas overlooking the Mediterranean. I felt like a movie star. Dollsie loved going to the flea markets, where she once managed to lose Nan for half a day, much to my delight.

The most memorable trip of all was Venice. We stayed at the Cipriani, a glamorous hotel located on its own island off the Grand Canal. In the mornings we would be dragged to churches and museums, where Dollsie made us memorize the names of artists and paintings with the fervor of a drill sergeant, and in the afternoons, we would nap and lounge by the luxurious pool, then dress and take the *vaporetto* to Piazza San Marco for the evening *passeggiata* and dinner in a cozy *trattoria*, followed by gelato and a gondola ride. It was the beginning of a lifelong fascination with Venice and all things Italian.

Dollsie managed to lose Nan on that trip too, but she was found hours later in a butcher's shop. Along with Dollsie's mother who had flown over from Miami, Georgie, the fat Russian prince, had also joined us, and although I did not know who he was at the time, later I would wonder if he and Dollsie were already lovers by then, and whether Dad knew, and what he thought about Georgie tagging along. All I remember of him on that trip was his stutter, which had us all on the verge of hysterics every time he opened his mouth, Dollsie leading the charge.

All drama aside, those three years spent between Vincy and Gstaad were the happiest I have ever known. In Vincy, I felt like Dollsie must have felt in Cuba, master of my own domain. I played in the vineyards, hid in the gardens, picked cherries and walnuts off the trees, and invariably got sick from ingesting my loot. I loved the cows and the sheep that grazed our fields, and the pigs and horses that Mina and Rolf kept at Mimorey. Most of all, I loved working in the vineyards during grape-picking season, helping the *vignerons* to collect the grapes off the vines and then—my favorite part—stomping on them in the huge vats, barefoot, my toes squishing the purple pulp, the strong scent of the grapes mixed with the pungent smell of sweat coming from the bare chested men. I felt heady and a bit overwhelmed by this first brush with sensuality.

Dollsie and Dad were gone a lot, but I barely noticed. Tata was there—when she hadn't been sent away—along with our governess Carol and the rest of the staff.

On Wednesdays, when school finished early, Mina would take me to the movies, and then we would go out for tea. She was a wonderful storyteller, with her deep and dramatic voice, and a great listener as well, seeming to follow every word with a look of rapt attention—her trademark expression. She invariably pretended to be fascinated by whatever dumb movie I made her sit through or whatever ridiculous story I told her, or whatever petty complaint I recounted about Dollsie or Anton or Nan.

Dollsie and Dad, in keeping with their reputation as the perfect couple, never argued openly. I could only recall ever hearing them fight one time, when, ear pressed against their bathroom door, I had overheard Dollsie screaming at Dad, calling him a moron and an idiot and wimp, and Dad responding calmly (like he always did when she had one of her outbursts) "I'll leave anytime you want me to". I was seven or eight at the time, and the conversation, Dollsie's shrieking and Dad's deadly calm tone, terrified me. I never mentioned it to anyone, not even Mina or Tata.

I did not know at the time that Jacques—a Russian émigré who had grown up in Paris and come to America penniless, subsequently making a small fortune—had opened an office in Paris shortly after our move to Switzerland. Dollsie would disappear on "shopping trips" on a regular basis, returning with extravagant gifts for us.

This was, after all, the seventies, and people like my parents, with too much money and too many choices—and too young to handle it all—had grown bored with their traditional and predictable lives, and were looking for something different. Living in a repressive, Calvinist society only encouraged everyone to go wild; to have affairs and break all the rules. Although Dad was successful, he detested the atmosphere of the banking world. He often wondered about what would have happened had he pursued his dream to write and teach. Whenever he could, he would escape by going off to Esalen, a nudist colony in California which he had discovered during his separation from Dollsie, where people went to find themselves by joining gestalt groups, engaging in "primal screaming" and "rebirthing" and experimental touching, along with massage and meditation and exploration—sexual, emotional, spiritual—all in an effort to get in touch with whatever seemed to be missing from their lives. To fill the void.

I did not know then that all of it—the château, the chalet, the parties, the trips—was Dollsie's attempt to give us a fairy tale existence, at least for a while. For she knew that one day it would end. While she was busy building a fantasy life for us, trying to reclaim some of what she had left behind in Cuba, she was also struggling to find her own identity; to make sense of her own life and to make the right choice. I did not know that her heart was torn—not between two men, but three—Dad, Jacques, and Georgie.

And then, after three years glorious years spent in Vincy and Gstaad, everything changed. Much to Dollsie's chagrin, we had to give up the château because the owner, having served his years of extradition, had been pardoned and was returning to take possession of his home and lands. We moved to an even grander property which was closer to Geneva and right on the lake. It was famous for having housed President Woodrow Wilson during the League of Nations conference, and later, after us, President Reagan during his summit with Gorbachev. Dollsie brought over her friends Mica and Chessie—fashionable decorators from New York—to jazz the place up, but it never felt like a home the way Vincy had. It was formal and elegant, but also cold, austere. Living there felt like being a courtier at Versailles.

Nan and I lived on the top floor, along with Tata and the other servants. Anton's bedroom was on the second floor, next to Dad's study and their bedroom. For some reason, he was not allowed up on our floor unsupervised. Something had happened between my brother and sister that I was only vaguely aware of. Like much else in our family, it was not discussed.

Anton was taken out of Le Rosey after Dad found out that the school had installed a helicopter pad for the sheiks and emirs when they came to visit their children, and he and I were both placed in Florimont, a rigorous all-boys Jesuit school in Geneva. Life all of a sudden seemed very serious. I got my first taste of how cruel and perceptive other kids can be. I learned what every gay kid learns: how to endure. I hated every minute of it: the conformity, the sports, the rigidity and competition.

During lunch break, I would sneak out and go seek refuge at the Hare Krishna compound which, funnily enough, neighbored the Jesuit academy. It was surprisingly easy to sneak in and out of school, and I loved going to the compound and being with the happy, smiling men and women with their bald skulls and pony tails and exotic food and flowing, colorful garments. I felt accepted there, welcome. I didn't have to worry about being different.

At the age of nine, I was no longer carefree, on my way to becoming a lonely and insecure child. I turned to Tata and Mina for solace, and the unconditional acceptance that I could not find elsewhere. Tata loved me fiercely, and although I called Dollsie "Mummy", it was Tata that I always turned to for comfort and consolation.

A few months after settling into the new house, Dollsie left to go to back to the States for a while. We were told that it was because she needed to have an operation. When she returned six weeks later, she seemed different, in a way nicer, less demanding, more even tempered. She was either out a lot or locked away in her room. Life became quieter. Family dinners, which Dollsie insisted on having in the formal dining room with fancy china and the whole bit to teach us proper etiquette, became somber affairs. Whereas before, Dollsie had always dominated the table and talked incessantly, she often sat there quietly now, only saying something when the quietness became too loud, and often she would leave the table in tears for no reason that we could fathom. Even Tata became somber, suspecting, no doubt, what was to come.

On Wednesday afternoons, when school got out, instead of going to the movies with Mina, Nan and I would often be taken to visit Prince Georgie and his children, who detested us as much as we did them. Dollsie and the prince would drop us off at the movies, and then pick us up afterwards. They were often late, sometimes very late, and the four of us would wait outside the theater, a little afraid and wondering where they were. It was only a few years later that

I would find out the cause of their tardiness, when Tata, in the middle of one of her fits of rage over what *la señora* had done to "destroy such a beautiful family," revealed to me in shattering detail what had gone on between Dollsie and her two Russian lovers, and how those events had led to the divorce.

And then came Easter and our last visit to Gstaad. It rained for days, as often happens in April. The snow had melted and we skied through what was left of it, wanting to savor every last bit, now caked in mud and rapidly turning to slush. On Sunday, we went to Mass and then to lunch with Mina and Rolf, and after they departed, Dollsie and Dad sat us down to tell us that they were getting divorced. We had seen *The Way We Were* on a weekend trip to Paris a few weeks earlier, and Dollsie explained to us that, just like the couple in the movie, she and Dad loved each other very much but would no longer live together. We would move back to New York with Dollsie—"just for a year, to see how it goes"—and Dad would stay in Geneva, along with our beloved Tata, who would look after him.

The fairy tale was over. As our taxi pulled out of Genthod to take us to the airport—almost exactly four years after we had first landed—I did not know what lay in store for me, but as I looked out the back window and saw Dad, Tata, Mina and Rolf waving goodbye sadly, smiling bravely through their tears, I knew what I was leaving behind.

Tata was never the same again. Something snapped in her when we—her niños—left. I noticed it when I returned to Switzerland the following summer, and the summers after that. I saw it in her fits of crying that would erupt at any moment, in the vehemence with which she would tell me all these terrible things about Dollsie, exacting her revenge by spilling all her secrets. I heard these stories, laced with bitterness and regret and condemnation, and that's when I began to despise Dollsie. Not only had she wrecked our lives, but she had wrecked Tata's as well.

On the way to America, we stopped off in London, to visit Allison, an American friend of Dollsie's who had married a gay English Lord. We spent a few days visiting the city, then went to their country estate, where Dollsie got bucked off a horse the first day while showing off her riding skills and broke her collarbone. We had to delay our flight to the States for weeks, waiting for her to recover. I fought with our governess, a Portuguese woman that had been hired to help us "adjust", I fought with Nan, and I fought with Dollsie. It was a miserable time.

Instead of being a peaceful moment of transition, Dollsie's way of easing us into our new life, it set the tone for what was to come.

I have often wondered if Dollsie believed her own fairy tale, or if she just pretended to believe it for our sake. Did she just play the game until she could no longer play it anymore, until she could no longer pretend? I have spent most of my life judging her for leaving Dad for another man and for breaking up the family; making it my mission to make sure that the guilt she carried like a cross too heavy to bear always remained firmly in place.   Now that she's no longer here, now that all that guilt and shame have become irrelevant, I see things differently. I understand how lost and confused she was, and I marvel at her tenacity and strength to keep it all going for as long as she did.

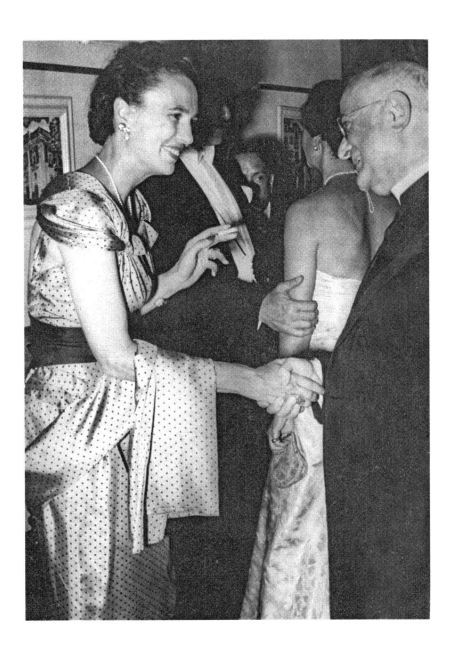

SIX

PASO DOBLE

Mina is in her usual spot when I arrive at La Gottaz, the nursing home where she has chosen to take up residence, leaving the splendid property she had shared with Rolf for the past four decades without a second glance. She is sitting in the reclining chair and looking toward the window as if something in the distance holds her attention. It pains me to see her here, willingly confined to this impersonal room, without any of her belongings or wardrobe or any of her beloved Impressionist paintings that she had amassed after the war, buying them up for next to nothing from cash-starved collectors. She had not wanted to bring anything with her, retreating into a Zen-like renunciation of all things material. How depressing to end up like this, after leading a life so grand in scope, so rich, even if she felt that she somehow wasted it—had "read it away," as she said—letting it go by without ever doing anything important.

Jessamine (which she had later changed to Jasmine upon marrying my grandfather, who thought it sounded too American) had been born in Buffalo on the eve of the First World War, and had spent most of her childhood there. After attending Miss Porter's School, she set sail for Europe aboard the Mauritania with her brother Paul and her cousin Ginger. Mina and Ginger would attend L'Hermitage, a finishing school in Paris, while Paul was sent to Le Rosey.

In 1931, she and Ginger were presented at court to King George and Queen Mary, and soon after, while attending a lunch at Le Rosey, she met Andre, my grandfather, a dashing and refined man from a prominent family in Geneva which had been around almost since the days of Calvin. They, too, had once been wealthy, but nothing compared to the Schoellkopfs, whose fortune was relatively new and derived from the mighty Niagara Falls (or the *Creek*, as they referred to it), which Mina's grandfather had been the first to harness into hydroelectric power. Mina knew right away that she would marry Andre, but her father needed some convincing. His forebears having left Germany to become prosperous in America, he was reluctant to allow his daughter to move back to the Continent to marry someone who, by all appearances, would not be able to take care of her in the manner to which she was accustomed. But he eventually relented and consented to the marriage, and at the age of nineteen, she left Buffalo for good without a backward glance.

Andre had turned out to be a difficult husband, exacting and critical and domineering, a perfectionist who never quite reached his goal, but Mina had enjoyed her life as a diplomat's wife, in Paris, Washington, and Cairo, where Andre had been appointed Swiss Ambassador. King Farouk still ruled, and the lavish lifestyle was like nothing Mina had ever experienced—the immense palaces, the multitude of servants, the exquisite entertaining, the exotic sights, the refinement and generosity. Buffalo had seemed far, far away, and until the end of her days, she would look back on her years in Egypt as the happiest time of her life.

And then, at the age of fifty-three, Andre had died of peritonitis. Mina suddenly found herself alone for the first time in her life, a widow in her mid-forties with a son in college and the means and freedom to do whatever she wished. Her mother and brother had encouraged her to return to Buffalo, but after all her years abroad, she knew that going back to that provincial life was not an option. She opted for Paris, a city which she had always found magnificent, but surely never more joyous and carefree than during the fifties, post-war.

During our outings, I would often ask her about her years as a merry widow in Paris, which had remained a mystery, the one chapter of her life she would never discuss with anyone. She would just smile evasively and shift the conversation back to me, asking me about my life in Paris, living vicariously as I entertained her with my latest stories, perhaps remembering that brief period of her life where she, too, had felt free, unencumbered by husbands or family.

After seven years in Paris, Mina decided that it was time to marry again, to regain some stability and purpose. She had met Rolf during her time in Cairo, and had reconnected with him when she rented his home one summer. Soon after, without much thought, she consented to marry him. They had shared the same bed for three weeks, after which she had kicked him out because he snored too much. That set the tenor for the rest of the marriage, which she often referred to as a "forty-year mistake."

Whereas Rolf had always been petrified of old people, illness, and death, Mina saw the end as a blessed relief. She feared that she would last and last and last, becoming increasingly impatient and frustrated and—for the first time in her life—bitter as she witnessed the daily decline of all her faculties, the slow renunciation of the independence and autonomy which she had always treasured above all else.

"Welcome to the *mortuaire*," she says by way of greeting. As I predicted, she is more upset by my tardiness and preoccupied with Dollsie than with anything having to do with Rolf's death. She is agitated about having to plan the funeral, and tells me she cannot bear the thought of "all those people" (by which she means his daughter, her husband and the devoted staff of Mimorey who had tended to them for almost half a century) attending the service. Even in death, she does not want to give him more attention than she feels he deserves.

After making sure that Walt is okay—tied up to a tree in the shade, with a bowl of water—I help Mina into her wheelchair and roll her down to the dining room, the small one off of the main *salle à manger* where the rest of the "inmates"—as she refers to them—eat. Mina prefers the smaller salon, where she can avoid having to run into anyone she knows—like "that awful Prince Georgie", Dollsie's ex-lover. She appreciates the irony of ending up in the same home as the man who had married her best friend's daughter and then had proceeded to help ruin her son's marriage.

Now that her eyesight and hearing are almost gone, she doesn't much see the point in saying hello to anybody, whether she knows them or not. Privacy is paramount. For Mina, who has always taken pride in her beautiful manners and impeccable social skills, being courteous in her present circumstances means ignoring those around her, pretending that she is too blind to see who is at the next table, and too deaf to hear their greeting. As we enter the room, I exchange a "*bonjour monsieur, bonjour madame*," with those at the neighboring tables.

"Who on earth are you saying hello to?" Mina asks me, with her characteristic mixture of curiosity and impatience.

We speak to each other in English, as we always have (despite having been married to two Swiss men and having spent the vast majority of her long life in Europe, she still sounds very much American, her accent a mixture of her native Buffalo twang and her mother's aristocratic southern drawl). Because she is hard of hearing, she speaks extra loudly, while the others in the small, intimate salon eat in silence, trying to ignore the conspicuous American snob who never says hello to anyone. They all maintain the same implacable facade, staring stonily at their plates.

I, too, try to remain implacable, unfazed by her appearance, which has deteriorated further since the last time I saw her a few months ago. Mina, the most elegant lady I have ever met, always perfectly coiffed and stylishly dressed in the latest Paris fashions, has let herself go. Besides the obligatory daily toilette performed by the attendants, and the weekly visit from the coiffeuse, it is clear that she just doesn't care anymore, and knowing Mina like I do, it makes me sad.

True to form, after waiting impatiently for the waiter to take our order, Mina starts right off by lecturing me about going to Gstaad.

"I know that you and your mother have had your difficulties over the years— Lord knows she is not an easy woman—but I'm very worried about this problem she is having and your place is by her side."

That closes the topic as far as she is concerned, and we spend the rest of lunch just trying to get through it. I watch her eat her meal with difficulty: the hearing aids in both ears; the shaking hand struggling to get small bites from the plate to her mouth; the embarrassment she no doubt feels by having me witness her declining faculties. I think back on our escapades to London, staying in swanky hotels like Claridge's and Duke's and cramming as many plays, restaurants, museums, and shops as we could into a weekend, connecting in ways that went far beyond grandmother and grandson, exchanging revelations about our lives and relationships that we had never shared with anyone else in the family. How we savored those moments, just the two of us, both of us feeling as if we were escaping from our lives, the dullness of hers, the perpetual chaos of mine.

After wheeling her back to her room and settling her back into her easy chair, I reluctantly set off for Gstaad, with Walt sitting next to me, forever patient, never questioning the unpredictability of his days and the long journeys. We should be there by four, at the latest, if I manage to not get lost, as I tend to do on my annual treks to Gstaad (despite the fact that I have been traveling the same route since the age of six). My classic Freudian slip, my gift to Dollsie:

by missing the exit for Bern—the same damn one every time—I end up lost somewhere in the canton of Fribourg, thus delaying my arrival and shortening the already all-too-brief forty-eight hours I had planned on spending with her.

The last time had been just a few weeks earlier, when I had gone to spend her sixty-fifth birthday with her and Greasy, her mother, who was visiting from Miami. I usually avoided going to Gstaad for these occasions. Dollsie invariably got smashed and spent the evening telling one and all about how sad it was that she had to throw herself her own party, and how grateful she was that at least one of her four children had bothered to show up. But I figured it would be a good way of killing two birds with one stone—always my strategy of choice when dealing with family. I would get to see Greasy, and I wouldn't have to spend too much time alone with Dollsie (though with her, you never had to worry about being alone together for long: she needed a lot of people around her, to feel alive).

I hadn't noticed anything wrong with her then, and much to my surprise, she was not drinking. In retrospect, that should have been a sign that something was up, but at the time I was just relieved that there would be no awkward moments, especially after what had happened the previous summer in Saint Tropez, when another drunken incident in a restaurant in front of my friends had led to another explosion on my part, followed by another year of non-communication (the script was sickeningly familiar by now).

I knew that it was an effort for her not to drink in front of me, and she did so with only the slightest hint of resentment. I was grateful to her for staying sober. I would not have to spend the weekend counting how many drinks she consumed, as I had been doing since the age of fifteen, which only made her drink more, out of defiance and denial. The visit had been almost pleasant, which was the most I could hope for when I was around her. No incidents, no rage, no drunken conversations, no bitter regrets.

I manage not to get lost this time, having mapped out the route as an extra precaution. The day is crystal clear, soothing to the soul. Switzerland, too, is experiencing the heat wave, but from inside the car, with the cool, inviting lake and the snow-covered mountain peaks shimmering in the distance, it's easy to forget. As I drive, I listen to Wayne Dyer, my pop-psychology "guru", reciting his guided meditation on tape, "The Power of Intention." I had attended a seminar with him a few years earlier at a spa in Arizona, and had felt it to be life-transforming, at least for a while. I haven't yet perfected the art of meditation—and I'm not sure that Wayne would advise putting it into practice on the highway—but I figure it might help clear my mind of all the bullshit and prepare me for Dollsie. My *intention*, I resolve, is to focus on staying calm when I see her, and to show support instead of engaging in our usual passive-aggressive paso doble. I will not regress like I always do and slip into what one of my therapists in California had labeled the "blame-shame-and-complain" cycle that dysfunctional families revel in. I would "stay chill" and not let her get to me.

I find my way to the clinic in Zweisimmen, a village about twenty minutes away from Gstaad. I pull into the parking lot and let Walt out to run around for a few minutes before finding another shady tree for him. I figure I won't be long; I will just pop in to say hello and make sure everything is okay, then use the dog as an excuse to head to the chalet for the night. I've been so focused on my own "process" that the possibility that she might actually be seriously ill hasn't occurred to me.

After smoking a cigarette, I walk into the clinic which seems deserted in the off-season—empty of the skiing accidents that usually fill its halls. I stop to ask for directions at the reception, and as I approach her room at the end of a long corridor, I can hear her familiar voice chatting away on the phone, and I pause to listen before entering, both irritated and relieved to hear her sounding completely normal.

SEVEN

MISS DOLORES

"Anyway," as she is explaining to whoever is on the other end as I enter the room, "yesterday, a few hours before the party, as I was doing my rounds, checking up on everything at the last minute, I suddenly felt deathly ill. The people at the florist kept asking me if I was okay. 'Yes, I'm fine,' I told them. As you know, Hanya, I'm not one to dwell on physical symptoms. And I wasn't about to let anything get in the way of the party. So after the florist, I headed to the gym for my Pilates class—with that gorgeous Austrian boy teaching it—you know the one, yes, Hans—anyway, I'm changing and I suddenly feel as if I'm about to pass out cold right there in the ladies' locker room of the Belvedere Spa. Just like Pamela Harriman when she croaked in the pool of the Ritz in Paris. I felt this sharp, stabbing pain in my upper abdomen, where I suppose the blockage is. The kind of pain you can't ignore no matter how hard you try. The kind that literally takes your breath away. So I sat myself down on the bench and waited for it to pass, trying to take deep breaths, which only made it worse. Finally, I felt well enough to put my other clothes back on, realizing that there was no way on earth that I was going to be able to take that class, sexy Austrian or not. As I was putting on my skirt, the pain came again, like a sharp knife."

When I see her, I stop dead in my tracks. She is yellow, just like she said. Yellow all over, not just the eyes. I stand there for moment, registering it all with a frozen smile. Then I walk over to the bed and kiss her on the forehead, something I cannot remember ever having done before. I'm relieved that she is so deep into her conversation that she doesn't end it immediately, not even for my arrival. I'm pretty sure that my expression registers total shock, and I listen to the rest of the monologue in a daze, wondering what the fuck is going on.

"Well, my dear, I barely made it to the car. I thought I was going to croak right then and there. But I did manage to retrieve Sharif from that cute little dog house they have, where you can tie them up while you go work out—so civilized, only in Gstaad—and then somehow got myself to the doctor's office, where I collapsed."

Ordinarily, I would have followed the one-sided conversation with a mixture of amusement and irritation. If I had not been standing beside her, trying not to stare at her yellowness, I would have thought that she was just spinning another one of her dramatic productions; a heroic life-and-death tale starring the world's greatest narcissist as she attempts to attend the party against all odds. A Cuban version of Virginia Woolf's *Mrs. Dalloway*, Dollsie lived for her parties. But this time, maybe for the first time in my life, I believe every word she says.

"And that nice Dr. Rudi—So handsome, isn't he?—Not the brightest bulb in the patch but what can you expect—this is, after all, a small mountain village, no matter what anyone says, and everyone just goes to Geneva or Lausanne when anything serious goes wrong—which is exactly what I should have done, given the dump I've landed in—not a staff person in sight, Hanya. Anyway, he takes one look at me and says, in that divine accent, 'Now, Miss Dolores'—don't you love it?—'Miss Dolores you are *wery, wery* ill und you must go to the hospital at *vonce*.'

"'But Herr Doctor,' I say, 'that is just not possible! I must attend my party this evening at the Palace! I have been planning it for six months! And there are very important—*sehr importante*—people coming from all Europe to attend it! I must be there! Give me a shot or something to get me through it and I promise that I will check into the hospital in the morning, or even right after the party, if you insist.'

"Well, Hanya, he wouldn't hear a word of it. He insisted that I was critically ill and that my life was in danger and this and that and the other—very dramatic—you know how these people can be—and told me that I must get to the clinic at once. Before you know it, they appear with an ambulance to cart me off like I'm dying or something. I was furious! I tried to insist that it wasn't that bad, but you know how stubborn the Swiss can be—after all, we both married Swiss men the first time around—you know how they are. Just impossible!"

She looks over in my direction while feigning surprise, as if she is just noticing me there for the first time.

"Sergei! My darling! You came! I'll be right with you, Sergei. Yes, Sergei just arrived. Can you believe it? So soon after his last visit? I'm simply thrilled, and so touched," she says, as if it had been my idea. "Thank God my wonderful sons are coming to the rescue. He just arrived from Paris, yes. After going to your granddaughter's baptism in the Perigord or something. Oh, you didn't know about it? Your own daughter didn't invite you to her daughter's baptism? How awful for you. I'm sorry Hanya, I had no idea. Well yes, I know, but that's how they are these days, aren't they? I'm so sorry for mentioning it. Me and my big mouth. Anyway, he came to be with his grandmother Jasmine for Rolf's funeral and I begged him not to interrupt his plans to come see me, but he told me in no uncertain terms that he would not take no for an answer, that his place was by his mother. Yes I know; I am fortunate."

As always, I marvel at her ability to tell a bold faced lie about somebody with that person sitting right there in the room. No shame. It's one of the things that drive me crazy about her, but that I also kind of admire and emulate: her ability to create her own reality.

"Now," she continues after pausing to smile in my direction and motioning me to sit down, "enough of all this nonsense. I'm sure that I'm fine. If I don't catch herpes in this place. Disgusting. Now tell me everything! How were the flowers? And the food? Did Hernst do a good job? Did Empress Farah show up? She did?? How marvelous! I knew that the event would be a smash! I just knew it. Did she buy anything? Did Frédéric sell a lot at the party? I hope he doesn't think that just because I could croak any minute, that I'm not going to claim my commission! After all, I put that boy on the map."

She goes on like this for a while longer, absorbing every detail of the party. I can tell that the pain is intense and coming at regular intervals, like a punch, taking her breath away. I do not hear the rest of the conversation. I am stuck on the word "sons". I have not spoken to Anton in eight years, after another big fall out, but have heard that he is summering in Italy with his family. My younger brother, Dimitri, is in New York. Who is Dollsie referring to?

Although it had been her mission in life to show others how much her four children loved her and how devoted we were—a testament to the "sacrifices" she has made—deep down, she believed that she had ultimately failed as a mother, that she had wrecked our lives with her narcissism and her volatility and her rage and her drinking, the way her father had wrecked hers. The last twenty years had been one long campaign to salvage her reputation, both in the eyes of her children and the world at large. I wonder how much of her own P.R. she actually bought; whether deep down, she really did believe that she had been a good mother, a loving mother, despite everything.

But the one thing that Dollsie had always been certain of, and that she had imparted to us with fierce conviction from the day we were born, was that neither she, nor her ancestors, nor we, were in any way ordinary. She would often remind us of our aristocratic roots and her Spanish title (she claimed she was a Duchess) and our illustrious ancestors, grandees of Spain appointed by Isabella and Ferdinand to represent them in the New World as the first viceroys of Peru. These were the tales we were told at bedtime; like most Cuban families, ours had no shortage of myths.

Thus we heard endless stories about Fico, her grandfather, the son of a Spanish immigrant who had made a fortune in sugar and become a senator and one of the most powerful men in Cuba (according to Dollsie). How he and her grandmother Lolita would take her away from her parents every summer and whisk her off to Europe for three months, for the Grand Tour, along with the maid, the chauffeur, and traveling by separate accommodations, Fico's mistress.

Finally, she ends her conversation, and it's my turn. By now, I'm certain that Anton is on his way. I had vowed never to see him again, and for the past eight years, all of Dollsie's efforts to sabotage my resolve had failed. But she has finally manipulated me into seeing him, using this gallstone thing to guilt-trip us both into showing up without telling either one of us about the other. Classic Dollsie. I consider walking out of the room, getting in my car, and driving back to Geneva. But of course it's too late for that. Too late to leave. I feel trapped.

For a moment, she is off the phone, her attention focused on me. "I am so sorry. So sorry for all of this." It would become her mantra over the next ten months. Over and over. I am so sorry for everything.

The phone rings again, allowing us both to escape the moment. As she picks up, she gives me quick instructions for the trip the next day: what time I have to be at the clinic, what to tell the maid, what to do with her dogs Sharif and Czarina, and what I should pack for her day trip to Bern.

"We will be home by evening," she assures me again, "and you will be able to join Mina the day after, just in time for the funeral. If I feel well enough, I might join you!" she adds. I mutter something in response, trying to sound upbeat and positive.

"I am so sorry!" she says again, as she takes the call and I rise to head out, "I feel so guilty that you had to interrupt your summer to come all this way," she tells me in her classic stage whisper, obviously more for the benefit of whoever is calling than for mine.

Driving to the chalet, I realize that we are both in drama mode, which is par for the course when we are together, and which allows us to slip back into famil-iar territory so as to escape the scary and unfamiliar situation at hand: Dollsie is sick. Very sick. Her eyes and skin are yellow and she is in pain and her suf-fering is audible, a sharp, smothered sound that she emits every time she pauses to catch her breath. A sound that I have never heard before. She no longer reminds me of Ingrid Bergman or Lauren Bacall or Sophia Loren or Grace Kelly or Catherine Deneuve or any of the other glamorous dames of her generation with whom she had been compared and claimed kinship throughout her life. Without the make-up—"the face," as she calls it—and with the yellow eyes and complexion, her features contorted in pain and fear, she looks just like any other ordinary, frightened old lady. What a concept. I'm stunned.

EIGHT

CHALET ALBOSCO

I walk around in the dark, searching for a cigarette. The chalet smells like Dollsie, an overpowering scent, invasive, demanding attention. Despite its various occupants, the place hasn't changed much in the past thirty years. A mixture of traditional Swiss bucolic and mod-seventies decor. Dollsie's cows are everywhere: on the walls, on plates, glasses, mugs, napkins, towels, sheets, ashtrays, pitchers, salt-and-pepper shakers, butter trays, marmalade jars, vases, napkins, on table cloths and on the welcome mat... Cows on every surface and in every room. Dollsie had been obsessed with cows since the day we had moved to Switzerland, referring to them as her "girls". She loved their big dumb gaze and their heavy, leather cowbells decorated with alpine flowers, their imperturbability and placidity. When she ventured forth into a pasture to greet them, it reminded her of her childhood and the summers spent at her grandfather's cattle ranches in Cuba.

I climb the stairs up to Dollsie's room on the top floor to collect her things for the next morning. Once again, I marvel at her capacity to transport her entire life from Miami to Switzerland every summer, and then back again. So much stuff—clothes, make up, shoes, papers, jewelry, beauty products—and yet she manages to "contain the multitudes" in three average-sized wooden closets. Nothing about Dollsie is average-sized, but like everybody else who left Cuba in the diaspora brought on by Castro, she has learned to adapt.

Dollsie and Dad had found the chalet shortly after we moved to Switzerland.

It stood at the top of a hill overlooking the town, right down the road from Le Rosey, which moved to Gstaad in winter so that its students could master skiing and cultivate the après-ski life of their parents. It had just been built, and the owners let us choose the name: Chalet Albosco—The chalet in the woods—a Cubanized version of our last name. Dollsie and Nan and I installed ourselves there each winter—from December through Easter—and Dad drove up on weekends to join us.

I attended the village school, along with the locals children and the children of celebrities who had homes in Gstaad—people like Elizabeth Taylor and David Niven and Roger Moore. Even at that age, I was starstruck and somewhat jealous when these famous parents would come to pick up their fortunate offspring.

In the mornings we would attend class, and in the afternoons, weather permitting, we would hit the slopes of the Wassengrat, the Wispielen and the Eggli, the mountains encircling Gstaad. There I discovered the exhilarating feeling of riding to the top of the mountain on the chair lifts, then losing myself on the way down, confident of the terrain, fearless enough to sail over the jumps, arms outstretched, eyes closed. I was not afraid to fall in those days, and if I hurt myself, which I invariably did at least once a season, twisting a knee or an ankle, it was the price to be paid for this freedom, and the attention it afforded me made me feel special, almost heroic. I was proud of my recklessness, which I saw as fearlessness. Gstaad was the kind of place where no matter what you did, no matter what happened in the confusing and chaotic world of our parents and their friends, one always felt safe. Safer than I have felt anywhere ever since.

And free. I had never felt so free.

But more than anything else, it was the ski instructors that caught my attention. They were so handsome and radiant, and I loved to watch them in motion, their hard bodies gliding gracefully down the hill, so effortless, no matter how steep the slope or how rough the conditions. They were so brave, so fearless. I wanted to be just like them.

High atop a hill and dominating the village stood the Palace Hotel, a Disney-like castle with tall turrets and grand salons. The indoor swimming pool was covered at night and converted into the dance floor of its infamous discotheque, Le Greengo, Gstaad's version of Studio 54. When it wasn't too cold, Dollsie would take us skating and then to Charlie's Tea House, overlooking the rink, for *goûter*, which consisted of pastries and a huge, delicious mug of steaming hot Ovaltine. On weekends, I would hit the slopes with Dad and Anton, and Dollsie would take the chair lift up the Wassengrat to meet us for lunch at the Eagle Club, a members-only ski lodge that was the epicenter of Gstaad's social life. She had attempted to learn to ski, taking private lessons with an old instructor favored by her set named Rudi, but after spending entire afternoons descending a mountain which took most people twenty minutes, she had abandoned her efforts. But that would not stop her from missing out on the Eagle, where everybody who was anybody gathered every day for lunch. After a long leisurely meal, she would take the lift back down while the rest of us set out on our afternoon runs. Anton would often take off on his own, while Dad would patiently make his way down the slope with me close behind. Then we would take a T-bar or a chairlift back up the hill for another run or two or three, not wanting the afternoon to end. I loved these rare, precious moments alone with Dad.

In the evenings, the chalet would be bustling with guests and cocktail parties and buffet dinners for twenty or thirty. I would wait by my bedroom window, wondering who would show up. It all seemed impossibly glamorous and elegant to my eyes; these young beautiful grownups from all over the world, some of them famous, living in cozy intimacy in this beautiful little town in the mountains. I couldn't wait to grow up and become one of them.

For my birthday, we would go on horse-drawn sleigh rides through the mountains, then for cheese fondue at the Olden, Dollsie's favorite restaurant. Six weeks later, as spring approached and the ski season drew to a close, we would pack up our things and head back to Vincy to finish out the school year in the village school. It was a surreal existence, this fairy tale that Dollsie had created for us.

Thirty-four years later, as I amble through the dark looking for a cigarette, it all still feels so familiar. Although little has changed in the chalet, everything else had, and part of me still resents Dollsie for making us leave all this. I had never accepted the idea of her moving back into the chalet after the end of her second marriage, acting as if nothing had happened, as if she could pick up where she had left off. I have visited Gstaad as little as possible since then; never yielding an inch, stubbornly refusing to give her the satisfaction of allowing that any of it might ever be reclaimable.

Dollsie, in turn, lamented my stubbornness, my adamant refusal to never let anything go, to never "give her a break." She was not trying to reclaim the past, she insisted, she was just grateful to be back in the place where she, too, had been happy and young and beautiful. At her zenith, with a handsome banker for a husband as tranquil and safe as the mountains that surrounded us, beloved by all, before she had given it all up *for that man.*

"The biggest mistake of my life."

Still, as I wander around the chalet in the dark, without the distraction of Dollsie's presence, I have to admit that it does still feel like home. The place seems eerily quiet without her—no phones ringing, no loud voice barking out orders at the Filipino maid—with only Walt and Dollsie's cows to keep me company. They are everywhere, inside the chalet and out in the pastures and on the mountains, grazing and gazing into the dark, quiet summer night. Dollsie would be pleased.

I go to bed, the same bed where, at the age of seven, I had found Dollsie astride Dad, after walking in on them early one morning. "You should have knocked!" I was told sternly, after which they both avoided talking to me for several days.

It was also the bed where Nan and I had watched Dollsie spread her legs and playfully invite her miniature greyhound to pleasure her, as if it were a game, enjoying the sensation and laughing at our bewildered expressions as we stood there, transfixed. It had happened more than once and over the years, I had spent many hours with therapists (secretly enjoying their looks of suppressed shock as I described the scene) trying to figure out why; why anyone would find it amusing to do that in front of her kids. It seemed so reckless. What had she been thinking?

I lie down, feeling overwhelmed by the past. As if time has stood still, as if, after all these years, I still haven't been able to move on. Walt waits by the bed until I help him up, heaving his front legs onto the mattress, then the hind ones. I am glad to have him here with me, taking up most of the bed, filling the emptiness. He just sits there, looking at me impassively in the moonlight. Chill out, he seems to be telling me, with those big, deep eyes that penetrate my soul.

NINE

LIVING OR LEAVING

The next morning, I gather Dollsie's things: the make-up—which she has itemized for me lest I forget something vital—a change of clothes, her industrial-size personal phone books (one for each continent), and some cash for the tips she likes to distribute to one and all with great benevolence. I manage to avoid her houseguest Frederic, the French jeweler, who is staying at the house. I haven't slept much, and the day promises to be a long one. But with any luck I will be out of there and back in Morges near Mina by nightfall.

Accompanied by Walt, I descend the brick path that leads down to the village for breakfast at the Rosti, where I can check my emails while having my usual Swiss breakfast: orange pressé, café au lait and a croissant. The day is glorious, refreshingly cool, a welcome surprise, the morning mist rising over the mountains.

After dropping Walt back off at the chalet, I set off for the clinic, trying to prepare myself for the long day ahead. Dollsie will be in full Dollsie mode, highly agitated and driving everyone crazy with her incessant demands and questions and her impatience; her modus operandi, especially when she is nervous or afraid. Although we have been assured that the procedure is a minor one, with no likelihood of complications, I know from experience that whenever Dollsie is involved, escalation is bound occur. She will be at her most imperious, doing everything she can to get the attention and special treatment to which she feels entitled, and usually receives, through sheer force of will.

As I enter her room, I find her on the phone again, telling the same story, as if she has been engaged in the same conversation since I left the previous evening. She is even more yellow today, which I didn't think was possible, and she looks very tired, worn down by the pain. I can tell that she is talking to him. She pushes the phone at me and I take it, resisting the temptation to just hang up on him. The conversation is brief. I tell him that she is okay and that I am on top of things, in the vain hope that he might decide to postpone his trip or cancel it altogether. Obviously the wrong tactic: he is the firstborn—as I have been reminded all my life—and as such, he is the *jefe de familia*; as a Latin male (which he very much considers himself to be, despite the fact that we are only a quarter Cuban) it is his role to be the one in charge in times of crisis. He responds coolly that even though he does not doubt my ability to handle the situation (I wonder how much sarcasm I am supposed to read into this), he is planning on being there, "in case anything goes wrong."

As they prepare Dollsie for the trip to Bern, I go looking for the doctor on call. I want to know how they have arrived at the conclusion that it is a gallstone and not something else. The night before, I had managed to track down my friend Ashley, a surgeon, who was on a bicycle trip through the Dordogne.

"Make sure they do an ultrasound before they remove the stone," she advised in her sing-songy voice, sounding more like a southern belle than a Boston surgeon. "Based on what you've told me, I don't see how they can be so sure about their diagnosis. I mean, they are probably right, but it could be a number of things. And if it isn't a stone, they need to find out before they go in there, so that they are prepared. Otherwise they could have a big problem on their hands."

But try telling that to a Swiss doctor. When I find him and voice my concerns, he assures me icily that yes, they are certain of their diagnosis, and that no further exams are needed. The procedure is an easy and quick one, and if there are any complications, they will be minor and due to the fact that she has waited so long to have this taken care of. The jaundice is entirely normal, given the circumstances. He seems eager to send us on our way. Dollsie has evidently been up for hours, driving everyone nuts.

We set off for Bern at nine on the dot, with me following the ambulance in my car, navigating the unfamiliar, winding mountain roads and paying extra attention not to get too close to the edge. Being somewhat absent-minded, especially behind the wheel, I have visions of missing a turn and plunging into some ravine.

As we arrive at the hospital in Bern, the ambulance pulls into the emergency entrance, and I drive around looking for a parking spot. After wandering the halls of the hospital, attempting to decipher the signs written in Swiss German, I find Dollsie in the waiting room of the day clinic, an open space with a dozen beds for people who are either awaiting or recovering from outpatient procedures. She has just been told that there will be a small delay. In the meantime they will get her settled in and run some tests. Dollsie requests a private room in case something goes wrong. A doctor is summoned. She asks when she will be operated on. I ask about the ultrasound. Dollsie repeats her request for a bed and a private room. The doctor replies that this is a teaching hospital (meaning, I gather, that we shouldn't expect any comfort or special treatment), that he doesn't know when the procedure will take place, that he cannot guarantee a room because a room will not be necessary, and that an ultrasound is not necessary either as the tests have already confirmed the nature of the problem. With that, he walks away before Dollsie can press her case. It is going to be one of those days; Dollsie is not accustomed to the word no.

We settle in, and Dollsie tries to keep busy and distract herself from the pain by heading out into the corridor to make more calls about the party, after being told that she cannot make them in the waiting room. She wants more details: who had come, who hadn't, which pieces of jewelry had sold, who had bought them, how much had been made, had the Palace been paid, had they given her a break on the bill... and on and on. In between calls she heads out to the courtyard, still dressed in her street clothes, to smoke. Then back to the nurse's desk to get an update on the surgery and to request a room. Every time a new staff member appears, she presses on with her campaign. Most of the nurses and attendants are Swiss German and do not speak French, which she chooses to ignore. She cannot fathom a Swiss person not speaking French, and despite all her summers spent in Gstaad, she has never bothered to learn the local language. I can't blame her; neither have I. German is not the most attractive language in the world and the Swiss German dialect is worse, even more guttural.

The hours wear on. Wishing that I had a joint that I could sneak out and smoke, I read my *New Yorker*, and watch the other patients, the doctors and nurses coming and going. Ever since my first extended stay in a hospital at the age of twelve while awaiting back surgery, I have been fascinated by hospitals. They remind me that I'm still alive, and that no matter what, that's a good thing.

As anticipated, the endless wait is turning into a major ordeal. The more agitated Dollsie becomes—fear and pain and anxiety and impatience slowly but inexorably precipitating her toward one of her eruptions—the more I distance myself, retreating into this other world of other people whose lives have also been turned upside down at a moment's notice. Their suffering, I can manage. As a psychotherapist who specializes in HIV and other health issues, I have been doing it for years. I can feel empathy and compassion for them, without reserve or fear of consequence. But Dollsie's world, I know from experience, I cannot manage. As she becomes increasingly worked up, I sit there, impassive, retreating into therapist mode.

She has never had much tolerance for being made to wait, and what with the pain and exhaustion, not to mention all the meds that have been withheld—the anti-depressants and tranquilizers that she has been ingesting for years—she has crossed the threshold and is rapidly progressing to a state of full-on hysteria. I can see the storm whipping itself into a frenzy, getting ready to unleash its waves of fury and destruction. Like a seasoned survivor of natural calamities, I recognize the signs and know when to run for cover. I feel powerless. All I can do is to keep asking for updates every few minutes, as she requests, and for something to manage her pain (and nerves), which they refuse to give her without the doctor's consent, who—as they explain over and over, their patience wearing thin—is held up in an emergency. No one knows when he might be available again, nor when the procedure might take place.

Anton calls to say that his flight has been delayed. Thank god for small mercies. With any luck, he won't arrive until after it is all over, and I'm on my way.

By mid-afternoon, after being there most of the day, Dollsie finally falls asleep, exhausted, and I slip out for a smoke. I'm beginning to think that the procedure will not happen at all that day, and that since there are apparently no available beds, we will have to schlep back to Zweisimmen, with Dollsie in agony and Anton in tow, and start the whole thing all over again the next day. I load up on caffeine and stroll through the halls of the hospital, peeking into the rooms whose doors are open. It is a quiet hospital, no visible drama here; hushed voices and cleanliness and dignified suffering in silence. No rushing around, no one making demands. No sense of urgency or impending doom.

Clinical. I envy that about the Swiss: their ability to maintain control, to make sure everything always works, just so. Being part Swiss myself, it mystifies me why my life had always felt so out of control, like a cuckoo clock gone haywire. What happened?

Just after five, Anton sweeps in, arms aloft, all two hundred and fifty pounds of him rushing toward her, ready for the big overpowering embrace that he is so proud of and that I have always found suffocating and slightly threatening. The only one of us to be born in Havana, he is in full macho/hero-come-to-the-rescue mode.

"Don't worry, Mumsy, I'm here now," he says, as he envelops her. The word Mumsy makes me want to puke. I marvel at their physical intimacy, so alien to me, and feel slightly repelled by it.

Dollsie gives Anton a blow-by-blow of all the indignities and ills she has suffered throughout the day, and her powerlessness—and by implication, my incompetence—to get anything done. And then things start happening: Anton explodes, Cuban style, his voice escalating, his large body trembling. A doctor is summoned, and before we know it, she is finally prepared for the surgical procedure, leaving them both feeling triumphant. That is how you take care of business. He has made it happen.

As she is taken away on the stretcher, she gives me a perfunctory squeeze and peck on the cheek, while I just smile at her, thinking to myself, "wheel faster!" And then she and Anton clutch each other again in some sort of Farewell Forever Embrace, right out of *General Hospital*. Dollsie, who has been crying since Anton arrived, lets out one final long drawn-out sob, knowing that she can finally let go, that at least one person in this uptight Swiss hospital can handle her wails of pain, her raw emotions and building hysteria.

Up until now, Anton and I have said no more than "hello" to each other, in the most civil of tones, with that perma-grin that is basically code in the family for "fuck you". After Dollsie goes into the operating room, he spends a good while on the phone—like mother, like son—checking in on his wife and his daughter, whom I've never met. It is so strange to be in this room with him after eight years. I observe him as he chats away and feel myself rapidly regressing to adolescence, wanting to run away from them both and seek shelter.

I can't think of anyone to phone except Giovanni, so I call him and that lasts about five minutes. He's a sweet kid but I've never had much to say to him and

I'm not much in the mood for phone chat anyway. Fortunately, I still have another *New Yorker*, as well as Wayne Dyer's latest book, *Manifesting Your Destiny*. I never go anywhere without something to read—my way of dealing with my own lack of patience—but if I whip out the book right away, Anton will take offense, thinking I am being hostile or something. Acute sensitivity to perceived slights, bordering on paranoia, is another family trait we all share. Beneath the arrogance and sense of entitlement, we are all as delicate as hothouse orchids. We are very good at picking up on signals, real or imagined. As Wayne Dyer says, we go through life looking for occasions to be offended.

I check my watch for the hundredth time that day: six p.m. She should be done in a few minutes, thank fucking God. And Anton is still on the phone, which is just fine with me. A young, ruddy doctor who looks like he has just gotten back from a long hike in the mountains comes in to give us an update.

"How did it go?" barks Anton, sounding more like he is making a demand than asking a question.

The man in scrubs turns out to not be the doctor, just a resident or something coming to tell us that they have not begun the procedure yet. They are still "preparing."

"Is there a problem?" I ask.

"Not at all," he replies with that congeniality that is supposed to pass for reassurance. "Everything is in order."

He disappears before we can ask anything else.

Anton settles into the couch facing mine in the waiting room. I fight the urge to giggle, a habit of mine when things get weird. Talk about small talk. What do you say to the brother you haven't laid eyes on in eight years, during which time you have been at war nonetheless, exchanging letters and emails and faxes, each carefully crafted to hurt, insult, offend, gain the upper hand, followed by short periods of truce-like silence. I had planned on only seeing him again at the obligatory family weddings and funerals. I resist the urge to ask myself if this might be one those occasions. Don't be a drama queen, I tell myself, don't go there.

I take a long, good look at him, noting with satisfaction that the St. Paul's squash champion whom all the girls had lined up to hug and kiss goodbye at graduation, and whom Dollsie had always held up to me as an example of everything I wasn't —the stud, the athlete, the popular one—is no more. Dollsie had always played us off each other, either out of a Kennedy-like desire to see us compete and conquer, or because she could wield more control that way. She had raised us in her own image, and had never been able to accept how that image looked when it was reflected back to her. The curse of the narcissist parent. Like the queen in Snow White asking her mirror who is the fairest of them all, Dollsie asked the question through her children, especially Anton. We were her mirror, and when she didn't like the answer we gave her—when we were less than perfect, fat, disrespectful, lazy, unpopular, clumsy, and spoiled—she made us feel her wrath. No matter how much she claimed to love us, and she did, it felt very conditional, entirely dependent on how we reflected her in all her incarnations.

I had feared Anton for the first ten years of my life, and except for a period of co-habitation at the family spread in Pebble Beach, had pretty much avoided him ever since. Like Dollsie, he occupied too much space and brought too much *sturm und drang* to my life. Now, he just seems like a tired, overweight, defeated businessman going through life like everyone else, just trying to make it all happen. He looks as ordinary as Dollsie in her hospital bed in Zweisimmen, and just as unthreatening. Like two old warriors who have been worn down by life's battles, neither seems invincible, nor larger than life. They seem all too human.

Anton is the one who finally breaks the ice.

"I heard about your plans to adopt a baby," he says. "That's great news! Soraya and I are also adopting a kid. A beautiful little girl we found in Guatemala."

By this point, I am wiped out. The last thing I want to talk about is the adoption process, which I am just beginning and which feels totally overwhelming. And being his mother's son, I know that he will just turn this into a drawn-out, dramatic story starring his heroic self. I am in no mood. But at least it's a safe topic. I tell him about the agency that has agreed to take me on and placed me on a waiting list, a process that will take roughly eighteen months, with lots of administrative hurdles and paperwork along the way. He nods with vague interest, and then jumps in to tell me about how he and his wife had gone about finding a kid in Guatemala.

"We wanted a girl, and we wanted her to be Latin, so she would look like us, and we wanted her to be a year or two younger than Anna, so she can can have a little sister."

"Cool," I say, resisting the urge to add: "A designer baby! Just like homos do!"

The adoption topic has run its course. I look at my watch again. It is getting late. Another hour has gone by. The procedure should be over by now. The halls are starting to quiet down, and the waiting room is almost empty. Anton is getting ready to hit the phone again. I walk down the hall to the operating room to try to find out what is going on. I wait in front of the swinging doors, and after a few minutes, someone comes through them and walks past me in a nervous rush. I attempt to intercept him, but the man doesn't speak French, or pretends not to. He just keeps going, looking preoccupied.

After waiting for him to come back, I return to the waiting room.

"I think there's a problem," I tell Anton.

"Why's that?" he asks, in business mode.

"Because what was originally supposed to be a simple twenty-minute intervention has now morphed into a two hour procedure. Something is up."

"Maybe they were just late getting started."

"Yeah," I say. "Maybe."

After another thirty minutes or so, the doctor finally emerges. Probably in his late sixties, he looks like he has just been through a major ordeal. His face and neck are covered with red splotches, his hands are shaking, and his scrubs are soaked through with sweat. How weird, I think to myself; how could a little gallstone be so hard to remove? They had told us that all they had to do was insert some kind of stent and then flush it out. No biggie.

"Hello, I am Herr Professor Steinegger, and ve must talk," he says, speaking in a heavy accent. As he leads us back to the sofa where Anton and I have spent the past two and a half hours, I think to myself, here we go. I have watched enough hospital shows on television to know what that means: nothing good.

"Is something wrong?" I ask. "Is she okay?"

The doctor explains that what they found when they tried to insert the tube to remove the obstruction was not a gall stone, but a much greater mass blocking the passage, almost certainly a tumor. They are not sure of its location, but they suspect that it is an "ampullary tumor", in or near the entrance to the pancreas. In addition, there is a serious infection raging through her body and she is rapidly approaching a state of "sepsis", because of all the stuff that has been backing up due to the blockage. And last but not least, her liver appears to be in the early stages of cirrhosis, whatever that means.

"To summarize," concludes the Professor, "your *mutter* is in *wery* critical condition and at this point *ve* cannot know *vat* her chances are."

"Chances of what?" asks Anton, who by now has lost all semblance of his usual I'm-in-charge composure.

"Of living," answers the doctor. With his accent, it sounds like "leaving", as in leaving the hospital, or leaving this earth. It comes to one and the same: living or leaving. Either way, it's not good news.

I have often wished for and fantasized about Dollsie's disappearance, and now that the moment may actually be at hand, I do not know how I feel, or how to react. It is hard to see past the guilt. Careful what you wish for. Hold on, I want to tell the doctor, back UP! This was supposed to be just a fucking gallstone. She's not supposed to be croaking because she has some damn tumor and because she decided to try to get to a party.

Anton pulls himself together. He has to take charge; it's the only way he can get a handle on this. "So what happens next, Professor?"

"*Vell*, first *ve* must decide *vat* to tell your *mutter*," he replies. "She has been under sedation for a *vile* now, and she *vill* be *vaking* up soon. *Ve* did not anticipate this, of course. Then after *ve* talk to her, you must decide what to do. She must be operated on *wery* soon, there is no question. Unfortunately she is too *veak* to undergo surgery today. The question is whether *ve* can stabilize her so that she can be operated on tomorrow or the next day. And you must decide of course *vhere* you would like that to happen—if she is in good enough shape to be moved. *Vether* you *vood* like us to do the operation here or *vood* prefer to make other arrangements."

"Operated for what exactly?" I ask. If she has a raging infection and a tumor and a liver that has imploded, where do you start?

"*Vell*," he replies, "her only chance at this point is for us to clear the passages by inserting a stent and draining away as much of the excess fluid as *ve* can, in the hope that this *vill* reduce the infection. But that is only the first step. *Vithout* it, *ve* can do nothing. Then, if that is successful and *ve* are able to stabilize her, you *vill* have to decide *vether* to have a surgical procedure known as the 'Whipple'"—which comes out sounding like "*Vipple*"—"*vhere ve* remove most of the pancreas and some of the surrounding organs."

"Pancreas?" I ask, hearing the word again. That sounds bad. I've always heard that pancreatic cancer is the worst kind.

"It is too early to determine, but *ve* think that the tumor is at the entrance of the pancreas. *Ven ve* find out exactly *ver* it is, it *vill* help us determine her chances. But at this point, *ve* cannot determine anything, because of the infection and all the matter that has backed up in her system. If *ve vere* to run the tests now, it *vould* only show confusion."

Anton asks the doctor how much time we have to decide about the surgery, and Herr Professor repeats that he has inserted a temporary stent and that they will insert another one tomorrow morning, "if possible". That gives us at most a day or two to decide. After that, it will be "too late".

"Things do not look good, I am afraid, but *ve vill* not know for sure *vat* the situation is until she manages to fight off the infection, and until *ve* get further results from the biopsy."

"So let me get this straight," says Anton, thinking in power points. "There are three problems: the infection, the tumor, and the liver. Any of the three could be critical at this point."

"Correction," answers the doctor, his accent making the horrifying news sound even more so. "Not 'could be'. All three ARE *wery* critical. I am sorry to insist on this point, but you must know that she is in *wery* serious condition. There is nothing more *ve* can do for today but let her rest and see if the body manages to fight off the infection *mit* the antibiotics, and hopefully the stent *vil* drain some of *vat* has accumulated and she *vil* feel some relief and be able to get some rest tonight. *Ve* have of course reserved a room for her."

We are led to the post-op recovery room, where Dollsie starts to stir. She slowly opens her eyes and looks around. Her drugged gaze pans from Anton to me to the doctor, and back again, in slow-mo, registering the shock and fake calmness in our expressions, the lame attempts to smile reassuringly. She knows that something is up, and that whatever it is, it's not good news.

"What's wrong,' she asks, her voice cracking, "Am I croaking?" She means this to sound like a joke, but the pleading, bewildered look in her eyes betray her panic and fear.

Anton and the doctor attempt to reassure her, launching into a gentle explanation of how there have been "complications". I just stand there, staring at her.

As fucked up as our relationship has always been, it has been relatively free of bullshit, at least from my end. I am not up to the task of pretending that everything is fine. She looks at me, as if waiting for me to give her the real lowdown. I don't know what to say, so I say nothing. She gets it.

"Let's go have a cigarette," she says, "As a matter of fact, I think I'll have two."

TEN

AFRICA AND ENRIQUETA

Dollsie is wheeled to her room—the room they had been so adamant about her not needing—and as soon as she gets there, she asks for her wallet and pulls out twenty francs which she hands to the attendant, pleading with him to take her outside to smoke. The bribe proves too tempting to resist, so down the elevator and out we go, stretcher and tubes and all. Dollsie is back in charge.

The anesthesia has not quite worn off, and she keeps trying to work out the sequence of events, but the only fact which seems crystal clear to her is that the C word has been mentioned and she knows she's fucked. The rest of the doctor's explanation has gone unheard. Anton tried to soften the blow, but once the word tumor was mentioned, there is no going back. From now on, there is Dollsie Before Cancer, and Dollsie After Cancer. The moment feels like a tectonic shift, once of those moments that change all the moments to come, until you run out of moments. Cancer is her new reality, and by extension, ours: mine, and Anton's, and Nan's, and her beloved last-born, Dimitri's, and everyone else in her extended orbit.

For if every family is like a constellation, Dollsie has always been at the dead center of ours: a bright and shining troubled star presiding over all. We bounced around her, keeping a safe enough distance from her fiery light so as not to get singed again, but imagining with great difficulty what the universe would be like without her. I had done whatever I could to keep as far away from her as possible, seeking refuge wherever I could, and now I find myself by her side, plunging into the chaos.

She is at the beginning of a journey that I have already embarked upon. I feel joined with her; I understand what it is to live hard, burn out and self-destruct. To live life too fast. I have faced my own mortality and now it is her turn. I can help her face hers. And perhaps she can help me. I begin to feel like a son again.

Still, it seems incomprehensible, the notion that this woman—so vital, so beautiful, so full of energy and love for life, so manic—could be running out of life.

"How do you feel, Mother?" I ask, once we get back to her room. Anton is out in the hall calling every person he can think of. It is another family trait we all share: coping with calamity by keeping endless lists, lining up task after task after task, creating a semblance of order and a permanent distraction. As for me, like many gay men of my generation who have faced the prospect of death since we started fucking, my way of coping is to turn to sex and drugs. I am beginning to wish I had some of both right about now.

"I feel perfectly fine and everything is going to be fine," she affirms, with all the conviction she can muster in her drug-induced haze, trying desperately to sound like the old Dollsie, the pre-cancer Dollsie.

"Actually, I'm feeling quite peculiar, almost in a pleasant way. Was that morphine they just gave me? I feel a little loopy. Like my Cuban *tias*. Did I ever tell you about my crazy aunts, Africa and Enriqueta?"

She launches into a story that I have heard a hundred times; like so many of her tales of life in Cuba, they have been told so often and so dramatically that they have become accepted family lore whose veracity no one questions, taking on the invincible aura of a Greek myth. This time, I welcome the distraction.

"Africa and Enriqueta were my grandfather Fico's ancient sisters and they lived at the other end of the sugar mill, hidden away in their own *casita*, with the black tatas who had cared for them their entire lives. I wasn't allowed to visit them—or know they even existed—and the only times they were ever seen were during special occasions—birthdays and saints days, Christmas and Easter, and the weddings of course—when they would be made presentable. But I always wanted to see them when they weren't presentable, when they were doing their crazy things and talking their crazy talk, with Enriqueta running around clucking like a chicken and Africa forever sewing her invisible wedding gown.

"And so every week, as soon as I received my allowance, I would use it to bribe Tirso, Nanny's beloved chauffeur, to take me there. I would bring them gifts: cookies that I had stolen from the kitchen when the servants weren't looking, and chocolates from France, and flowers that I had picked myself, and always one of the beautiful dolls that Fico and Nani had collected for me during their trips to Europe in the summer.

"How I loved my Fico!" she rambles on, in her post-anesthesia haze. "Every summer he would take me away from Mother and Father and my brothers and their drab middle class lives. 'You are better than them,' he would tell me. 'You are my princess, my queen.' I have looked all my life for another man who would treat me like that. Your father was like that, minus the *cojones*, of course. If Fico had been alive, I never would have left your father for that creep, Jacques. He would not have allowed it."

"Years later, when Fico was dying, I asked him what had ever happened to Africa and Enriqueta, and how they had gotten their names. He looked at me with uncomprehending eyes. They had disappeared into oblivion. What a sad life."

"That's a beautiful story, Mother," I say, with genuine sincerity, surprised at how deeply the story resonates this time. Anyone who knows Dollsie knew to take these childhood tales—and all her other stories, for that matter—with a huge grain of salt. But the facts are beside the point; in her morphine-induced altered state, she has found new meaning in this oft-told tale, something we can both latch onto for a while.

"I've been very fortunate, you know. If I'm dying, I must stay grateful."

"You are not dying, Mother," I say, trying to sound convincing, unfamiliar with this new terrain of communication between us. Although I've counseled hundreds of patients dealing with life and death issues, I can't recall ever trying to comfort my own mother before.

"Come on, Sergei, they haven't told me as much, but it's obvious. Your poor brother is about to collapse, and that Professor looks like he's been through Hiroshima, and you haven't said anything at all, which has always been your way of saying everything. And you kissing me on the forehead? That the first sign of tenderness you've shown me since you were a little boy. Something is terribly wrong, that's for sure."

I don't know what to say. Anton is back in the room, still on the phone, intent on letting the whole family know before I get a chance to talk to anyone.

He is her "warrior," as she had once explained to us after taking a course in Jungian archetypes, and I, her "poet philosopher", the "European one": un-athletic, refined, tortured, brilliant, yet totally unprepared to deal with the real world and how to "get ahead". The perpetual dreamer.

She had never been capable of loving her four children equally and consistently. Perhaps because she loved each one of us too much and too intensely, especially her sons. There was always a favorite, and one that was on the shit list. A good guy and a bad guy. There was always someone in need of rescuing and intervention, punishment and absolution. There was always someone in need of Dollsie.

"Have you managed to reach Nan?" Dollsie asks Anton. "Poor Nan, so far away. And what about Dimitri? My poor little baby. Why haven't you put me on the phone with him yet? I want to talk to my daughter and to my baby. Now."

We haven't been able to reach either one, and since I know that Anton will keep hitting the redial number until he gets through to them, I decide to head back to the chalet. Walt is waiting, and I use that as an excuse to get the hell out of the hospital. I don't want to spend the night with the two of them. I have been there all day, now he can take over. I need to disconnect, absorb what has transpired.

As I try to focus on the curvy, unfamiliar mountain roads, pitch dark and surprisingly soothing, Ashley returns my call from the French bed & breakfast where she has stopped for the night after biking all day. I update her on the day's events. She had been right on point; the only one to think that this might not be what they thought it was, that it might be something far worse. She had tried to prepare me.

"Is she okay?" she asks, in her soothing southern belle baby girl voice.

"You tell me." I answer.

"Oh sweetie, I don't need to tell you what you already know. It's probably pancreatic cancer. Which means that she's got about nine months, no matter what you do—chemo, radiation, surgery... I'm sorry, honey."

"Gee, Ashley, please don't feel you need to mince words around me. I can take the bad news."

We both laugh. We know each other well. We had met in the halls of boarding school, looking for weed on a Saturday morning, and after getting kicked out a few years later she had gotten her shit together and had gone on to become a brilliant surgeon while I had gone through the motions—doing just enough to get by in life.

I know she's right. From the moment the doctor gave us the news, maybe even from the moment I saw her for the first time laid up in the hospital bed in Zweisimmen, I've known that Dollsie is going to die. I have been there before. I know what being terminal looks like. I know it long before she or anyone else in the family can accept it, and I am grateful to Ashley for preparing me for what is to come. While Dollsie and the others will spend the next nine months wavering between hope, despair, and a great deal of denial, I stay anchored in the reality that my mother is most probably going to die, and that I can help her during this process. I, who have probably caused her more pain than any man in her life save for her father, withholding love and hating her and judging her for all the imperfections which I now embody; who has taken great pleasure in punishing her and making her feel shame and guilt at every opportunity; who has done everything possible to avoid her at all costs; I can now make things right—for the both of us—just by being there for her, by accompanying her on this journey. Because I am less attached to her than the others, and because of my experience with illness and hospitals, she can count on me to tell her the truth, when she asks. But more than that, she will not die thinking that one of her kids hates her. I owe her that much. And I owe it to myself, as well as my future child.

But first we need to get her back to New York, so that she can be operated on at Memorial Sloan Kettering, New York's famous cancer institute (also known as the Roach Motel: where you check in, but you don't check out). We will meet with the doctor and the surgeon in the morning to make some decisions based on how she is doing, and then we will need to make all the arrangements to get someone in her condition from Bern to Zurich, and then from Zurich to New York. If she can make it, as the doctor had repeated several times.

After getting lost twice, I arrive at the chalet well after midnight. Walt comes out to greet me, as do Dollsie's two miniature greyhounds, Sharif and Czarina (aka Dumb & Dumber). Frederic the jeweler is either asleep or not home, thank God. That's the last thing I want to deal with: being grilled by one of Dollsie's social friends who, like Anton, would be on the phone the next morning, informing all of Gstaad.

I suddenly remember that at the end of my last visit a few weeks earlier—which feels like eons ago—I had hidden some weed in one of the miniature copper pots that hung on the beam above the dining room table. I step up on a chair, praying it's still there, and to my immense relief, I find it. I retrieve some rolling paper from my toiletry kit and prepare a joint, comforted by the ritual. Accompanied by the dogs, I set off for a walk down the moonlit path leading down the hill to the village. I know this road so well. Like the chalet itself, it is part of the landscape of my childhood, and every step, every smell, every view, brings back memories, flooding the senses and releasing the tears. It was in this chalet that my childhood had ended, and here I am, walking along the same path, certain that my life is about to change once again.

The moon shines over the mountains that surrounds the sleepy village, the snow covered peaks and the glaciers of the Diablerets reflecting the moonlight in the distance. All is quiet and dark, except for a few lights coming from the Palace up on the hill, which is at its most majestic at night. I can understand why Dollsie had been so determined not to miss her party. A queen never abandons her castle.

PART TWO

THOSE LITTLE TOWN BLUES

ELEVEN

BLACKOUT

Dollsie and Anton consider staying in Bern and having her "growth" removed there (studiously avoiding the C word) so that they can resume their respective summers in Europe without interruption, still under the delusion that this might turn out to be a minor inconvenience. But during the night, her stent becomes dislodged, with no one on shift who can put it back in place, leaving Dollsie in a state of great discomfort and panic until morning. By the time I arrive, she has decided that we should get her to New York as soon as possible, and is already on the phone, making arrangements.

The rest of the day goes by in a blur as we make calls to New York and San Francisco, with Nan coordinating the travel details, including finding a nurse who can fly with us at the last minute, and Dimitri using his dad's pull to line up doctors and a bed at MSK. We get everything done just in time to depart the next day on Swissair, out of Zurich. There's no telling how long I will be gone, so I arrange to have Giovanni come from Paris by train to retrieve Walt and the car at the chalet, and take them back to Paris.

The nurse that Nan has found to travel with us shows up at the hospital the next morning. Dollsie takes one look at her and declares, in her distinctive stage whisper: "I am most definitely not getting on any plane with some twenty-year-old hippie for a nurse." After I point out to her that she does not have much of a choice, Dollsie and the nurse and I leave the hospital in Bern in a taxi bound for the airport in Zurich. The ride lasts an hour and a half, Dollsie moaning in pain every time the taxi hits a bump or takes a curve, and by the time we get there, she is already a mess.

As we are checking in for our flight, the officials at Swissair inform me that I won't be able to enter the United States without a U.S. passport or visa. I explain to them that I am a U.S. citizen but that I have left my American passport in Paris, never imagining that I would need it, and that since I didn't have time to return to Paris to retrieve it I am traveling with my Swiss passport instead. With this bit of news, Dollsie's anxiety level—already high—heads into the stratosphere, and after much pleading on her part—bordering on hysterics—they finally let us board. We'll worry about what happens in New York when we get there. I feel confident that I will be able to convince the immigration people that this is an emergency that warrants an exception. "Fat chance," says Dollsie.

The flight is uneventful. We are both medicated enough to avoid the enormity of what is happening and get through the trip (I had helped myself to a Xanax from her stash). I think back on all the voyages we've taken together, the long flights to places like Russia and China (where, at Anton's prompting, I had tried cocaine for the first time while standing on the Great Wall) and Nepal, where we stayed in a tree house at a fancy lodge, waking up at three in the morning to go trekking for tigers. In Katmandu, I had bought a sizable amount of hash, smuggling it into India inside of toothpaste tubes. Once we arrived in New Delhi, I stashed my treasure in some wood carving I had found at the flea market, and asked the concierge at the hotel to ship it to me at boarding school. That was my genius plan. I figured I would have enough to sell throughout the Spring semester, and would make a small killing. Fortunately, the package never arrived, indeed probably never made it past the front desk.

In Nepal, I also came down with serious case of food poisoning from eating tomatoes (just to spite Dollsie, who had told us not to), and I dragged myself through India, getting sicker by the day. The only high point of the three week trip as far as I was concerned had been the dinner party we had been invited to by the Maharani of Jaipur in the gardens of her magnificent palace. These trips, as chaotic as they were, were her greatest accomplishment as a parent. She had not succeeded in creating a permanent home for us, but instead, she had shown us the world.

And here we are again, zonked out, on a long flight home, which this time feels like "destination unknown."

As we approach JFK, Dollsie checks her make-up one last time. During the last two days, she has gotten the hang of applying her powder and lipstick and mascara, with needles strapped to her arms and chest and tubes dangling. But after the long flight, Dollsie is in bad shape. She looks terrible and no amount of makeup can cover her suffering and exhaustion, and she knows it. The trip has practically finished her off. Throughout the long flight she has alternated between panic and martyred resignation—her default mode in times of crisis—worrying aloud about the "German hippie" getting her through the trip in one piece—with the woman sitting right next to her—and about the ambulance not being there to meet us, and about there being no room for her at MSK, and about the doctor she had insisted upon—the world famous Dr. Burger—not being available. Although she doesn't say it, I know that since "the children" are in charge for once instead of her, she has the gravest doubts about what fate awaits her upon landing.

Her main concern is that Dimitri—her "baby"—will fall apart when he sees her. That's why she insists on changing before landing, putting on her favorite beige Armani suit and doing the best she can with her hair and face. In this family, appearance is everything.

As we pull up to the gate and wait to disembark, a couple from Ohio returning home after their first trip to Europe—as they explain to us at great length, blissfully unaware of our total lack of interest—wish Dollsie well and ask her if this is her "last stop".

"My 'last stop'?" she answers, winking at me and suppressing her raucous giggle, "My last stop? You bet it is. I'm on my way to Sloan Kettering!" she exclaims, with mock cheerfulness, leaving the couple speechless. I do my best not to burst out laughing as Dollsie makes her grand exit off the plane, holding on to me and Helga the hippie, who carries the tubes connected to Dollsie, along with her medical bag.

We are met at the exit by an airline official waiting with a wheelchair and are escorted to the front of the immigration line, which Dollsie appreciates. She has always loved and expected VIP treatment, especially if it involves cutting lines. She is the first to pass through, then Helga, and then it's my turn. I produce my Swiss passport.

"Where is your visa, sir?" asks the agent.

As I attempt to explain to the officer the situation, Dollsie reaches her foot out from the wheelchair and kicks me as hard as she can, hissing "*Callate la boca!*" (shut up!) and giving me a dirty look. Another agent shows up and asks me to follow him. Dollsie had urged me to lie and tell them that I had lost the passport, and as usual, she was right. I can tell that I'm fucked. This is post-9/11, and they aren't taking any chances.

"Officer, I am traveling with my mother who is very sick, and we have an ambulance waiting to take us to Sloan Kettering for emergency surgery," I say, with all the humility and deference I can muster.

"Your mother and the nurse are free to leave with the ambulance, but as for you, I'm going to escort you to the immigration office, where you will most likely be held until we can deport you back to Paris for traveling with an illegal passport."

"Illegal?" I ask, incredulously.

"U.S. citizens are not allowed to hold other passports, sir."

"But Switzerland is a neutral country!" I exclaim, dumbfounded, almost adding: "Who gives a fuck?"

Dollsie, who has managed to hold it together for most of the trip, finally breaks down. She begins crying hysterically (as usual, I wonder how much is genuine and how much for effect), alternating desperate pleas addressed to the agents with furious looks of *I told you so!* hurled in my direction. The agent remains impassive. Dollsie and Helga are sent through, and as she is wheeled off, I try to reassure her that everything will be fine, that I will get out of here in no time, and that Dimitri will be waiting for her at the hospital. But she's having none of it.

"Don't leave me alone with this hippie!" she cries out. "What if there is no ambulance? What if no one is there to meet us at Sloan? What if you end up in jail? I told you not to mention your American passport. I begged you. If you had just said that you were Swiss, or that you had lost your passport, they would have let you through," she says, not minding the officer and everyone else who is following the scene with rapt attention. "Why must you always be so obstinate? I told you to keep your mouth shut!"

I watch Dollsie disappear through the sliding doors into the baggage claim area, sobbing, with Helga, who has not said more than a few words since leaving Zurich ten hours earlier. I wonder when I will see her again.

I am escorted to a waiting room where dozens of people—mostly African and

Middle Eastern—wait for their turn. Some of them look as if they have been there for hours, if not days. There seem to be only two agents on duty, and I envision being stuck in this gloomy room for twenty-four hours while Dollsie goes through life-threatening surgery. I wonder if I might even be incarcerated and flown back to Paris. It feels unreal. I try calling and texting Dimitri several times, but for some reason, I can't get through.

I ask the agent at the reception desk if I can skip to the front of the line, given the circumstances. To my surprise, he agrees and I am brought up to an inspections officer who sits at a desk on an elevated platform, as if he were some kind of judge looking down on a criminal in court.

"What is *this*?" he asks, holding up the red passport as if it were a big bag of cocaine.

"Sir, that's my Swiss passport," I answer, trying to keep cool. "I apologize—I know that I'm not supposed to travel with another passport—but my mother had to be flown to New York for emergency surgery, and I did not have time to return to Paris to retrieve my American one."

"How did you get this?" he asks, practically seething.

"My father is Swiss. We get one automatically when we are born," I reply.

"Are you aware that holding a second passport from a foreign nation is considered treason?"

Treason? The guy has got to be kidding. I suppress the urge to laugh in his face. "No, Sir, I was not aware of that."

"And you have evidently renewed the passport several times, is that right?"

"Yes, sir," I answer, becoming more obsequious by the moment, wondering where this is heading.

"Let me ask you this," he said, his demeanor softening slightly after a long pause. "Have you ever taken the pledge of allegiance?"

The what? What the fuck?

"Uh, no sir, I don't think I have. I was born in this country. I thought only immigrants take the pledge," I say, almost adding, "Have you?"

"Alright, sir, given the circumstances, you may proceed, but we will keep and destroy the passport," he says, making a big show of reaching for his scissors.

Whatever. Keep the fucking passport, I think to myself as I make a big show of thanking him profusely, *à la Dollsie*. After retrieving my suitcase and going through customs, I head outside where I find Dollsie waiting, her six large

Vuitton bags stacked beside her. She has a look of horror on her face, which is matched by the expressions of the nurse and the ambulance attendants who have obviously been having some kind of altercation with her. I know that look all too well. Dollsie can be quite terrifying when she goes at it.

"I told them that I refuse to budge until my son appears," she exclaims, sounding as imperious as she can under the circumstances.

"Sir, we have a problem," said the ambulance attendant. What now? I think to myself. "There is no way that all three of you and all the bags are going to be able to fit in the ambulance."

Dollsie had insisted on having her entire summer wardrobe packed up, knowing that she would probably not be returning to Gstaad anytime soon. The Filipino maid had been put in charge of that task, along with Dollsie's friend Claudine Kalashnikov ("Yes, that Kalashnikov!" as Dollsie would say whenever anyone enquired, "gun money") who had taken detailed instructions from Dollsie over the phone about what needed to be packed and what was to be done with the chalet and its staff.

"We will take your mother and the nurse, and you can follow us in a taxi with the luggage."

"I refuse to go without my son!" repeats Dollsie, raising her voice another notch.

"Mother, this is no time for a sit-in," I tell her, on the verge of losing it myself after what I've just been through. "I told you not to bring all those bags. We could have had them sent later. The nurse has to go with you in case something happens. Don't worry, Dimitri will be waiting for you, and I'll be right behind you in a cab."

"My baby, I want to talk to my baby!" she wails, as they transfer her to a gurney and load her into the ambulance.

By the time I find a cab large enough to transport her huge suitcases, the ambulance is long gone. I try to reach Dimitri again to give him the heads up, but I still can't get through. I then try calling his father, Jacques, who, being a notorious hypochondriac, knows all the "right people" and has managed through his connections to secure a bed and the right doctor for us at MSK. No luck reaching him either. I ask the cabbie if I can use his cell for an emergency, and I try both numbers again. Nothing.

The traffic into the city is heavier than usual. It takes us over two hours just to reach the Triboro Bridge. As we start to cross it, I notice that there is no traffic coming from the opposite direction. Instead of cars, hundreds of people are crossing the bridge on foot in the middle of rush hour. I can't believe my eyes. I ask the driver what is happening. He is just as puzzled as I am, and he scans the radio stations for information.

I wonder if another terrorist attack has occurred. It has been almost two years since the last one, and today's date is August 11th—a month shy of 9/11. I also wonder what has happened to the ambulance; by now it should have reached the hospital, but with whatever is going on, who knows?

Once we manage to get over the bridge, we find chaos. The traffic lights are dead, and the intersections have become free-for-alls. Hordes of people pour out of the tall buildings and flood the sidewalk, scattering in all directions, some in a daze, many panicking. What the fuck is going on? I ask myself again. It is more than a little scary.

We make our way to the hospital, but the main emergency entrance has been cordoned off by security guards, and there is no way to gain access with the taxi. The driver agrees to drive around the block until we find another entrance, and after dropping me off with all the bags, he takes off.

So many people are trying to leave the building that it is almost impossible to enter. I stand there on the sidewalk, with the seven bags, trying to figure out a game plan. I am tempted to just leave them there while I go look for help, but I know that there will be hell to pay if they disappear, which of course they will, this being Manhattan. I spot an elderly hospital attendant with an empty wheelchair, and he agrees to let me have it. So I pile the suitcases on the chair and we venture forth into the dark, crowded lobby, dodging the exiting crowds.

"What the hell is going on?" I ask him. He explains that there has been a massive power failure, cause unknown, and that the whole city had gone "dark." Most of the hospital is in the dark as well, with just a few generators running to provide minimal lighting and keep some of the medical equipment going.

He leaves me in the middle of the lobby, and after parking the Vuitton-laden wheelchair in an out-of-the-way corner that looks relatively safe, I set forth down the long hall. All over, people lie in stretchers, in pain and in shock, some crying and calling out for help, but mostly just sitting in silence, dumbfounded by this latest calamity. At the end of the dark hall, I come upon a large sitting area, which is being used as a temporary triage center. And there I find Dollsie, laid out on her stretcher, with Dimitri and her friend Martine beside her, all of them completely freaked out.

"Sergei, thank God you made it!" Dollsie cries out. "We've been stranded here for hours and no one knows what the hell is happening, and these people won't even let me have a glass of water, much less a cigarette. Or some actual medical attention— which, as I've explained over and over, is what we just flew across the Atlantic for," she says seemingly oblivious to all those around her. "Thank God you are here. Take me out to smoke. Now."

I am desperate for a smoke myself, so we negotiate the crowded hallways and make our way back outside, Dimitri following, speechless. He's clearly in shock at Dollsie's appearance and the unexpected turn of events. Everywhere we look is pandemonium. We walk by the spot where I've left the bags.

"Are those my bags, sitting there unattended?" Dollsie shrieks.

"No, Mother, they must belong to someone else who is checking in today with six Vuittons," I answer with exasperation, mixed with a certain relief that Dollsie's priorities have remained intact. I take it as a good sign that in the midst of everything that is going on—no electricity, no attending physician in sight, and no working elevators to get Dollsie to her room on the VIP floor—she stays focused on her cigarettes and her precious luggage. She is still with us.

"Dimitri, go get the driver. I'm not moving from here until those bags are taken care of. We'll wait here until you come back, then we'll go smoke." Dollsie is *back in the saddle*, as she likes to say. By my calculations, we have been on the move for eighteen hours since leaving the hospital in Bern, and for all her agitation and pain and exhaustion, she seems to be holding up. More than that, she is taking charge: a good sign. There is nothing like a crisis to get her going.

Helga announces that she is leaving, having already put in two extra hours when her contract only calls for door-to-door service. At first, Dollsie is too stunned to answer, but then she lets loose. "I told you it was a mistake to hire that hippie!" she hisses loudly at me, as Helga departs. "Imagine abandoning a helpless woman in these conditions. Typical. They're all that way." I couldn't figure out if she was referring to Germans or hippies, or both.

"Now you boys go find out what is going on with my room before I croak on the spot with all these unattractive, bizarre people lying around all over the place. God only knows what infections they're spreading to everybody as we speak!"

Dimitri and I leave her in the care of Martine, who is decked out in some slinky outfit and stiletto heels. A French-Bulgarian cabaret singer in her fifties who is married to an elderly rent-a-car magnate, she and Dollsie have been best friends for years, but I am meeting her for the first time. She reminds me of a cross between Eartha Kitt and Marlene Dietrich. A vampy aging sex kitten.

Dimitri and I are both relieved to have a moment alone. He has always been my favorite sibling, even though we are only half-brothers. I can imagine how hard this is on him, still in his twenties and having to face his mother's mortality. He struggles to hold back the tears.

"Dude, what's up with Martine's outfit?" he says with forced jocularity, shifting to safe territory. "Her dress is totally transparent and practically hitched up her ass."

I laugh, for the first time in days. It feels good to have someone with whom I can let go.

"And what's up with the fuck-me-now heels?" I add, "Is she planning on straddling one of the residents while she's here?"

"Dude, I wish this was a joint," he says, puffing on his cigarette. "Mom looks fucking terrible. I had no idea."

I reach up to hug my six-foot-three brother, the baby of the family, impeccably dressed in his custom-tailored Italian suit and tie. The heat is suffocating, both inside the hospital and out on the street, but he keeps the jacket and tie on for Dollsie. It is what she expects of him: composure at all times. Whereas the three of us from her first marriage had always gone out of our way to "rebel" (as she put it whenever we did something that went against her expectations for us) Dimitri—who, as far as she is concerned, is the only good thing to come out of her leaving Dad for Jacques, has grown into the kind of son she had always hoped for: handsome, perfect manners, devoted to his mother, and leading the kind of social and professional life appropriate to someone of his background and breeding—living on Park Avenue and weekending in the Hamptons, frequenting the Health & Racket Club and the Bath & Tennis, attending benefits. Doing normal things with normal people—"P.L.O.'s," as Mooma called them— People Like Ourselves.

Dollsie had tried desperately to make sure that her other children turned out the same way, but she had failed miserably, on all counts. If she had "never left your father for that man," Anton would not have ended up out there in "La-La

Land," with a disastrous first marriage to the crazy Colombian, followed by a second marriage to another nut, a "channeler" who claimed to have a direct line to none other than God himself. The one who had turned Anton into a California husband, doing yoga, sweating in teepees, and according to Dollsie "running around the house doing everything that the wife is supposed to do in the first place." (As if Dollsie had any clue what a wife did. The extent of her housekeeping usually involved picking up after a late night dinner party, drink in one hand and cigarette in the other).

And if she had never left Dad, as she told us often, Nan and I would not have turned out gay—"such a silly word to begin with"—especially not her poor, sweet daughter, living out there in Berkeley with her "partner", feeling guilty about her privilege, spending her weekends picking mushrooms and kayaking with children "with special needs", as she insisted on calling them, with her sanctimonious political correctness. Always going on about how rude it was to call people fat or stupid or black or Mexican. Dollsie loved her dearly but she could be so tiresome, especially with the whole "recovery" thing. Ever since *The Accident*, when she had run over her girlfriend ("the truck driver" as Dollsie referred to her) in New Orleans during a drunken binge, Nan had stopped drinking. And although Dollsie would never have told her so to her face, she secretly believed that, as far as Nan was concerned, a drink or two now and then wouldn't be such a bad idea; it would make her a little more amusing. A little less *pesada* (heavy).

But I sensed that she felt that she had failed most of all with me. I, who had graduated from Georgetown "summa cum" (actually it was only cum laude, but with Dollsie, you always had to allow for inflation) and who had gone on to complete two Masters; who had shown such promise early on in my brief publishing career, but had ended up opting for an easy, decadent life frittering away my talents and my trust funds in Paris, Ibiza, Mykonos, Saint Tropez and every other gay Mecca on the planet, frequenting nightclubs and doing drugs and "fornicating with every Tom, Dick, and Harry." And always so angry and harsh and downright rude, especially for someone who came from a long line of diplomats. And still alone, after all these years.

Never mind that I had arrived in a city where I had few connections and had managed to make a life for myself, building a thriving practice and running an organization for English-speaking people with HIV/AIDS living in Paris. She was happy to boast about my achievements when she was at a dinner party—"my son the most brilliant young psychotherapist in Paris"—but deep down she couldn't help but feel that we had mutually failed each other.

She blamed herself for all of it, but at least Dimitri had turned out normal, and for that she was grateful.

Of course, I was convinced that she knew me not at all, could only see me as an extension of herself. Like any child of a narcissist, all my life I had tried to get her attention, rebelling against this image she had of me while cultivating it, not knowing whether I gained more satisfaction from the perverse pleasure of proving her right or the exhausting effort to prove her wrong. I had learned at an early age, like most children of dysfunctional families do, that I had been assigned a role—one that made me the fall guy for all the family's problems. No matter what I did in life, my family would always see me through the prism of that role.

After wandering through the half-lit, crowded halls, Dimitri and I find a doctor who seems to be in charge, and we brief him on our situation.

"Doctor," says Dimitri, assuming a take-charge voice like Anton, wanting so much to come to the rescue and to make everything alright for his beloved mother, "We just flew our mother in from Switzerland for an emergency procedure called the 'Whipple,' to be performed by Dr. Burger, and after being in transit for fifteen hours she has been stuck here in the lounge for several more hours. She tends to get a little hysterical when she runs out of patience, which I can promise you is imminent. And trust me, doctor, you don't want her going postal with all these people around."

The doctor, a young resident evidently overwhelmed by the situation at hand, replies that he and the others have already been alerted about her case, and that a room has been reserved on the coveted nineteenth floor—the VIP wing—but that the elevators are still out and that until power is restored, there is no way to get her up to her room.

"We have examined her and we do not feel that she requires urgent care," he concludes, to our astonishment. "And we have paged Dr. Burger several times, but we have not been able to locate him yet."

It seems like several more hours before Dollsie is taken up to her room. I decide to leave her with Martine and Dimitri and head out. I'm done. But before I go, the resident on call has me fill out some paperwork, and asks me about her medical history and what medications she is taking. I whip out the list that the doctor in Bern has written up:

- Wellbutrin, 150 mg, 2 pills 1x/day
- Trazadone 50 mg, PRN
- Xanax .25 mg, PRN
- Colace 100 mg, 1 tab 2x/day
- Carafate 1 gm, 1 tab 2x/day
- Xantac 300 mg, 1 tab 2x/day
- Senoside 8.6 mg, 2 tabs at night
- Advair, 2 puffs 2x/day
- Combivent 2 puffs 3xday

Significant Health Problems:
- Asthma
- Depression
- Anxiety
- Moderate to heavy smoker.
- Moderate to heavy alcohol intake.

Past Surgeries:
- 2 uterine suspensions, appendix, tonsils, two Morton's toes,
  2 benign spinal tumors, 1 benign breast tumor, 1 tubal liga-
  tion, 1 clavicle fracture, 1 breast reduction, 1 face lift.

"She's on all these meds?" he asks me incredulously.

"I guess so," I answer, shrugging.

With that, I make a bee line for the exit. I start walking in the direction of Dimitri's apartment on the Upper East Side, about fifteen blocks away from MSK. By now, it is evening. The power is still out and the city has emptied out. There are no cabs or other vehicles running down the long avenues; something I've never seen in New York. Terrorism has been ruled out; the blackout is due to a power failure at some electrical plant out in the Midwest somewhere that no one had ever heard of. No one knew when power would be restored. And the notion that it depends on some power grid in the Midwest is baffling.

I have never felt at home in my native city, and after living in so many places, I find myself right back where I started, with Dollsie in a hospital room right across the street from where I had been hospitalized for a back problem as a teenager—and where Raphael had died six years ago. I walk up Lexington in a daze, the usual deafening noise of evening traffic replaced by the sounds of conversation coming from cozy candle-lit sidewalk gatherings. People huddle in front of townhouses and apartment buildings. They seem friendlier than usual, relaxed and surprisingly intimate. After all, they have been through worse. I am reminded once again of how excluded I have always felt, how utterly apart and disconnected. Rootless.

Once I reach Dimitri's building, I take the service stairs to his apartment, grateful that it is only three floors up and that my luggage has already been delivered to his building by his driver and taken up to the apartment by the doorman. Once inside, I use my lighter to navigate the foyer and living room in search of a candle. I find two on the dining room table and light them. I haven't had anything to eat or drink since the plane but all I want to do is find Dimitri's stash and smoke a huge joint and pass out. He's told me he keeps it hidden in a chess game on the top shelf of a closet so that Rosario—the maid/spy placed by Jacques and Dollsie to report on his every move—won't find it.

I'm not familiar with the apartment, so I make my way from room to room using the candle to light the way until I find the right closet. Bingo. It seems like a huge triumph after the crazy day. Has it only been five days since I wandered the quais of Lake Geneva on a carefree summer night, in search of a joint and a little company? I am grateful for the joint, an old familiar friend which at times, like tonight, feels like a savior. I stretch out on the bed, knowing that the joint will push me over in no time. Blackout.

TWELVE

YOU'LL GET YOUR PONY
WHEN YOU LOSE TEN POUNDS

For a moment, I don't know where I am, and as I head to the kitchen to search for juice and coffee, I check out Dimitri's apartment; a small two-bedroom in a typical pre-war Upper East Side building for which he no doubt paid some ungodly amount. As I look out the window of his sleek living room, I notice for the first time that right across the street is Buckley, the school I attended after we moved back to the city. Those years had been the worst of my life, and I had Buckley—and Dollsie—to thank for that.

After moving back from Switzerland, we settled into an apartment a few blocks away, on 78th and Park, found by Dollsie's friends, who were thrilled to have her back even if they didn't quite understand how she could have left Dad for "that man".

A few weeks later, I was sent off to a camp in Colorado, The River Ranch. I had never been to camp before, and I dreaded the prospect of finding myself stuck in a cabin with a bunch of smelly bullies, forced to participate in activities which would make me look ridiculous. But much to my surprise, finding myself away from Dollsie and the rest of the family proved to be a wonderful thing. I enjoyed cabin life, and quickly adapted to the routine. Every morning at breakfast, the director, a friendly guy who ran the camp with his Swiss wife, would call out the list of available activities for the morning and afternoon sessions, and we would sign up for whatever we wanted. I invariably chose the same two: making jewelry in the morning and riding in the afternoon. I hadn't been near a horse since breaking my arm while riding in Gstaad three years earlier, and I was surprised to find myself on a horse again, but I found the Western saddles comforting, because I had something to hold on to, and I loved the cowboy counselors who led the rides, singing and telling stories. Sometimes, there would be three-day excursions to choose from, fishing trips and rafting trips and horseback riding and hiking trips, and I always opted for the riding. We would be on horses all day, traversing fields and forests and rivers, and at night we would set up camp.

I was fascinated by this new world, the ritual, the male bonding, sitting around bonfires and roasting hot dogs and marshmallows, watching the way the fire light flickered on the handsome, nearly grown-up faces of the counselors as they told terrifying ghost stories, making them come to life. At bedtime, I would set my sleeping bag by the campfire while the others settled into their tents. At age ten, I still wet my bed, and while I had grown adept at rising at dawn to change the sheets and hide the evidence before the others in the cabin awoke, I knew that it would be less easy to hide in a tent. On those camping trips, I was often the only one sleeping outside, and sometimes I would wake up in the middle of the night, drenched by the rain and soaked in my own urine and utterly miserable. Still, I would not move into the tent, fearing that the others would notice the smell. I would huddle in my sleeping bag, trembling with coldness, and wait for morning to come.

Apart from this nightly trauma, it was a wonderful summer. Dollsie would call twice a week and berate me for taking jewelry classes, going so far as to ask the director to forbid me from signing up for this activity, to no avail. I loved being far away from her. I felt free, whether riding bareback through the wide expanses, or shooting the rapids, or eating whatever I wanted to at mealtime, or dressing up on weekend nights, which were always busy with movies and dances and other activities. When it was dance night, the counselors would primp themselves with macho pride, making lewd comments about the girls they would meet and what would happen. My cabin mates and I would imitate the ritual, and all week I would look forward to those moments during which we all dressed together and prepared ourselves for an evening of conquest, not realizing, as I only did much later, that what I loved most was watching these sixteen and seventeen-year-old boys on the verge of manhood preparing for the age-old, primal game of seduction. They were so strong, so handsome, so normal. I basked in their maleness and I wondered if I would ever be like them.

After camp was over, I joined Dollsie in Miami for the month of August. We stayed with my beloved grandmother, whom I had baptized "Greasy" at a young age, because of the cream she lathered on her face like butter at bedtime, her hair curled in toilet paper and bobby pins. The name had stuck. She lived on Key Biscayne—an island off Miami—in a house that Dad had bought for her and my grandfather a few years after their exile from Cuba. Shortly after they had settled in, John died of emphysema, in his early fifties. She had lived in the same house ever since, on Gulf Road.

Key Biscayne in those days was almost wild, with the largest preserve of mangroves in the northern hemisphere. In summer, Cuban families would rent bungalows on the beach where they would hang out drinking and discussing politics while the kids were left free to explore the island. Many years later, most of the mangroves would be destroyed by Hurricane Andrew and in their place, huge condominiums were built, one by one, taking over the quaint beach front hotels until the island was no longer recognizable. In the past few decades, huge Scarface-type mansions had sprung up everywhere, built by South American expats—drug runners and corrupt ex-ministers and other assorted crooks—seeking a safe haven for their families and their cash, transforming understated Key Biscayne into a replica of whatever nouveau riche aspirational lifestyle they had left behind.

In the mornings, I was sent off to sailing camp at the Key Biscayne Yacht Club, an activity which I hated because of the heat and the mosquitoes. In the afternoons, I would seek refuge at Nani's, Greasy's mother, who lived right behind her in another house purchased by Dad. We would watch television as she scratched my back with her long, beautifully manicured nails. Her favorite show was The Jeffersons and she would giggle like a little girl, amused at the thought of watching black people on television—an unfathomable notion to her, but then, as she always said, America was not to be understood. Sometimes I would stay for dinner, and her son Alberto would join us. He lived with Nani and he reminded me of Archie Bunker. The three of us would split an entire chicken, and I would watch fascinated as Nani devoured half of everything: the chicken, the peas, the mashed potatoes, and the key lime pie, my favorite. I marveled at her great appetite—she was probably hungry for everything that she had lost and left behind in Cuba—and I wondered where it all went in that frail little body.

I avoided the other kids on the key, who were like Anton and the other bullies who made fun of me in school or at camp. My only friend was Claudia, who had just moved to Miami with her family from Spain. We became best friends. It was a friendship that lasted ten summers until the accident in Italy, which I can still now visualize as if I had been in the burning Jeep with her. But that was later.

After Labor Day, Dollsie, Nan and I returned to New York to begin our new life, and Anton went off to St. Paul's. That first year, I attended the French Lycée, which Dollsie explained would only be for a year, by way of transition, after which I would be placed in an English-speaking school to receive a proper American education.

I was happy at the Lycée. Its international character reminded me of my school in Gstaad, and because the kids were from all over the world there were no cliques, and no established norms of behavior which I was at risk of violating. No one made fun of the way I dressed or talked, and although they did mock me during sports, it was not in the same cruel way as the boys had made fun of me at the all-boys school in Geneva. There were more girls than boys in my class, and I liked that. My best friend was an Italian boy called Simone, whose father was a famous movie producer in Rome (ten years later, in an odd twist of fate, he would find himself in that same Jeep with Claudia, and would almost lose his life trying to save hers, pulling her out of the flames before the jeep exploded.)

Considering the tremendous change, it was a happy enough year, except for weekends when Dollsie would make me attend a sports club, to "toughen you up" as she said. She told me that next year I would be attending an American school, and that I would have to be more manly, more athletic, or they would keep making fun of me, calling me a sissy and a fag. The prospect of it loomed over me all year.

Every Saturday at eight a.m., the sports club bus would pick me up in front of our building, and would proceed up Park Avenue picking up other boys along the way. We would drive through Harlem before crossing the Triboro Bridge, and I would stare in fascination at this other world that seemed so foreign to me. I would sit in the back of the bus, talking to no one, dreading the day that lay ahead. In the mornings we would play soccer or football, then we would break for lunch, and in the afternoons, softball or capture-the-flag. As far as I was concerned, they were all equally traumatic. I was always the worst in any given sport, and the last to be picked for the teams. In soccer, they would always stick me on defense, and when I saw the ball headed my way I would freeze in terror, praying that it would change course and head somewhere else. At the last minute I would kick blindly at it, usually missing the ball entirely or sending it off the field, or worse, kicking it to a member of the opposing team. In football, I would do just as I was told, running in the same direction as the others, oblivious to what was happening or what I was supposed to do. In capture-the-flag, I was always the first to be captured, with the other kids yelling: "Capture the Fag!" I didn't mind at all being the first one, because it meant I could just sit there for a while and not worry about anything. In softball, I could barely hit the ball, never mind the rest, but I liked it better than the other sports because I wasn't the only one to fuck up.

The hours would pass very slowly, and I would shut out the mocking voices of the other kids by moving into my own internal fantasy world. This was the world of *Bewitched*, where I pretended I was part of the family, along with Samantha, Tabitha, Endora, Doctor Bombay, Aunt Esmeralda and the other witches and warlocks. By wrinkling my nose I could escape the field and the threatening ball in perpetual motion, and the voices and faces that made fun of me, and enter a world of magic. A world of power, a world of medieval pageantry and strange brews and poetic spells. I would play out elaborate scenarios in my mind, grand conferences that took place on a cloud or in some exotic land like Siam. Conferences at which the very nature of magic would be debated, the rules determined and the transgressors punished. I would always be congratulated for the restraint I exhibited in the use of my powers, and by way of recompense I would be appointed to some exalted post, like Grand Duke of the Children, or Chief Ambassador to the Mortal World.

It was a world that mirrored Dollsie's fantasy world, and that lasted for many years. Even now, I rejoice when I come across *Bewitched* on television, feeling as if I've run into old friends, the kind that had gotten me through some very hard times. Later, the fantasies changed, but they were always there to rescue me from the tedium and pain and utter confusion of daily living. Of trying to be normal and sane and steady in a world that had appropriated these words and declared them rigid and fixed and inviolable. The kids continued to laugh, to call me names, but I had power, the power to escape.

The following year, in April, Dollsie married Jacques. He had been chasing after her for almost ten years and had finally prevailed. I didn't mind much. It was the occasion for another one of Dollsie's fabulous, exciting parties, and Jacques seemed nice enough. And I felt like I had known him for a long time, not realizing how or why until a few years later, when Tata had told me that as a child, Dollsie would take me to visit him at his apartment, and then Tata would bring me home, while Dollsie remained for "tea"..

The ceremony was held in the living room of the apartment that Dollsie had rented for a year, while waiting to marry Jacques. It was a strange wedding; no one seemed to smile, and Greasy was the only one of Dollsie's family to attend. Years later, when Dollsie took Anton and me out to lunch one day to belatedly "spill the beans" on her decision to leave Dad and marry Jacques and what had led up to that, she told us that on the day of the wedding, she had tried to escape through the service entrance of the apartment at the last minute, and that earlier in the year she had had a change of heart and had asked Dad to take her back. But after consulting with Mina and his shrink, he had declined. A woman was like a dog, the shrink had told him; once the dog bites someone, it's going to happen again. So she had decided to marry Jacques, no doubt with a sense of impending doom, knowing that she was about to make a big mistake, but that it was too late to turn back after what she had put us all through.

That night, a reception was given in the sprawling duplex across the street that Jacques had bought in anticipation of the long-awaited wedding. The large apartment on the corner of 79th, in the only all-Jewish building on Park Avenue, was still for the most part, undecorated and unfurnished, and thus ideal for a big party. In a picture of the two of them taken that night, Dollsie is dressed in a flowing rust-colored gown, her hair up in a chignon, held in place by a wreath of gardenias. Between the hairdo and the heels, she is at least six inches taller than Jacques. Their faces are twisted into an awkward grimace which is meant to approximate a smile, their expressions revealing, even then, the enormity of the mistake. The photograph is like a road map to their seven-year marriage; it's all there.

A month and a half later, after school let out, the four of us—Jacques, Dollsie, Nan and I—set off for Europe for our first family vacation. Our first stop was Paris, where we checked into elegant adjoining rooms at the Plaza Athenée. The next morning, while Nan and I were eating the elaborate petit déjeuner continental that had been delivered to our room, I glanced up at the high ceiling and decided to try a neat trick I had seen in a movie on television the night before. I placed a pat of butter in the middle of my linen napkin, and with a swift motion flicked it up to the ceiling. I wanted to prove to Nan that the trick couldn't work, that there was no way the butter would reach the ceiling, much less stay stuck to it. But much to my horror it had. As I anxiously stared upward praying for gravity to bring the butter back down, Jacques walked in from their adjoining room. Noticing the direction of my gaze before I could avert it, he spotted the butter right away, which by now had begun to spread across the pristine white ceiling, illuminated by the elaborate chandelier.

Jacques calmly turned around, walked back into their room and said something to Dollsie, and in she came, swinging her belt in the air, furious and outraged that I would do such a thing. After a few slaps and pinches and half-hearted lashes with the belt, and swearing up and down that I would pay for this out of my allowance until the end of my days, the crisis passed and we set off on our day of sightseeing, which typically consisted of visiting the museums and the expensive jewelry shops on the Place Vendôme .

After Paris came Athens, where, after a few days of rigorous sight-seeing, we embarked on a cruise of the Greek islands. I was fascinated by Greece, and it was there that the nature of my sexuality began to dawn on me. For a long time after, I would dream of Santorini: its dramatic, steep cliffs that one climbed up by donkey and its surreal sunsets and its music. I would dream of being there with a beautiful Greek boy, one of the many I had seen during our rushed tour of the islands.

Dollsie and Jacques fought the entire month, and I was relieved when the trip was over. After stopping over in Switzerland for a few weeks to see Dad and Mina and Tata—our first gloomy, post-divorce visit—I was sent off to camp again.

The River Ranch was less fun the second year, mainly because I quickly became the target of a gang of boys from New York whose main source of pleasure was to mock and humiliate me, chiefly by inventing names that reflected my athletic ability and general demeanor. In addition to the predictable ones, like Fag and Gay Boy and Fatso, there were more creative ones, like Sir Gay the Gallant Knight. I wasn't sure where they had developed these notions about me, but I did not doubt their veracity. Still, I hated them like I had never hated anyone, and I couldn't wait for the session to end.

Much to my horror, I discovered that all of these boys attended Buckley, the school that I would be attending in the fall. When I heard this, I ran to the phone and called Dollsie, panic-stricken, pleading with her, begging her not to make me leave the Lycée. But to no avail. "No son of mine is to be a sissy. Look at your brother! Already on his way to becoming a squash champion! A real man. If you were like him, these boys would leave you alone. Learn to fight back!"

The last night of the camp, an apocalyptic event occurred, so dramatic and devastating that it made me feel as if everything I had been through that summer had been for a reason. While all of us were gathered in the dining hall—which stood atop the hill, overlooking the rest of the camp—to enjoy our last evening together and celebrate the end of our session, a storm moved in, seemingly out of nowhere, filled with lightning and thunder. It rapidly grew in intensity and precipitated a massive mudslide. We watched in terror as waves of mud baring huge boulders and branches and other detritus slid down the mountains surrounding us, engulfing and smashing all that lay below, including the cabins and stables. It turned out to be a providential celebration, for had it been any other night, we would all surely have been killed.

We spent the night in the dining hall and woke up at dawn to witness the devastation that the storm had wrought. Few of the cabins were left standing; most had been destroyed by the mudslide and the ensuing flooding of the Colorado River. All our possessions had been washed away (which only added to the excitement, as it meant buying a whole new wardrobe when I got home). The stables, too, had for the most part been destroyed, and much to my horror dead horses lay strewn about. I had ridden every day for the past month, and I had become attached to several of them. They helped me overcome the loneliness. I ran from the stables in tears, terrified that I might spot one my favorites among the bloated carcasses. I was devastated.

Later that morning, we boarded the bus for the five-hour ride to Denver, from where we flew back to our respective destinations. As I sat next to the Buckley boys on the way to the airport, I couldn't help but wish that some of them had been in their cabins the night before. I pictured them being washed away, along with all the hate and venom they had spewed upon me all summer and that surely awaited me at my new school.

Despite protesting bitterly until the very last minute, telling Dollsie that I had finally found a school where I had friends and didn't feel out of place, she refused to let me stay at the Lycée, certain that it would never prepare me for a good boarding school, never mind a decent college. I had to attend an American school to improve my English, as well as my athletic and competitive skills, which, she told me, were essential if I expected to get anything done in life. I knew that the real reason was that she didn't like me the way I was, and wanted me to change, to be more like Anton, to fit in.

That first day in class, I found myself right next to two of my tormentors from camp: William McLanahan and Bart Johnson, who, as my luck would have it, happened to be the gang leaders, as bullies often are.

"Look who's here!" Bill shouted to his friends as I walked in, "It's Gay Boy!"

The others laughed, and I knew at that very minute that my life at Buckley would indeed be miserable. I spent three years there. Three years during which I managed to make two—and only two—friends, both of whom were so unpopular as to severely limit their choices. Three years of low grades, disciplinary problems, and sports. Endless afternoons on the field where the others, who were far more athletic than anyone I had ever been in school with, marveled at my complete lack of coordination. Rigor Mortis, they called me, because rather than risking ridicule by doing something wrong, I would do nothing, standing in place frozen while the balls went around me, and the others shoved and berated me, and the coaches lambasted me. When I got home in the evenings, more of the same awaited me from Dollsie.

My fantasy life went into overdrive. By now, I was King of the World Council of Witches and Warlocks. It had been decreed that every Buckley boy and his family would find themselves in perpetual, eternal hell; that they would wake up one day without money, without their blond hair and blue eyes and athletic bodies, without their apartments on Park Avenue and their houses in the Hamptons. Without everything that supported their conviction that they were the Chosen Ones, the Perfect Ones, and that anyone who deviated from their standards was a freak of nature.

And a freak I was. I knew they were right about that: fat, stupid, with a weird accent and weird clothes and weird hair that I parted in the middle (Dollsie had warned me that the kids would make fun of me for the hair, which only made me more adamant about wearing it that way) and from a weird country that no one had ever heard of. And such a "fag" when it came to sports. Like the time in gymnastics when I hadn't been able to hang on to the rings long enough to land on the mat, and had ended up spraining my ankle. Or the time in hockey when, because I was in the way as usual, someone had slammed into me so hard that I had lost my breath and been rushed to the hospital. ("What is it now?" Dollsie had exclaimed in exasperation as she met me in the emergency room for x-rays, "When will the histrionics stop? You simply must toughen up!")

In addition to my athletic inabilities, my low grades, my unpopularity, and my lack of masculinity, Dollsie was always on my case about my weight. I was only about ten pounds overweight, but she made me feel obese, telling me it was one more thing that would prevent me from being happy in life. She would instruct the school to serve me a special diet, so in addition to all the other stuff that made me feel different from the others, I would have to sit there with my special plate of faggy diet food. It was deeply humiliating, and I hated her for it.

Weight was such a big deal for her that she tried everything to get me to lose it. At first, it was: "You'll get your pony when you lose ten pounds". Although I had always wanted my own horse more than anything else in the world, my need to stand up to her overcame that desire, and I never lost the weight. The following year, I no longer wanted a pony, I wanted a moped to tear around the back roads of South Hampton, and she adapted her refrain: "all you have to do is lose ten pounds—make that fifteen, because you've gained more weight—and you will have the moped of your choice."

To sabotage her, I would steal money from her purse every night and while taking her miniature greyhounds for a walk—one of my chores—I would go to the pizza parlor around the corner and ingest two or three slices, sometimes four, making friends with the other regulars, regaling them with invented tales about my family and home life. Dollsie never did figure out why I wasn't losing weight, and although I felt that I had won that battle, I have spent most of my adult life combating the same demons, never happy with the way I look, always seeking to lose those however many pounds to reach the magic number and find myself transformed and desired by all. I have binged on food and sex, futilely attempting to reign in my impulses while seeking validation through the eyes of another, wanting to feel wanted, to feel attractive and loved. To feel thin.

Life went on with its various set pieces, with Dollsie playing the leading role and the rest of us supporting characters. Like Thanksgiving on Park Avenue. As usual, Dollsie would invite every stray cat she could think of, so the "family gathering" always consisted of thirty or forty people. It was her way of avoiding intimacy while feeling magnanimous. Out would come the blue Ming dynasty china that she had acquired during her first trip to China, along with a prodigious buffet spread and a profusion of Latin maids in uniform to serve it. Usually, by six she would be tanked and ready for the remaining hangers-on to leave.

On one such occasion, she had spent hours trying to convince one of her friends, Pedro Menocal—a painter known for his portraits of Cuban society—that he and his ex-wife were terrible parents, and that they should let her adopt one of their sons. Finally, Pedro had stormed out, furious, along with the remaining guests. As if things weren't messy enough, Dollsie suddenly remembered that she had seven tickets to the musical "Cats" that evening, so we were rounded up and on went the coats and out we went, searching high and low for taxis. We arrived fifteen minutes late. Dollsie stumbled in and presented the tickets to the usher, who, after examining them with his flashlight, told her "Ma'am I'm sorry but these tickets were for last night."

"What do you mean last night?" she roared majestically, doing her best Liz Taylor in *Cleopatra* imitation, "I specifically requested them for Thanksgiving eve."

"Yes, ma'am. Thanksgiving eve was yesterday."

The rest of us squirmed, desperate to turn around and get the hell out of there before Dollsie made a complete fool of herself, but she would have none of it. Amazingly, the usher eventually relented, powerless against her drunken onslaught, and we were allowed to watch the show, even though it was completely sold out. There we were, six kids and a very inebriated Dollsie, all decked out in our holiday finery, sitting in the middle of the aisles watching "Cats". By intermission, she decided that she was bored, and so we all departed, much to my relief.

To this day, I can't listen to the music from "Cats" without experiencing a vivid flashback, and I still wonder and marvel at Dollsie's ability to actually talk someone into letting seven people come in late to a Broadway musical and watch it while sitting in the aisles.

In the evenings, when Dollsie and Jacques went out, I would sometimes entertain myself and Nan by dressing up in Dollsie's extravagant outfits, couture dresses in outlandish shapes and colors with labels like Givenchy, Yves Saint Laurent and Adolfo. I would select a pair of shoes to match the outfit, just as I had done for Dollsie in Vincy, and sometimes would apply some of her make-up. Thus costumed, I would parade around the apartment doing hilarious imitations: Dollsie in a rage, Dollsie drunk, Dollsie being seductive, being a so-cialite, Dollsie trying to act twenty years old. I suppose that part of me wanted to be her on some level, to take on her identity, while at the same time mocking her and everything she stood for. This went on for several months, until one of the maids caught me in the act one evening and promptly reported the incident to Dollsie, who confronted me that night at dinner, in front of Jacques and Nan. I denied it passionately, feeling the color rise in my face, deeply ashamed. Nan, seizing the moment, called me a liar and confirmed the maid's report.

The following week I was sent to a child psychiatrist. It was a windy, rainy day in November, and the damp cold seeped through my bones as I made my way over to the West side after school. The walls of the doctor's office were covered with African masks, like the ones my parents had brought back from Kenya which had precipitated many a nightmare in my younger years, as I awoke to find them looming over our beds. I spent the entire session telling the doctor everything I hated about my mother: her severity, her screaming, the whipping and other brutal punishments, her fights with Jacques, her coming home every night drunk from her dinner parties and me waking up in the middle of the night to hear her vomiting in her bathroom, which was next to my room. At the end of the hour, I came out to find that the rainstorm had become a snowstorm, and there was not a taxi to be found. I walked home across the park, crying, feeling a sense of despair and loneliness unlike any I had ever known. I fanta-sized about being mugged, held at knife point, abducted and murdered. That would show her. The world was dark and I was a miserable person and things would never change, so what was the point of going on?

Years later, I would think back on that afternoon often and recognize that it was then that thoughts of suicide had taken root. They would persist through-out the next three years, becoming firmly entrenched in my fantasy life. I would compose farewell notes, sometimes even write them out. They would be addressed to Dollsie, blaming her for my miserable life, for my death, and expressing the sincere hope that she would feel guilty and sad for the rest of her life. I hated her so much.

But much as I thought about suicide, I was always stopped short by two things: the ugliness and/or pain and/or embarrassment of most methods, and the grief and heartache that my death would bring to the three people I truly loved: Mina, Tata, and Greasy. Had it not been for them, I might have found a way.

When I finally arrived home from the shrink that day, after walking in the snow for an hour and freezing cold, Dollsie was waiting for me in her *peignoir*, drink and cigarette in hand, fuming, like Joan Crawford in *Mommie Dearest*.

"It's no use my sending you to expensive doctors to get help if you're going to sit there and lie to them. The doctor just called and told me about all your lies."

I couldn't believe that the doctor had ratted me out. Even at that age, I sensed what a staggering betrayal it was, and I was outraged.

"I suggest you go to your room and spend the evening thinking about why you have to lie so much, and why you are always right and everyone else is wrong: your teachers, the boys in your class, your sister, your father, me... We all seem to have it out for you, and you're in no way to blame. I suggest you think long and hard about whether that's reasonable, Sergei."

She didn't slap me or whip me this time, but her face, twisted with rage, and her voice, were more terrifying and hurtful than any belt she might have used. I would always remember that face and that voice, and I knew that the scars would take a lifetime to heal. Even now, I wake up sometimes in the middle of the night, bewildered, lost and alone, like a little child frightened by the nightmare he has just had. The ritual nightmare involving some horrible, devastating conversation with his mother. Even now.

Dollsie became pregnant that year. She announced it to us at the end of the summer, when we returned from Switzerland. By then, Tata had been "let go" and had retired to her native village in the north of Spain. Before leaving, she had filled me in on Dollsie and Jacques' history, so I had mixed feelings about the announcement, but I soon became excited at the prospect of a baby brother or sister.

It was a difficult pregnancy, not only for Dollsie but for all of us. She was almost forty, and had been drinking and smoking to excess for years. She spent most of her term in bed, with her wine and cigarettes, eating and crying. (Years later, she would claim that her "drinking problem" had started during the pregnancy, and that she had been encouraged to do so by her obstetrician, in order to help her "relax".)   I had never seen her so helpless, so weak. She started to pluck hair out of her scalp, creating a bald spot which I found deeply disturbing. But I also secretly rejoiced in my newfound freedom—being able to do my own thing without her constant vigilance and reproach.

Dimitri was born on April Fool's Day, and when Dollsie returned from the hospital with him, I felt as if I had found my salvation. This baby would love me and spend time with me and look up to me. He would not hurt or criticize or reject me. This baby would be my friend.

Little Dimitri kept the family happy for about a year. Jacques was overjoyed to have a son at last, and Dollsie was so thrilled to have her figure back that she promptly flew to Paris to order herself a new wardrobe. During that time, she seldom fought with me or Jacques, who had become like an ally to me. Although he had never had children of his own, he had turned out to be a pretty decent stepfather, taking time to do things with me on weekends; kind and attentive without trying to take over the father role. I was so happy to have a little brother that I didn't mind school as much.

Deliverance came during the spring of my second year at Buckley, when I was in seventh grade. It was the second day of baseball practice, a sport I had never played before. I had actually managed to hit the ball once that day, and as I walked back to the bus I was feeling a little bit hopeful; baseball might turn out to be a sport I could actually do, and who knew, I might even enjoy it. I liked the pace of it, the slowness. It left me plenty of time for day dreaming.

As I walked back to the bus after it was over, someone ran up and jumped me from behind. I fell to the ground and felt a sharp, excruciating pain in my lower back, which ran down the back of my right leg. I said nothing, and fighting the tears, I slowly stood up and boarded the bus. Back in the locker room, I dressed with difficulty, then began the seven block walk home. After two blocks, I found that I could no longer walk. I sat down on the corner, wondering what to do. I was afraid of calling Dollsie, knowing that she would call me a sissy and get mad at me for interrupting her day. I tried to walk another block. Halfway through, I collapsed. Someone came out of a store and helped me up. I went into the store and asked to make a phone call.

"Mummy?"

"Yes, Sergei, what is it?"

"Mummy, I can't walk."

"What do you mean you can't walk?"

"I can't walk! Someone jumped on me today and I can't walk. I'm at 76th and Lexington."

"I'll be right there, honey, don't worry," she said, sounding concerned. She could tell that I had been crying. I was comforted and surprised by her reaction.

The next few months went by in a blur. I did not go back to school, spending weeks in bed, first at home and then in the hospital. There were many consultations with orthopedic surgeons, neurologists, child psychiatrists, anesthesiologists and physical therapists; dozens of tests were run, including x-rays, spinal taps, and a myelogram. That one was the biggie, the one I had been dreading. Dollsie lied and told the nurses that I was epileptic so that they would give me a shot of Demerol, even though it was against hospital policy. Bliss followed. As they inserted a needle the size of a pencil into my spine, I watched the proceedings on a screen and listened to the attendants exchanging recipes. I floated, floated, floated... After the test, I had to lie on my back for twenty-four hours without moving an inch.

Surgery was scheduled twice, once to remove a tumor, the second time for a spinal fusion. The first operation had been called off the evening before when the tumor did not show up on the myelogram. The second was cancelled after Dollsie decided to switch doctors, sensing that the one I had was perhaps a little knife-happy.

While awaiting surgery, I spent a month in the hospital. My roommate looked like a deformed dwarf, with bones growing in strange places and a myriad of other illnesses which kept at least a dozen doctors in a state of permanent excitement. He had gained national attention because of the severity and rarity of his case; the experiment of the year. I was more than a little freaked out by his appearance, but we became friends. Dollsie would bring in other children on the ward—cancer patients and others dying of mysterious, terrifying diseases—and although she never came out and said it, I could read the message in her eyes loud and clear: "Look at these children. This is suffering. This is pain. You have no right. No right to complain and sit around like you do. Recover!"

I grew to love and hate hospitals, finding my refuge there but aware that it was a strange, twisted place for a thirteen year old to hide in, and that it came at a price. Mina arrived from Switzerland, laden with sympathy and gifts. Dad came too, for a few days, and talked to me about what I was putting Dollsie through. He told me about psychosomatic symptoms, and said that maybe having a tumor was not such a bad thing, especially if it was benign. The other kids at school just had measles and mumps. I got to have a tumor.

His message confused me. I felt like I was being told that I had invented my back problem to get out of school and to get back at Dollsie, and that I should ease up on her because it wasn't her fault. To this day, I don't think that either of them ever believed that there was something actually wrong with my back. They probably thought that the diagnosis I had been given, spondelolesis, a congenital dislocation of the vertebrae, was just something that the doctors had come up with to explain and legitimize my psychosomatic symptoms.

I was relieved when Dad left. He was always good about showing up when you needed him, but once he did show, it never felt like he was entirely there. He reminded me of Chauncey Gardner, from the movie "Being There," living in some parallel, placid universe. Perhaps all those years with Dollsie, whose presence was so totally overwhelming, had made him feel invisible. Or perhaps it dated back to his childhood, to the feeling of abandonment he must have experienced when he had been sent by his parents to Buffalo to be cared for by relatives for the duration of the war.

I took my final exams in the hospital bed. Dollsie administered them, and books in hand, she would fill in the questions I didn't know the answers to. I was released shortly after school ended—perfect timing—and was fitted for a body cast, which I would have to wear throughout the summer and fall. It was made out of plastic, and even though I was allowed to remove it at night, it was extremely uncomfortable—not to mention embarrassing—having to walk around in something that looked like a girdle. I spent that summer in Florida, mostly on my own as usual, swimming and doing physical therapy and watching old Bette Davis movies in bed. And eating, always eating.

By September, the beginning of eighth grade and my third year at Buckley, my back had healed—at least for now—and I was allowed to abandon the cast. Fortunately, the doctor felt that it was important that I keep swimming and going to physical therapy throughout the year, so while all the other boys played soccer and hockey and all the other sports that had plagued my existence, I went off to swim every day at Marymount, a nearby women's college that had a pool on the top floor.

Initially, this routine of swimming alone was bliss compared to what I had endured before, but I soon grew bored of doing endless laps every day. It dawned on me that there was no reason for me to keep coming, since no one was supervising me. And so, with a little guilt and much ingenuity, I began attending movies instead. At first, it was just movies in the neighborhood so that I would be sure to make it home on time. Gradually, I began to spread out. Sometimes I would have to leave early to make it home on time. Even if I was a little late, Dollsie would not notice; she was usually busy with her volunteer work in Harlem, or her course work or with the baby, or fighting with Jacques, or getting ready to go out.

The following spring my back gave out again, and once again I was hospitalized and spent the last few weeks of school in bed, preparing for finals with tutors who came to coach me. This time, I had a room to myself, and friends would come to visit, sneaking in cigarettes and other contraband. Dollsie had no patience for my symptoms and when I was finally released after school was let out, she decided that it was time for a change of environment. She had not wanted me to go off to boarding school in the fall, believing that I wasn't ready to assume the responsibility, and that I would only go further downhill without her around to keep an eye on me. But for once, Dad stepped in, no doubt sensing my despair, and told her that he would hold her responsible for whatever happened to me if she made me stay in New York. So Dollsie finally relented. I was accepted at Taft, a prep school in Watertown, Connecticut, and I spent the summer counting the days. Buckley was behind me, and soon Dollsie would be out of the way too. I could not wait.

THIRTEEN

A SERIAL KILLER
AND A MEXICAN

As I walk to the hospital, life in Manhattan is back to its usual summer vibe. Power has returned to many parts of the city, and as it is August, the traffic is still light. New Yorkers, carefree and in good spirits, trade war stories from the day before, proud to have survived yet another cataclysmic event. This time, I enter MSK through the main lobby, now fully lit and chaos-free, and ride the elevator to the nineteenth floor.

Dollsie seems better. Being on the VIP floor has definitely done wonders for her mood. It feels like staying at the Ritz: large suites with nice views of the East River and the city, lots of staff running around—just the way Dollsie likes—and an elegant lounge for families and guests appointed with antiques and a computer. There is even a private dining room with a fully-stocked pantry for entertaining.

"Mother, you're looking great. Nice digs!" I say, sounding as cheerful and upbeat as I can, relieved to see that the day might be less dire and traumatic than yesterday and the days before that.

"Yes, isn't it marvelous?" exudes Dollsie, positively upbeat. "Did you sleep well? I met the nicest Filipino nurse, thank God. They really are the best. Her name is Baby. She used to take care of Dorita Matheson, you remember her? She croaked here, too. Dorita's daughter Elenita made the arrangements. So kind of her. You must send her flowers for me, please."

"Sergei," she continues, shifting into familiar drama mode, "you will never believe what happened. The doctors came by to see me this morning, and when I asked them when I would be seeing Dr. Burger, they informed me that he had slipped his disk while trying to climb up to his apartment yesterday—the elevators being out on account of the power thing—and that he would be arriving here soon—not to see me, but to check in as a patient! I knew we should have stayed in Switzerland. The whole reason we came was to see this man who they say is the world's leading expert on ampullary tumors, or whatever the hell it is that I've got. A lot of good that does me now!"

"Yes, Mother, how totally inconsiderate of him to fall down the stairs of his dark building when you've come all this way to be operated on. Downright rude!"

"I see you must be feeling better too," Dollsie says, laughing, "back to your snide self! So anyway, they sent me this very odd man, a Dr. Caluzzi or something, but I've been making calls and I hear that the only one who should ever be allowed near me, if I can't have Dr. Burger, is some Chinese man by the name of Wu or Liu or something. So I request to see him but instead they send me someone else, a very nice Mexican man. This place is like Ellis Island! Not that the Mexicans ever entered the country through Ellis Island!

"I'm counting on you and Dimitri to get me the Chinese doctor because that Caprisi or whatever his name is looks like a serial killer, and excuse me but—and I don't mean to sound racist—you know I love the Mexicans as if they were my own people—but I am most certainly NOT being operated on by one of them. And don't look at me like that. I am not prejudiced. But one can only imagine what kind of medical schools they have in that godforsaken country!"

"Mother," interrupts Dimitri, who has spent the night with Dollsie in her suite and is by now as exasperated as I have been during the past few days, "for the tenth time, the guy's name is Gonzalez and I checked him out. He was born in Los Angeles and went to Harvard Medical School. Is that good enough for Your Highness?"

"Well, whatever. I can't believe I've come all this way to be operated on by a serial killer and a Mexican," she replies, with grim finality.

She is back in Dollsie monologue mode, not listening to what anyone is saying, and I take that as a good sign because it means that the pain must be under control.

"Now Sergei," she continues, as if moving on to the next item on her To Do list for the day, "I don't know what on earth you told those doctors when they did their intake yesterday, but they keep asking me if I'm experiencing any tremors or any other symptoms of alcohol withdrawal. The "DT's," they call it. I had to ask what that meant. Delirium tremens! What happens to alcoholics when they stop drinking. I nearly hit the roof! And then they asked me about what pills I take. I would hope that you didn't tell some total stranger that I am a boozer and a pill popper. And then they asked me about my 'multiple marriages'. I told them, 'I've been married twice, thank you very much!' You make me sound like Liz Taylor! I also told them that I just need my Xanax and my Paxil and whatever they are giving me for the pain, and that I'm not some alcoholic/drug addict, but of course they didn't believe me. I have you to thank for that!"

"Mother, I only mentioned..."

"I knew it! Well, if that isn't the pot calling the tea kettle black! Speaking of pot, did you smoke your little joint last night? Or two or three? Anyways, thank you for making me look like some kind of junkie. Now they won't give me ANY of my prescriptions. They claim that I am taking too many pills. I hardly think this is the time to worry about that, and besides, I really don't see how it's any of their business.

"Now," she continues, turning toward Dimitri after pausing to catch her breath, "Here is a list of everything I need from my bags." She pauses again, and gives us one of her dramatic looks. "We are in for a long haul, boys. A very long haul. This ain't going to be no picnic. So prepare yourselves."

You're telling me, I think to myself, wishing I could have some of whatever they gave her. Those must be some good meds. Propped up in bed, with her coffee and phone and phonebook, CNN on in the background, she looks like she's ready to attack the day. As if she's in the midst of planning another big event. I'm not sure I'll be able to keep up with her, barking out orders at the nurses as if they were part of her own personal staff, requesting appointments with the in-house hairdresser and manicurist and priest—"in that order!" It's difficult to imagine that a large tumor is blocking the entrance to her pancreas.

I go to look for Dr. Gonzalez—aka "the Mexican"—and find him at the nurses' station, talking to Dimitri, who is trying to wind up his shift so that he can head home to shower and change before going to the office. He's not thirty yet, but Jacques is grooming him to take over the company, and for both of them work comes before anything. "The Jewish thing," as Dollsie refers to it. Although her failed marriage to Jacques had brought out her anti-Semitic side, she does admire the work ethic. "Kind of like the Swiss and the Germans, but more ruthless," she would say.

"As I was telling your brother," continues Dr. Gonzalez, after introducing himself, "your mom seems to be out of danger for now. We're going to be running tests all day, but the infection seems to have receded. That was a very close call, I must tell you. I am not sure that I would have let her travel in this condition had I been the one in charge over there. But she is still in no shape to be operated on. Or at least, we can't be sure that she is. We have to monitor her liver, and run some more tests, to determine if she is strong enough to undergo this type of surgery, should you choose to go ahead with it. The "Whipple" is a major procedure. One of the biggies. We basically take out as much as we can— her pancreas, parts of her intestine, her gall bladder—and then we have to redo all the plumbing. And that's assuming that the cancer hasn't metastasized to the liver. That is the first thing we have to check out when we open her up, because if the cancer has already hit the liver, there's no point in doing the operation."

I look at Dimitri, who is fighting to hold back the tears. I've already explained most of this to him, more than once, but it doesn't register until he hears it from a doctor. "What do you do in that case?" he asks, his voice cracking.

"We just sew her back up. Nothing to be done, I'm afraid. If the cancer has spread to the liver, then it is basically inoperable."

I glance at Dimitri again, and I know that we are both visualizing the same scenario: Dollsie waking up from surgery to more bad news, and us being the ones who would have to deliver it to her.

"Assuming you can go ahead and operate, when would this be done?" asks Dimitri, shifting back into business mode, his zone of comfort. He is trying to play it cool, but the look of fear in his eyes betrays him. He is freaked out of his mind, the gravity of the situation beginning to sink in as the shock wears off.

"Well, after what happened yesterday, all the surgeries that were supposed to take place need to be rescheduled and on top of that, we are one man down, with Dr. Burger laid up. But we will get to her as soon as we can. Probably Monday or Tuesday. She needs that time to rest up for the surgery anyways. We will see how she is doing after the weekend. There is no urgency for now, unless of course something changes."

"What are her chances? Assuming the surgery goes well," I ask.

"Well, if we open her up and see that the tumor has spread to the liver or to other organs, and that we can't operate, then her chances are not good. But if we are able to successfully remove the tumor, then she has a decent chance of beating this, depending on its shape and its exact location."

I am not sure whether I believe this last part, after what Ashley told me. Further research on the internet has confirmed that people with pancreatic cancer rarely live beyond a year. And I'm weary of these places; of doctors who put patients through these killer treatments and instill false hope all in the name of research. But I decide not to challenge his assertions in front of Dimitri. There will be plenty of time for that later.

Dimitri takes off, and I call Giovanni to find out if he has made it to Gstaad yet, and when he will be heading back to Paris. I wonder when I will get back to Paris myself. I have only been gone about a week or so—I'm beginning to lose track of time—but it already feels distant to me. As if it belonged to another chapter of my life which has now concluded. Part of me had been feeling this way all year. Everything seemed to be winding down: my practice, my relationship with Giovanni, my social life: even Walt was slowing down. Perhaps it was all in preparation for this. Transition time. The calm before the storm.

I walk back down the hall to Dollsie's room, peeking inside the other rooms as I pass them, curious about the other patients on this VIP wing. I can't help but wonder what celebrities, CEOs and foreign potentates might be on this floor. Dollsie has fallen asleep, with her compact case and lipstick, her hands poised in midair. She looks old and harmless, this raging dynamo who has exhausted me all my life with her terrific energy, her manic eighteen-hour days, and her mega personality.

I approach the window to check out the view. The room overlooks New York Hospital across the street, and beyond that, the East River. Only six years ago, I had stood in another hospital room across the street, on a similar VIP wing on a high floor, watching the tugboats placidly drift by as my best friend Raphael lay in a morphine-induced coma, wondering how long it would take him to die.

FOURTEEN

BE A MAN

I grew up in a family with major emotional barriers and few physical boundaries, where everyone was always walking around naked—Dollsie, Dad, my siblings—and although I was always slightly repulsed by this, it felt normal. I remember one summer in Key Biscayne—I must have been five or six—when Dollsie would sunbathe nude and parade around the pool, showing off her privates which had been trimmed in the shape of a heart, enjoying the looks of shock from her mother and the rest of us.

Dollsie claimed that her psychology courses had taught her that there was nothing wrong with nudity, and furthermore, that "mild incest can be a positive growth factor"; a phrase she would often repeat just to provoke a look of disgust on my face. I could never figure out exactly what she meant by that, but I had spent enough uncomfortable hours in bathtubs with her and Nan—where she would "tickle" our genitals with her toes and make constant references to my "cute little pipi"—to know that on some level, she meant it.

At the age of fourteen, I had begun to question my sexuality after stealing a Hustler Magazine from the neighborhood store. As I came to a spread that featured a hot blonde couple fucking on a beach, it suddenly dawned on me that I was staring at the man and not the woman, that I was fixated on his penis, not her breasts or vagina. I thought to myself, with a mixture of fascination and thrilling horror, Oh my God! I'm gay! This epiphany had sent me into a daze which seemed to last for weeks as I contemplated the enormity of the revelation.

Dollsie, sensing that something was up, sent me to see Dr. Ralph, a Park Avenue society pediatrician who proclaimed himself an "expert" in everything related to adolescent behavior. When I told him that I thought I might be attracted to men, he protested.

"You've just convinced yourself of that so you won't have to compete with your older brother and his success with women," he said. "And so you won't have to feel inadequate around strong women like your mother. It's like telling me you are a pandophile: someone who is attracted to pandas. It is meaningless."

That summer before I went off to boarding school, a cousin came to visit from France. She was five or six, and I was put in charge of her while Dollsie recovered from her boob lift. My first summer job. She was a precocious child, coquettish and needy. Finding myself alone with her all day and left to our own devices, it quickly dawned on me that I could use her as an experiment to prove to myself that I was "normal". I attempted to molest her several times, trying to make her do the things that I had seen in movies, but I never got very far, no doubt due to my ambivalence. Testing my attraction for her and finding it wanting, I devised other ways of tormenting her, like pretending to lose her in supermarkets and drug stores. I felt empowered. I also felt deep shame.

And yet, as I realized years later after lots of therapy and time spent working with abused Hispanic kids in California during my first internship—in an attempt to understand why I had done what I had done, while healing the wounds by making things right—I was treating her exactly as I had secretly fantasized about being treated. My sadistic behavior was a mirror image of the masochism I longed to experience, transforming what I had always known—a domineering and abusive mother who lacked boundaries, an absent father, a terrifying brother, and no friends—into a desire to be used and abused. To relinquish all power and belong to someone; the classic gay fantasy. My cousin had been my guinea pig, and I had used her to try to figure out my manhood while wishing we could trade places, wishing someone would do to me what I was trying to do to her. It was very fucked up, and it set in motion the shame and sexual compulsion that would come to fuel a lifetime of sex addiction; self-destructive, impulsive, forever pushing the boundaries.

On the flight back to Paris with my cousin at the end of the summer, Dollsie noticed that her lips were swollen, and asked her why. My cousin responded that I had kissed her violently while saying goodbye. As soon as they landed, Dollsie called me, furious and demanding to know what had happened. I denied everything. Dollsie didn't believe me, but the rest of the family did, including my cousin's mother, her grandmother, and Mina, all of whom affirmed that the child had always had the most vivid imagination, which they attributed to her not having a father. They preferred to live in denial rather than confront this distasteful episode. I was off the hook.

Fifteen years later, when I moved to Paris, I found myself next to my cousin at a family dinner one evening. While the others carried on their conversations, I turned to her and finally apologized for everything I had done to her that summer. I wanted to express the guilt and shame I had carried around all these years, the attempts to expiate my crimes through my work as a therapist, but she cut me off. "I remember it well," she told me, "and I don't want to ever talk about it again."

Much to my surprise, we went on to become friends, and it was with tremendous relief that I attended her wedding a few years later, followed by the baptism of her child. I had not ruined her life after all.

After a great first year at Taft, where I discovered drugs and the theater—two modes of escape that would stay with me for life—and finally made friends, I made it my mission that summer to get my junior driver's license. Since my attempts to prove my manhood with my cousin had failed so abjectly, I decided that learning how to drive might do the trick. I yearned for freedom, for independence, and fantasized about running away with Dollsie's precious Mercedes convertible, her wedding gift to Jacques, which she had appropriated for herself a year later.

In order to practice for the upcoming test, every night, after Dollsie fell asleep, I would steal the car keys out of her purse and take the car for a spin. The night before the exam, as I was speeding around Key Biscayne feeling like a *man*, I put on my left blinker but at the last minute decided to turn right, causing a car to smash into me. Panicked, I took off, with the other car in pursuit until I finally pulled over. After much pleading with the driver not to report me to the police—explaining that it would jeopardize my chances of getting a license anytime soon—he let me go, after making sure that his vehicle had sustained no damage.

I drove Dollsie's car sheepishly back to Casa Del Mar, and once I had pulled into her space in the garage, I got out to survey the damage. To my great horror, there was a huge dent in the rear left fender. I went upstairs and entered the apartment quietly, replacing the keys in her purse. It took me a long time to fall asleep, as I envisaged Dollsie's reaction, her wrath and the consequences that lay in store for me.

The next morning, I was awoken by Dollsie shaking me. "Sergei! Sergei! Wake up!" she shrieked, in a panicked voice. "Jacques is going to kill me. I went out last night and apparently I must have had one too many because someone smashed into me without me knowing it. It's going to cost a fortune. He's going to have a FIT! You have to help me come up with a good story. I'm going to tell him it was a hit-and-run. That someone is out to get me because of my controversial refugee work. Do you think he will believe me?"

I breathed a huge sigh of relief, and helped her come up with a more plausible story. I couldn't believe my good fortune, and I set off for my driving test, confident that my luck would hold out and that I would pass on the first round. I didn't.

That fall, I had my first real sexual encounter. One afternoon, while I was home from Taft on a weekend break, I decided to go to a movie theatre on Broadway in the middle of the afternoon. The movie that was showing was *The Rose* with Bette Midler. I don't know why I thought that something would happen. Where I had gotten the notion that men had sex in movie theaters? The place was mostly empty. I sat behind a swarthy man and after exchanging glances with him, he came to sit beside me. He took my hand and put it on his bulge. My heart was racing a mile a minute, like the first time I had smoked a joint a few months earlier. He unbuttoned his pants and gently pushed my face down on him. Somehow I knew what to do and I went at it avidly, thrilled and terrified, unaware of the people around us.

The manager came and asked us to leave. Terrified that I would be arrested, I ran out of the theater and all the way home. I avoided looking at the doorman and elevator man as I rode up to the apartment, and once inside, I headed straight for the shower, where I spent half an hour scrubbing away the evidence. Did I feel shame or guilt? I don't think I did. But I did feel dirty, and I knew that something major had happened, something that I would never come back from. I could finally confirm that I was gay. To this day, every time *The Rose* comes on the radio, I still feel a rush and a pang of anxiety.

In the next few years, there were more visits to movie theaters during my weekends off. On the eve of my seventeenth birthday, on my way home from a black tie soirée at Doubles—a club in the basement of the Stanhope where Dollsie and her friends socialized and encouraged their offspring to do the same—I was picked up by a man walking down Lexington. He looked Filipino, and told me that he was a doctor. He politely invited me to his apartment, and I accepted, my heart pounding, knowing full well what was about to happen, at last. After putting on some classical music, he undressed me and fucked me. It hurt but I knew that it was supposed to; I was doing what I needed to do to become a man. After it was over, I left, feeling initiated. I had finally lost my virginity.

Meanwhile, at Taft, I went through four years of dating girls for whom I felt nothing, all the while falling in love with my male friends. We lived in a world of close intimacy, of sleeping and showering and partying together. Out of this grew fantasies which seemed natural enough in my own mind, but which I knew would be considered grotesque were I to share them with my friends. During those years, I never made any attempt to seek out others at school who might share my preferences. Even when I was drunk or high, I always remained aware of the potentially disastrous consequences of any move on my part. These were boys that had been raised with an overwhelming dose of heterosexuality, and trained to regard any deviation as perverse and disgusting.

But through the bonding ritual of marijuana and other drugs, I found myself with the first group of friends I had ever had in my life. For the first time, I belonged. During break or after classes we would sneak off campus and go get high in the graveyard or in an abandoned viaduct. At night, we would shove wet towels under the door and take turns passing the bong. We graduated from pot to coke and mushrooms and LSD. During weekend breaks, my friends and I would gather in New York, drop some acid and wander around the city hallucinating, watching in amazement as the lights turned into psychedelic wonders. I felt as if I had plunged into the depths of my soul; I knew myself for the first time. Everything was beautiful and perfect and no longer fucked up. Until the day, during senior year, when I spent the afternoon hanging out my window, contemplating leaping to a tree whose branches had come alive and were beckoning me, promising me that I could fly, that I would not fall. Feeling the eternal pull between self-destruction and self-preservation—a tension which would mark my life. I resisted, and after coming down off that trip, vowed never to do acid again.

1983 was a year of transition for all of us. Nan went off to The Madeira School in Virginia, Anton moved to California after a rocky few years in Manhattan, and Dad retired from the bank and moved to Buffalo with his wife to take over the family business, thus closing another chapter of our Swiss life. And Dollsie—after putting us all through seven years of hell—finally left Jacques and their vast gloomy duplex on Park Ave. to move back into "19 East," the same building we had lived in before moving to Switzerland. As with Gstaad, she was trying to turn back the clock, to erase this nightmare chapter of her life as if it had never happened, to get back to a time before her grand plan had become unraveled.

I graduated from Taft and moved to Washington to attend Georgetown University, where I had miraculously been accepted thanks to Dollsie's connections, despite my mediocre grades and my suspension for cheating on the final of my Modern China class (which happened to be taught by the headmaster), a school wide scandal that implicated several students and threatened to jettison our college prospects. Anton, too, had been caught cheating during finals of his freshman year at Princeton, and had not been "asked back." Besides the shame this brought upon the family, especially my grandmother, who worshipped at the altar of her deceased husband's legacy as a football legend, it also shattered Dollsie's illusions about her perfect firstborn son, and now that I, too, had been caught violating the Honor Code, Dollsie couldn't help but wonder what people would say about her failure to raise us with the proper values.

There had been some family pressure for me to attend Cornell University, where Mina's father had donated the Schoellkopf Field back in 1915, but after four years in the boonies, I was eager for a more cosmopolitan environment where I could at last begin to explore my sexuality.

That was also the year I turned eighteen. As soon as I arrived at Georgetown, two things happened, almost simultaneously: I came out, and AIDS made its "coming out" as well. My first Saturday night on campus, I snuck away from the dormitory meet 'n greet to go cruising. Excited and thrilled and terrified at the prospect of finally being able to fulfill my desires and live my sexuality openly,

I ventured into several bars that I had studiously looked up in gay guides, and ended up meeting a cute young black guy and getting it on with him in his car, as oblivious to the passers-by as I was to this mysterious, scary disease which had begun to devastate gay meccas like San Francisco and New York.

During my first weekend home I decided to break the news Dollsie over dinner at Mortimer's, the über WASP hang-out on the Upper East Side. You went there to be seen. Eating was beside the point. I figured that it was a good choice; since the place would be filled with "her crowd" she wouldn't allow herself to make a scene—unless she got drunk, of course, which was always a distinct possibility. Once she hit that first margarita, there was no stopping her.

Nan was there too, and I knew that she had already started dabbling with girls at Madeira, an all-girls school in Virginia (famous for its headmistress, Jean Harris, who had killed her lover, the "Scarsdale Doctor"). As I revealed my big secret, taking perverse pleasure in the reaction it provoked in her, Dollsie attempted to maintain a brave and neutral face throughout dinner, saying all the right things and pledging her love and support. A few hours later, however, she stumbled into my room, completely smashed, and with great seriousness and deliberation, said to me: "I just don't understand the big fuss, Sergei. After all, a hole is a hole!"

The very next day, she took me to see Pierre, her beloved French hairdresser, who was dying in the hospital. We put on gloves and masks to enter his room, and there he lay, weighing maybe fifty pounds. I stared at him, aghast, hoping the mask hid my expression. The exuberant, happy homo with his outrageous leather outfits and scandalous tales—whom I would observe with thrilled, forbidden fascination when he came to the house to do Dollsie's hair—had turned into an unrecognizable, bony creature; a veritable cadaver with a look of terror in his eyes and the smell of death emanating from his every pore. On the way out, Dollsie stopped me in the hallway, turned to me, looked me deep in the eyes, and said, "That's exactly what will happen to you if you are not careful."

Shortly after, I came out to my godfather, Maito, who a decade earlier had walked out on his wife and two sons after belatedly and brazenly declaring his preference for men. He lived in Litchfield, Connecticut, with his lover who made wigs, and the Jack Russells they bred and raised. While at Taft, I had spent many weekends at his place, lying awake at night, hoping that one of his guests might jump me. As with the teachers at Taft and the priests at Georgetown, these fantasies were never fulfilled.

When I told Maito about coming out to Dollsie, he said: "Well, my dear, I hope she didn't act surprised! After all, she was the one who used to dress you as a girl during your first few years and tell everyone: 'This is my gay son, the one who will never leave me for another woman.'" She would deny the story until her dying day.

Dollsie asked me to consult a psychotherapist in Washington, "just to be sure", and after trying out one or two I settled on a warm, heavy woman who knitted and drank Tab during our sessions. It didn't take me long to realize that I had chosen her because she was the very antithesis of Dollsie. After a few sessions, she told me that as far as my sexuality was concerned, she could confirm that I was indeed gay, and a very well-adjusted gay at that. My parents had done something right. But then she added:

"Now, if you want to hang out and do some Mom therapy, we've got a couple years of work ahead of us, because—excuse my French—that's one fucked up lady. She sure did a number on you."

So I followed her advice and stayed for two years. She was the first therapist to point out that knowing what was wrong with me was the easy part; I had been told all about that all my life. Our challenge would be to find out what was right with me. It was a credo that would stay with me throughout my own years as a therapist.

Six months later, I decided to break the news to Dad. I thought he would be cool with it; after all, both he and Dollsie had raised us with an open mind when it came to their gay friends. Instead, over dinner in Georgetown, he launched into a monologue, the longest I had ever heard from him in my entire life: "It's like playing golf, Sergei. Golf is a game for right-handed players, with right-handed golf clubs. If you're left-handed, you're at a severe disadvantage, because there are very few left-handed clubs and very few people who can teach you how to play a good game of golf that way. So you like screwing men? Fine. What's the big deal? A lot of men think about it and sometimes even try it, but then they move on. No need to ruin your life by walking around with a billboard announcing that you're 'gay.'".

On and on he went, and as dinner was drawing to a close, flabbergasted and not knowing what else to say, I asked him: "So do you wish I hadn't told you?"

"Sergei," he answered with exasperation, "that's like asking me if I wish you hadn't kicked me in the balls. When you told me you had something important to tell me, I got on a plane to come see you because I thought you might have a brain tumor or something. I'm not sure which is worse. I know I certainly didn't need to come all this way to hear this!

"My advice: go out and fuck every guy in sight. Get it out of your system, then move on. Because if you choose that route, there isn't going to be much for you to do with your life, besides being a hairdresser or a decorator or a florist."

After that, I didn't speak to Dad for six months. Our writing correspondence, which could be as frequent as daily, ground to a stop. We gave each other the silent treatment—our default mode when we were upset—and I swore I would never speak with him until he apologized. Which eventually he did, and we went back to exchanging letters, which later on became faxes, and then e-mails. Although we often corresponded almost on a daily basis, nothing of any great depth was ever exchanged. Feelings were avoided, platitudes encouraged. It felt more like corresponding with a congenial uncle and at times it could be downright boring, but I felt closer to him when we wrote each other than when we saw each other, and I knew he felt the same way. When we were together, we kept our distance. It was only when we were apart that we could feel close.

Later that fall, Claudia, whom I had been close to for ten years, died at the age of eighteen, two months after surviving a car crash in Italy, when the old jeep she and her friends had been riding in lost its breaks and plunged into a ravine, where it caught fire. The others had been bounced out of the jeep unscathed, but Claudia—the only one wearing a seatbelt—had remained stuck inside. By the time her friends were able to get her out, she had suffered third degree burns over ninety percent of her body. After she was transferred back to Miami, I went to visit her as she lay dying. I stood helpless before her agony, stroking her beautiful, angelic hair and face, the only parts of her body to have been spared the flames. She died a few weeks later, the blood oozing from her skin. I had lost my first friend and with her, the dreams and visions we had conjured for our improbable, wistful future together.

Death seemed to be all around me. For the next several years, I wondered if every man I slept with would give me AIDS and kill me. Especially the black man I met and went home with during one of my first terrified outings to the gay bars in Washington. After he had finished fucking me, he told me that he was Haitian. It was like delivering a death sentence. Back then, everyone "knew" that AIDS came from Haiti so for several weeks, I was convinced that I was going to die.

In time, the danger became a part of the thrill. Not because I sought it, but because it was real. For the next four years, I would spend my weekends frequenting the gay bars and clubs of the nation's capital—Blow Buddies and Tracks and Lost and Found—looking for Mr. Right, drinking enough to convince myself that I'd found him before we even left the club together, falling in love by the next morning, and moving on to the next conquest the following weekend. It felt wonderful to be desired, and the sex, I told myself, was just a gateway to something else. Being picked up by a hot guy, often older, made me feel special. It made me feel loved. It made up for all the validation that I hadn't gotten from the males in my life.

I suppose that this troika of sex, love and death was no different for me than for every other gay man of my generation. We stepped out of the closet into this liberating, terrifying world where every time you met a guy, you wondered if you would have sex with him, fall in love, and/or die. For a while, we managed to convince ourselves that AIDS was something that happened to others—to all those old scary men who had been around in the seventies; the clones with their tacky mustaches and tight jeans and the color-coded handkerchiefs in their back pockets that denoted their sexual preferences, the ones who went to bathhouses and had sex with dozens of men in one night, thousands in a year. We were not like them; we were just normal college kids doing what our straight counterparts were doing.

But then, inevitably, one of the boys I knew, Steve Champion (I will never forget his name), a gorgeous Cuban guy a few years ahead of me at Georgetown, got sick and died within a matter of weeks. We were all deeply shocked. Rumor had it that he had gotten fucked by hundreds of men while spending a semester abroad in Paris. So it could happen to us after all.

I spent the following summer in Paris myself, living on a barge on the Seine and attending a course in French cinema. When I wasn't in class, I would cruise the Jardins des Tuileries and venture into the clubs. I met many men that summer, and I wondered if I, too, would end up like Steve Champion.

I graduated from Georgetown with a 3.9 grade average for my senior year, almost a perfect score. This was nothing short of a miracle, given that until

Georgetown, I had always been in the C+/B- range. To celebrate, the entire family had flown in: Greasy, all my siblings, Dad and his wife, along with Jacques and Dollsie's current beau, Jack Warnecke. All of Dollsie's men—the three Jacks, as we called them. She had also invited a Cuban couple whom she knew socially. There was no reason for them to be at the dinner except for the fact that the husband was the highest Cuban appointee in the Reagan administration, which Dollsie thought would add social luster to the event.

The dinner took place in an elegant French restaurant in downtown D.C., whose name I have long since blocked. Dollsie proceeded to get rip-roaring roaring drunk and spent most of the meal taunting my helpless stepmother, referring to her repeatedly as "Nanook of the North", leaving everyone at the table aghast. It was the longest meal of my life.

Finally, it came to a blessed end, and as we waited outside for the Cubans' limousine to pull up, Dollsie started to pee, right there on the sidewalk, as she puffed nonchalantly on her cigarette. I was the first one to notice the puddle spreading beneath her feet, soon followed by the emissary's wife. She stared, completely horrified, as it slowly dawned on her what was happening: this elegant woman whom she barely knew was peeing on the sidewalk right in front of the restaurant, and would soon be getting into their plush, government-appointed limousine for the ride back to the hotel.

I had long ago nicknamed Dollsie "the lady who pees where she pleases"; she had a habit of relieving herself wherever she felt like it, totally oblivious to whoever was around her. We had witnessed her peeing court-side while watching a tennis game at the Wellington Polo Club in Palm Beach; off boats; on beaches; and—her specialty—on towel-covered beach chairs. We had learned at a young age to never sit in Dollsie's chair, because you were certain to land in urine-soaked towel.

So I was used to her peeing. But watching that Cuban lady as she stared at Dollsie relieving herself on the sidewalk in all her finery definitely took it to a whole other level. For months, I seethed with anger and shame. Why had she done this to me? She claimed that ever since her "difficult pregnancy", she had developed a bladder control problem. But I have always suspected she did it for the same reason that she "let" the greyhounds service her in front of her children: her narcissism had reached such a plateau that she took a perverse thrill in showing off how oblivious she was to the rules by which others lived, and how willfully unconcerned by whatever effect her reckless actions might have on us, her children.

Following graduation, I interned for a family AIDS clinic at Albert Einstein Hospital in the Bronx. These children were at the forefront of the AIDS epidemic, and many of them didn't know what they had. One little girl, Celeste, who had been in and out of hospitals all her life, finally discovered the cause of her multitude of illnesses when she was walking by a newsstand one day and saw a picture of herself on the cover of Newsweek, with the headline: "Children Living With AIDS". Every day, I would take the subway from the Upper East Side up to Morris Parkway in the Bronx, and observe and interact with these families in crisis. For two months, I played with dying children and talked to their desperate mothers, who were often dying themselves. Those two months undoubtedly changed my life.

Meanwhile, Dollsie had also immersed herself in the world of pediatric AIDS, doing fundraisers and volunteering at Metropolitan Hospital in Harlem. It was as if we had both decided, independently, that if we contributed enough to the cause, I might be spared. We were joined in our magical thinking, too terrified to raise the subject with each other, but deeply committed to doing what we could to help.

Our efforts were rewarded when Dollsie and I were invited by Nancy Reagan to bring Celeste to the White House for a photo opportunity to show the world that these kids were not contagious, that they deserved love too. Nancy walked in looking immaculate. She went straight up to Celeste and her grandmother, and embraced them with open arms. I was so taken aback by how genuine and warm she was that it threw me off my game, and by the time she came over to shake my hand, my palms were drenched. As she retreated, I noticed her wipe her hand against her skirt with all the subtlety she could muster. I was mortified, as was Dollsie, who gave me a look confirming that I had committed the faux pas of the century.

It was my second encounter with the Reagans, my first having been during their second inauguration, when I had been one of the waiters chosen to serve at the luncheon in the Rotunda of the Capitol. The day was so cold that the inaugural parade had been canceled. But we had been there since 5 am, frozen. I was assigned to Ron Jr.'s table, only a few feet away from the dais where Ronald and

Nancy were sitting, and by the time the lunch started, I still felt stiff from the cold. My hands could barely function and I wondered how I would get through the five course meal, served with gloves. The first course landed on everyone's plate fine, but by the second course, I had become distracted by the pageantry and the enormity of the occasion. Ron Jr. leaned over to flirt with some admiral and bumped into me just as I was attempting to serve him a piece of salmon. I missed the plate by a few inches and stared in horror at the piece of fish, laying there on the elegant embroidered table cloth for all the world to see, wondering what to do, as both hands were engaged. Ron smiled flirtatiously and picked up the fish with his fingers and dropped it in his plate, winking and whispering at me as he did so, "Don't worry, it used to happen to me all the time."

But I was sure that others had noticed, including Nancy and everybody else in the room, and was not surprised when the catering calls stopped coming from Glorious Foods.

After graduation, I stayed in Washington another year, to complete a Masters in English and write a novel, which would serve as my thesis. I moved to Dupont Circle, aka the Fruit Loop, and was thrilled to at last find myself living on my own for the first time, and in a gay neighborhood. Unencumbered by roommates or studies, I went on a rampage that year, yet somehow managed to complete both the novel and my degree.

Hoping to get my novel published, I returned to New York for the summer and landed a job with a neurotic, hysterical photographer married to a famous author who seemed to think she was as much of a bitch as I did, locking himself in his office on the top floor of their townhouse and interacting with her as little as possible. Instead of getting my novel published, I landed a job as an editorial assistant and found myself living in New York once again, a place where I had never been happy and had never intended to return.

During the day I would put in long hours as an editorial assistant, and then I'd come home and spend most of the night reading manuscripts. The first six months, I lived in a basement studio in the West Village, and then, with Dad's help, I bought my first apartment, a one-bedroom on the top floor of a brownstone with a roof garden in the heart of Chelsea. I was hyper-aware of what was happening all around me, especially at night, and I had trouble cutting it off and going to sleep. I soon discovered that you didn't have to go to bars to pick up men; you could hook up over the telephone. It was anonymous and dangerous and intense and thrilling. More often than not, I wouldn't find anybody, so the calls would go on all night, and the phone bills would go up and the exhaustion would set in, more or less permanently. The pattern was set in motion: if there was sex to be had I didn't want to be left out, and I was determined to find it so I stayed up as long as I could trying to make it happen, looking for connection and penetration and love. I developed a life-long insomnia that would rear its ugly head anytime I was in a major city where temptation abounded.

Then I met Raphael. He was twenty-four at the time, a year older than me. He worked for Dollsie's decorator, a pretentious closeted queen from South America who had come to Manhattan to reinvent himself. He had developed a clientele of super wealthy Latin Americans and nouveau riche oligarchs from various parts of the globe. Raphael, also Chilean, had also come to Manhattan a few years earlier to seek his fortune, and he had found it in the form of a seventy-year-old man named Peter, who came from an old German/Jewish New York family—the kind that seemed more WASPy than Jewish. They lived in a penthouse on Fifth Avenue and on weekends, we would either go to Peter's farm near Princeton, New Jersey, or stay in the city, doing ecstasy and going out clubbing. When I was on "X"—known as the love drug—I would invariably fall for the first guy that came on to me, and quickly disappear.

When we weren't out partying and cruising we would often find ourselves at some gay soirée, composed of older men who had achieved or inherited some measure of wealth or power—known as New York's "A Gays". They were surrounded by young, beautiful, ambitious boys who had come to New York to find such men. Dollsie was friends with many of the "A-Gays"—including Robert, a Sotheby's auctioneer who frequently threw these parties—so wherever I went, I was known as Dollsie's son. It was a bit unnerving. I felt like I had to live up to her reputation, while at the same time worrying that none of these men would hit on me, precisely because of her reputation.

Whether at these dinners or in the clubs, I never felt comfortable around the gay crowd in New York because it made me feel like I was back at Buckley, on the outside looking in, trying to gain acceptance to a club that wouldn't have me. As with Dollsie and the Buckley boys, for whom appearance and status were everything, the gay scene revolved around who had the hottest body, the best boyfriend, the power job, the killer pad and the house in Fire Island—the flip gay side of the Upper East Side/Hamptons social climbers. I didn't feel like I needed to compete when it came to most of these aspirational goals—being a "trust fund baby" gained me instant access—but the body image always got to me. Every time I would enter a room full of gay men, with their perfect New York bodies, I would feel like the fat, uncoordinated Buckley "fag" all over again.

On a weekend trip to New Orleans for Halloween with Raphael, I discovered bathhouses. I had always found the concept disgusting: the idea of walking around in a towel and picking up what I imagined to be scary, diseased old men. But being on ecstasy in a bathhouse in New Orleans during Halloween proved to be a different experience. Along with the scary old men there were also a lot of hot young ones, and the notion that I could enjoy more than one, that I didn't have to pick one and go home with him proved to be intoxicating. I spent most of the weekend in the bathhouse. We came back to New Orleans several times, enjoying the decadence and sense of freedom that came from being let loose in a wild city that wasn't our own.

In New York, things got more hardcore. The dancing clubs gave way to events like the Black Party, the first of the so-called "circuit parties" where gay men would come from far and wide to partake in what was essentially a drug-fueled mass orgy. I'll never forget walking into the space where the event was being held, an old movie theatre in the East Village. On the dance floor, thousands of men gyrated to the music, half-naked, while others ingested substances and got down and dirty, oblivious to onlookers. In the bleachers, one black man stood with his huge dick spilling out of his black leather pants, looking like a Mapplethorpe portrait, while men got in line, eager to service him.

Soon after arriving at the Black Party, Raphael shoved some powder up my nose, telling me it was coke. All of a sudden, I felt like I was about to die; as if my heart were plunging to the ground, taking me with it. Instead of coke, he had given me a drug called Special K, thinking my reaction would be amusing. After spending what seemed like an eternity in a near comatose state—otherwise known as a k-hole—I managed to find my way out of there and made my way home.

After two years in New York, I was beginning to feel burned out. I had thrived during my debut in publishing, but I wanted to go back to my own writing, and I knew that the sex and the drugs and the sleepless nights would eventually do me in if I didn't get away.

One day, as I was in the shower, trying to come out of my usual comatose state to get ready for work, one of my dogs, Tennessee, a chow chow, got into a fight with my other dog, Lucy, a sweet, odd-looking shar pei/lab mix. As I attempted to pull Tennessee off of her, he went nuts and attacked me, mauling my hands—first the right, then the left. It was several minutes before I was able to pry him loose by standing on the bed and dangling him in midair, until he finally let go. I managed to get dressed and ran out into the street, my hands wrapped in a towel, bleeding profusely. Several cabs sped by, before one finally stopped and took me to the emergency room.

I ended up spending a few days at St Vincent's hospital, then was transferred to St. Luke's, where I underwent surgery, almost losing the use of one of my hands, so badly had he bitten me. I spent most of the time in the hospital in tears, in great pain and overwhelmed by what had transpired. After consulting with chow experts as to what I should do with him, I finally decided to have him put down, a task which was left to my sweet dog walker, Matthew, a young Southern gentleman right out of a Tennessee Williams play who loved my Tennessee beyond measure. I can only imagine what it must have felt like for him to take that young, beautiful, ferocious dog off to be euthanized. I knew that I would not be able to face the gruesome task myself, but I couldn't run the risk of him attacking someone else.

A few days later, I was released from the hospital, and spent another week convalescing at Dollsie's. I was devastated, overcome with tremendous guilt. I felt responsible for what had happened—I knew that I had treated him much as Dollsie had treated us, with tough love and excessive discipline. I interpreted the freak attack and his untimely death as a strong warning that my life was slowly careening out of control, and that something had to change.

I quit my job at Doubleday, where my beloved and bewildered boss had just offered me a promotion, and flew down to New Orleans to attend Nan's graduation from Tulane. After a week of partying, she with her college mates and me on Bourbon Street and in the bathhouse, we embarked on a road trip across the country with our two dogs, smoking pot throughout the journey, stopping in places like Santa Fe and Phoenix, in search of the next destination, where I might settle down and become a writer, like Dad had dreamed of doing.

I had no idea where I would end up. All I knew was that I was heading West.

FIFTEEN

OFF TO THE BUTCHER

They finally schedule Dollsie for surgery three days later.

The day before, Dollsie decides she wants to attend Sunday mass in the chapel at MSK. I'm not sure she's up for it, but she insists, so down we go. As I wheel her into the room, I'm taken aback, and I can tell that she is too: patients in various stages of cancer are gathered in a circle. I take one look at them—their tubes, their baldness, their deathliness, their desperation and suffering, their hope and their faith—and I feel the tears coming. I do not want cry in front of Dollsie, I want to stay strong for her, to *be a man*, but I can't help myself. For the first time, looking at these people and what awaits us, I am overcome with grief.

Dollsie looks over at me, and squeezes my hand, as if to say, "It's okay, you can let go." I begin to cry uncontrollably. At first, I cry for Dollsie but then I cry for me, for the bitterness and anger that I've been carrying around all my life, this bitterness that I first felt toward Dollsie for leaving Dad to marry an older, richer man who had promised her the world. I hated her for leaving Dad alone and for destroying a family for the sake of personal fulfillment. Over time, those feelings had extended to every facet of my life, and now I feel them being washed away by the tears, leaving me drenched in regret but also free. Free from recrimination, free from the need to punish and the impossibility of forgiveness. For I realize that I can't heal my mother's shame, no more than she can heal mine. All we can do is be there for each other and do the best we can, not to try to repair the past—because how can you ever change something that has already happened—but to move forward, wherever that takes us. In that moment, I feel closer to her than I've ever felt before.

That night, Dimitri and I have a dinner catered for Dollsie's "Last Supper," as she refers to it. We order from her favorite restaurant, Mr. Chow's, and two uniformed waiters arrive with a huge spread which they lay out in the private dining room. Dollsie, in a lot pain, is nonetheless determined to put on a good show for us. She knows that it is the last meal that she will be indulging in for a long time, so she attacks the canard laque with all the gusto she can muster. We don't talk much about the operation. She takes it on faith that they will just "take the thing out" and that after that, everything will get back to normal. She has survived many other operations; she can get through this. She has not been informed of the possibility that the doctors might not be able to go through with the surgery once they cut her open.

She has spent the last three days making lists, just in case. Lists of her art collection and her valuables, who will get what if she "croaks on the table"; the cash gifts that she wants to bequeath to her many nieces, nephews, and godchildren; and instructions for where she wants to be buried and what arrangements need to be made, where she wants the reception held, and what caterers to contact. She has already spoken to her accountant and banker and estate attorney, as well as the Swiss lawyer who looks after her affairs in Gstaad. And finally, she has written us all farewell letters. Just in case...

Dimitri has taken to spending the night with Dollsie while I stay at his apartment, which suits me fine. There is only so much intimacy and face time with Dollsie that I can handle. I have spent the past three days making lists, too. I've decided not to go back to Paris; to stay with Dollsie, in New York or Miami or wherever she ends up, to be with her through this final journey. After twenty-five years of avoidance and animosity, I feel the need to heal some of the wounds, to make peace and achieve some understanding of this woman before it is too late. I don't want her to die with all this guilt, thinking that one of her children hated her. Or maybe, I don't want to be left with all the guilt once she is gone. I want to get closer to the person that I have spent my whole life running away from, perhaps to see what I've missed. I want to figure out why she and I have felt so much rage toward each other. I have been angry at her my entire life, and by extension at the whole world.

Most of all, I want to help her die with dignity. This much I can do. I've been dealing with illness and death for a long time. I can run interference for her with the medical establishment, much as she had done for me when I had been in and out of hospitals. I've notified my few remaining patients that I am taking a leave of absence to care for my mother and to await the adoption. Giovanni wants to join me in New York but I tell him that he should stay in Paris, and that he can continue living in my place, all expenses paid, until he finds a job. He hasn't worked since I have known him. He doesn't know it yet, but I'm ready to move on from him as well. But I'm not up for another break up right now, with all the accompanying drama and guilt. It's easier to just let him think that nothing has changed for a while longer. And I'm not ready to end my story with Paris yet. I won't miss it, but it's been my life for ten years. It is where I finally grew up. That love affair is almost over, but not quite. It's hard to leave Paris.

I have made lists of what needs to be done in Paris while I'm away, and what needs to happen in New York: doctors to be contacted for second opinions; living arrangements for Dollsie once she gets out of the hospital; and lists of short-term furnished rentals for me. Dollsie wants me to stay with her at Carlton House on Madison Avenue—she suggested adjoining suites—but that won't be happening. I need a place of my own, otherwise I will be swallowed up. And the adoption agency has informed me that I should establish residence in New York as soon as possible in case a baby comes up for adoption sooner than expected. Wherever I'm living has to meet certain requirements, and they need to conduct home inspections both here and in Paris.

During our "Last Supper", I tell Dollsie about my plans to stay with her until she "gets better".

"What about Paris?" she asks, in disbelief. "What about your practice and your beautiful house? What about Giovanni?"

"None of that is important. I want to help you through this."

"Okay," she says, after a long pause, "how much time do I have?"

"What do you mean?" I reply, taken aback.

"Sergei, darling, if you are leaving Paris and your practice and your lover for "Mommie Dearest"—as you've always referred to me—then I must be about to croak any minute. You just want to hang around to make sure they finish the job and put me six feet under."

We manage to laugh, Dimitri trying to retain his poker face as he navigates these unfamiliar waters.

Dollsie never makes it through her first moo-shoo pancake. She holds on for as long as she can, wanting to keep things as festive as possible, to show her gratitude and love, and to set an example of grace under pressure. After all, the party must go on, no matter what. But soon she is taken back to her room and the heaps of leftovers are packed up and put away in the fridge.

The next morning, we meet in Dollsie's room to accompany her to surgery. I find her dressed all in white, perfectly combed and made up, and holding a bouquet of flowers plucked from the many arrangements she has received over the last few days.

"Mother, what are you doing?" I ask, wondering if they have given her an extra dose of something.

"I am going to see the great Dr. Burger in his suite," she answers, adding grandly, "I am going to pay my respects before I go under the knife. My life is in his hands."

"Actually, Mother, it's not in his hands," I say, trying not to laugh at the sight of her. She gives me one of her looks and explains that since it has been decided that his two chief residents will perform the operation—the Italian serial killer and the Mexican—she in turn has decided to make a pilgrimage down the hall to Dr. Burger's room to beg him to oversee the operation by phone. And video if possible. She has been granted five minutes. So off we go down the hall, Dollsie looking for all the world like the bride of Frankenstein, or a tragic Tennessee Williams heroine about to greet her imaginary suitor. The nurses, doctors and patients watch mesmerized as she parades by, with Dimitri and me propping her up and rolling the IV stand beside her. Somber as the occasion is, he and I can't help but find this hysterically funny, and we avoid looking at each other for fear of losing it.

As we lead her into Dr. Burger's suite, Dollsie falls into a deep curtsey, bouquet in hand, as if she were being presented to the Queen of England. It's comical and touching; she wants so badly to make him understand that she is special, that she should not be allowed to die like all the others.

Dr. Burger is lying in bed, evidently in pain. I doubt very much that he will be overseeing the surgery in any way, shape or form, but he is playing along. He seems charmed, telling her that he will follow her progress every step of the way and that if they run into complications, he will insist on being wheeled down to the room immediately. They revel in each other's flattery and drama, laying it on thick.

"Really?" Dollsie says, practically batting her eyelashes.

"Really, my dear," he responds, with a Jack Nicholson leer.

It's tough keeping a straight face.

"Doctor, what are my chances?" she asks him, almost pleading.

"Well, Duckie, that depends on what we find and where we find it," he answers, in his upbeat, gruff voice. "I must tell you that if it is in the pancreas, well, you know, the chances aren't very good, I'm afraid to say. Let's just hope for the best."

"But why is that, Doctor, if they manage to get it all out?" she asks, with panic creeping into her voice.

"If we manage to get it all out, that would be wonderful, wouldn't it, Darling? But we still have to make sure it hasn't spread around to the liver and lymph nodes."

"And if it does spread, how much time do I have?"

"Oh, my dear," answers the doctor, suddenly exhausted. "It's too early to get into all that. Too early in the morning, and too early in the game. Don't worry, you are in the best hands possible. Better than these old meat cleavers of mine. And as I told you, I'll be watching over you every step of the way."

With that, we exit, and return to her room to await the operation. Martine makes her grand entrance, once again dressed to kill.

"Dodo!" she exclaims, with that fake cheerfulness that is already getting on my nerves.

"Don't you 'DoDo' me, you bitch!" replies Dollsie, willing herself out of her pain so that she can get properly riled up, "You evil, evil bitch!"

"But what have I done?" asks Martine, taken aback, in her French-Bulgarian vamp voice.

"I found out that you managed to get past security on the floor yesterday by claiming to the guard that you are my daughter!" Dollsie hisses.

We can't tell if she is genuinely upset or not, but Dimitri and I are enjoying the show, welcoming the comic relief of a cat fight before the big event.

"Honey," she continues, "just because you strut around town in stiletto heels and a transparent dress with your boobs practically falling out, it doesn't make you look like you could be my daughter. Not by a long shot!" She turns to us and adds, "Martine likes to think she is young, but she is over fifty. Well over fifty. She's barely ten years younger than me. How dare she claim she's my daughter? Ridiculous. And pathetic."

With that, the attendants arrive to take her down to surgery, and Dimitri and I follow, leaving Martine behind in the room in tears. On the way down, Dollsie tells the nurse—for the twentieth time—that she needs a lot of anesthesia, because of all the meds she is used to taking.

"I've had eighteen operations in my life, so believe me, I'm harder to dope up than a heroin addict."

"Don't worry," replies the nurse, patiently, "We will be sure you are sufficiently sedated. And I hope you followed your instructions and did not have anything to eat or drink or smoke this morning!"

"No, of course not!" replies Dollsie, lying. She had made Dimitri sneak her out of the hospital at seven in the morning so that she could have two cigarettes before they came to prep her.

"Off to the butcher!" she exclaims, as they open the doors to the operating area, beyond which we are not admitted.

We head to the lobby, which serves as a giant waiting room. Every fifteen minutes or so a family is paged to the front desk for an update. It feels like being in the airport, waiting for your gate to be announced. Although we are obviously eager to find out what is going on in the operating room, we know that if they page us too soon, it will probably not be good news; it would mean that they had opened her up, found that the tumor had spread or was inoperable, and then closed her back up. So every time we hear someone being called to the front we are relieved to hear that it is not us.

We take turns heading out for cigarettes and coffee, one of us always remaining in the lobby in case we are paged. Anton is still in Europe, Nan in California, and they call us every few minutes to ask for updates as do Greasy and many others. It's driving me nuts. I decide to shut off my cell phone and go smoke a joint outside, behind the hospital.

When I tell Dimitri where I am going, he looks at me like I've lost it.

"This isn't Ibiza, dude! You can't just go out and smoke a joint in broad daylight right outside the hospital."

"Watch me," I say, heading out. Old habits die hard. I walk up 70th Street in the direction of 1st Avenue. Every street and corner feels sickeningly familiar; I had walked these blocks as a pre-adolescent, going from doctor to doctor and hospital to hospital.

I wonder how things will turn out this time.

I head back to the waiting room after finishing the joint behind a construction site half-way up the block, feeling paranoid instead of relaxed, and wondering how I will handle any bad news. Hours go by without even an update. It feels like Bern all over again, except that this time no news is good news and I am with a brother that I can let go with, lean on. Dimitri is having a hard time handling this, which is normal given his young age, but he puts on a brave front and is determined to remain optimistic and upbeat throughout, for Dollsie's sake. He and I have always been close, but the last few days and hours have taken us to another level of intimacy. We are teammates, determined to see her through this ordeal together, come hell or high water. The only difference is that he believes that she will make it, whereas I harbor no such illusions. His love for her is astonishing to witness, and foreign to me. It is something that I have never experienced before, with anybody, and I wonder what it must feel like to love a parent so much, and how he does it without feeling crushed by her.

Finally, we are paged. We rush to the front desk. They have proceeded with the removal of the tumor. There have been no complications. She is in stable condition and is being taken to the post-op unit where she will spend the next twenty-four hours in the ICU. We are told to head up to her room to get some rest. They will contact us later in the day when she wakes up, or when the doctor is ready to talk to us. He has back-to-back surgeries lined up for the rest of the day so it might be a while.

Relieved, Dimitri heads out to get us some lunch and I go back to the room to make some calls, praying Martine is not still there. It is the first good news that we've had since the whole thing started. We still don't know much, but the fact that she made it through the "Whipple" and that they were actually able to remove the tumor is huge. I feel like the worst is over; no matter what happens, she won't have to go through anything like this again.

Dr. Gonzalez and Dr. Caluzzi come by to see us a few hours later.

"We are very pleased," says Dr. Gonzalez, "we were able to remove the tumor intact, and we did not see any evidence of the cancer having metastasized to the liver, or anywhere else for that matter, although we won't know for sure until we have done a biopsy of the lymph nodes we removed." They remind us that the next few weeks will be brutal; she will be in a great deal of pain and will not want to eat, exercise, or even move. But her recovery depends on it.

"Gotta get the new plumbing working as soon as possible," they tell us.

Dimitri and I head up to the ICU. We are shown into a large room where a few dozen patients lie, side by side, recovering from surgery, tubes coming out of every part of their bodies. The first patient we pass looks like he is already dead.

"Dude, where is she?" asks Dimitri, "I don't know if I can handle this."

As we walk to the end of the row, I spot her. She looks as if she has aged twenty years in a few hours, totally indistinguishable from all the other "old" people lying in the cots around her. She is unconscious and moaning in her sleep, in pain.

Dimitri leans over to kiss her on the forehead, the only space he can find that is clear of tubes.

"Dude, let's get the fuck out of here," he whispers to me, fighting back the tears, "before I boot all over the place."

Out in the hall, we debate whether to hold vigil in the ICU. The nurse assures us that there is no need, that we can stay in her room and that they will call us when she wakes up. So we head out for dinner, smoking a joint on the way, then come back to Dollsie's suite and watch television until we both pass out.

SIXTEEN

CALI DAYS

After traversing Texas, New Mexico and Arizona, with a detour through Bryce Canyon to sleep under the stars and awaken to the sun rising over the pink boulders, we landed in Los Angeles with our caravan of dogs and stuff. That first night, I went out on a date with a beautiful blond boy named Jeff whom I had met briefly at a party in New York. Not for the first time, it was love at first sight. My search for a new home was over. I would settle in Pebble Beach, where Dad had recently purchased a two-acre property with a breathtaking view of the Pacific. I would live in the guesthouse and write, and on weekends I would join Jeff in Los Angeles. It sounded perfect.

A month later, I set off on a cruise of the Greek Islands with Dad and his wife and my siblings and his wife's children. We had chartered a private yacht and while the trip had not been particularly smooth for the rest of the family, especially for my overweight step-sister who was mocked by Anton's spoiled slender wife, I had been happy that week. As we went from Santorini to Paros to Mykonos (which as Dollsie never failed to remind me, was where I had been conceived. "Which explains A LOT" she would add, chuckling at her own humor). I felt free, on the verge of discovering my destiny, much as I had felt when I would tear down those slopes as a child in Gstaad, arms wide open and eyes shut tight, ready for whatever might come my way. All those years of endless schooling were behind me, and New York as well, with its unhappy memories and dark associations, and in front of me lay California and my life as a writer and a boy called Jeff, who seemed as if he had stepped right out of Gatsby.

And yet upon my return from Europe, I felt myself sliding into an abyss. I broke things off with Jeff and took to my bed for much of the next two months. I figured that I was having a nervous breakdown, that my mind and body had come to a dead stop after two years of excess in New York, and I vowed to quit everything and go sober for a year. I started attending meetings of Narcotics Anonymous and Marijuana Anonymous and Sex Addicts Anonymous and Al-Anon, trying to find one that fit whatever it was that was wrong with me. I learned the language of the twelve steps. I went to church. I slept eighteen hours a day, and when I wasn't sleeping, I wrote.

At some point, I went to Los Angeles to house-sit for Anton and his wife. They had rented a beach front house in Malibu and I figured the change would do me good. One evening, Dollsie called, and we got into it. Exploding with pent-up anger, I let it all out: the long list of slights and grievances that I had been holding in since the age of ten. All the harm and pain she had inflicted; the physical and emotional and spiritual abuse. I told her that we had all moved to California to get as far away from her as possible, so that we could finally lead our own lives, free of her manipulation and grandiosity and rage.

"It sounds like you are angry," she responded in her cool, patronizing voice, after a long pause during which I could hear her lighting a cigarette. "How long do you think the anger will last? How much space do you need?"

"I don't know, Mom," I answered, my voice escalating, "You're the parent, the therapist, the cause—you tell me how long it will last!"

I wanted to tell her that I would be expressing this rage, one way or another, for the rest of my life. To tell her that she was the reason I hated women so, resented their concern and intimacy and love, experiencing it as if it were some form of bondage. And how that spilled over into my relationship with men. More anger and resentment and bitterness. I wanted to be done with it all.

Meanwhile, I had forgotten that the bath was running, and after I finally ended the conversation by slamming down the telephone, I discovered that I had flooded the entire house. In a panic (my terror of Anton had never quite abated), I rushed out to rent an industrial vacuum which would hopefully pump all of the water out of the house before Anton and his wife returned. The operation went on for days, the machine pumping out water, one room at a time.

I spent my nights at the bathhouse in Hollywood, watching with fascination as the men there took sex to new extremes. One guy, a gorgeous actor with a flawless body whom I recognized from a television series, would show up every night, undress, and lie down, leaving the door wide open for one and all to come in and fuck him. There was often a line at the door. I stared in fascination and horror. And I experienced some sort of epiphany: here was this beautiful man who had decided to self-destruct as a way of dealing with AIDS. Seeking immortality on his own narcissistic terms, greetings his fans in a bathhouse, "in position". It seemed to encapsulate the gay world that I had been perilously navigating since "coming out": beauty and sex and death and the eternal quest for immortality.

While in Los Angeles, I made an appointment to see the renowned Dr. Leo Rangell, an ancient Jungian psychoanalyst who lived in Bel Air and catered to the famous. He received me at his home, and looked at me with alarm when I asked to use his restroom. At the end of the session, after I had gone through all of my "issues" in great detail, he uttered his verdict:

"You are in danger and you better do something about it before it is too late."

That was it. "Duh!" I wanted to respond, as I walked out. So much for the famous Dr. Rangell. I returned to Pebble Beach feeling more nonplussed and depressed than ever.

I eventually met a therapist I could work with, Dr. Amy. She helped me get in touch with all that dissipated rage which had morphed into depression, and to direct it toward where it belonged: Dollsie. I cut of all contact with her and started to feel better. To get out of bed and do things. A few months into this period of recovery, Mina showed up from Switzerland to find out what was wrong with me. Raphael and Peter came to visit as well. They all convinced me that I was too young to be in a place like Pebble Beach—otherwise known as the Land of the Newly Wed and Nearly Dead—and that I needed to a change of scene so that I could jump-start my life again. A few months later, I moved to San Francisco.

I rented an apartment above the Castro with a stunning view of the city. I had always wanted to live in San Francisco—aka "Mecca"—but in 1991, it was not the place to be for a gay twenty-six year-old. AIDS was everywhere you looked, inescapable. I volunteered for several of the organizations that were trying to stem the crisis and take care of the thousands of men who had, in just a few years, gone from leading happy-go-lucky, professionally successful, intensely sexual lives to an existence that revolved around hospitals and medicine, incapacitation and loss of every kind, and then, inevitably, death. It seemed like everyone was either waiting to die or, having escaped the mysterious killer virus, avoiding having sex all together.

But I still went out and got laid often, in the hopes of finding a boyfriend and leading a "normal", AIDS-free life. It wasn't so much dying that I feared; rather, I was terrified of ending up like these men, who had once been attractive and had no doubt led successful lives with plentiful sex and who now looked like living corpses out of *Dawn of the Living Dead*. Delivering meals to these people in sketchy neighborhoods like the Tenderloin, where many lived in "last-stop" hotels, was not only a way for me to express my gratitude for having been spared by helping others—"there but for the Grace of God go I" came to mind every time one of them answered the door— but also a way of scaring myself shitless, like Dollsie had done to me with Pierre, her hairdresser.

I also continued in therapy—individual and group—and besides exploring all the fear and confusion I was experiencing as a young gay man living in this ambiance, I continued to unleash the anger that I had suppressed for most of my life, mostly toward Dollsie. The therapist, Don Clark, had spent time in Esalen, and being in group with him reminded me of what Dad must have felt like when he had been there.

For him, the encounter groups had been about finding a way to communicate, through simple eye contact and touch, to bridge the gap he had always felt between himself and others. Simple in theory, but seemingly impossible for someone who had always controlled his emotions, admitted no weakness, leaned on no one—although always ready to assist anyone who asked. It bothered him that he couldn't get close to people without breaking into a cold sweat. Hence the group.

For me, group therapy was also about letting go of whatever kept me from achieving intimacy with others. During a weekend group getaway up the coast, we acted out scenarios where we took turns impersonating our mothers. I had a hard time taking it seriously—gay men acting out their mommy fantasies—but it also hit very close to home, evoking memories of dressing in Dollsie's clothes, mocking her yet wanting to be her. In another exercise, we pretended to be lying in a casket at our own funerals while the others in the group eulogized us. My breakthrough came with the realization that my "D.O.C.'s" (drugs of choice)—weed & sex—were attempts to mask the rage that engulfed me. To escape it by whatever means. Sometimes, it frightened me: its tremendous capacity to hurt—myself and others—its fathomless, bottomless source. I wondered if it would ever exhaust itself. I became well-versed in the new age lexicon; the self-affirming, shame-denying, healing words of John Bradshaw and Pia Mellody and Alice Miller. I realized that until I re-discovered my "inner child" and learned how to have a relationship with myself—a healthy one—I would not be able to know and love and relate to anyone else. The process was under way.

The scars on my hands and wrist were still there. Every time i looked at them, I saw Tennessee, and myself that morning, covered in blood, helpless in the face of his rage. I had consulted a dermatologist to ask if something could be done, and she had told me that although they might improve over time, they would always be visible. I realized that was a good thing: it would be a permanent reminder of the force of my anger and the harm I had inflicted on myself (and others) for so long. I had been too harsh on Tennessee, treating him like I had been treated, punishing instead of teaching and taking my inner torment out on him, and he had reciprocated in kind. One day I would no longer see the scar, along with the ones left on my arm by Dollsie's pinches, and then I would know that I was healed.

A year after I moved to San Francisco, Nan followed and moved in with me, having just spent two years working as an intern in a refugee camp in Chiang Mai, Thailand. Her first night, we drove to Napa Valley to have dinner with friends, and on the way home, she asked me to take her out to the gay bars. I had had too much to drink, so instead of accompanying her I dropped her off in the Castro at the only lesbian haunt that I knew of. The next morning, I awoke to find her passed out in the guest room with a stranger.

Over the next few months, she and Lacey—the bartender she had picked up at the first bar she entered—became inseparable. Every morning, I would find empty beer and tequila bottles all over the house and in the car. Finally, not able to take it anymore, I asked her to move out. I did not want to bear witness to Nan's resurgent alcoholism, cultivated during her four years at Tulane. I had already been through it with Dollsie.

A month or so later, she called me from New Orleans in the middle of the night, her voice sounding panicked through a drugged haze.

"Sergei, something has happened. I don't know what to do."

"What is it?" I asked, trying to get my bearings.

"I ran over Lacey."

"You did WHAT?"

"I ran her over with the car. Twice. By mistake. We were partying in the Quarter, and then we decided to go home, and when I got in the car I couldn't see her, so I figured she had gone back to the bar. So I started the car, and heard her scream as I went over what felt like a bump. Then I freaked out and put the car in reverse and drove over her again. When I got out to look, she was under the car. Her leg was all mangled. So we went to the emergency room, of course—which took me half an hour to find even though I lived here for four years—and then after getting some medication, Lacey insisted on leaving, so we've been in this hotel for two days, taking pills and shots of tequila to numb the pain, and I don't know what to do."

After pausing to absorb this all and make sure I wasn't having a bad dream, I prevailed upon her to get on the next plane the following morning and bring Lacey back to San Francisco. I met them at the airport, and after taking one look at Lacey, who by now had turned green, I deposited her at the nearest hospital where she remained for five weeks, undergoing multiple operations on her leg to repair all the damage.

Nan continued to drink for a few months after that, then finally decided to seek help, realizing that she had hit rock bottom. But not before Dollsie had gotten wind of the whole thing, hiring a private investigator to fill her in on the details. By then, Lacey, not one to miss an opportunity, had sued my sister for a million dollars, which not only sent Dollsie into a panic, but Dad as well, along with the trustees and family lawyers. The case was settled in arbitration, and Nan entered a twelve step and gave up drinking.

Partly to get away from Nan, who had moved into the flat below, I moved out of the Castro and into Pacific Heights. I enrolled in the counseling psychology program at Santa Clara University. After working at the periphery of AIDS, all the while living it, I decided it was time to commit myself. I would become a counseling psychologist with a specialty in AIDS and health related issues, and family therapy.

Soon after embarking on this new course, during a weekend in Pebble Beach, I met an alcoholic from Texas named Duke and once again, I fell hard. I had been "in love" a few times before, but never like this. He reminded me exactly of Dollsie—with his charm and "social drinking" and narcissism and rage—and for the life of me, I couldn't figure out what the hell I was doing with him. And on top of that, he was a coke addict, the one drug which had always totally turned me off. We fought incessantly, our arguments strong echoes of the ones I had had so many times with Dollsie. This went on for two crazy years, as I commuted between San Francisco and Santa Clara for school and Santa Cruz for my internship and Carmel—often driving four or five hours a day to meet all my obligations to school and work and Duke.

In many ways, the two years I spent becoming a psychotherapist were the most intense of my life. While I found the course work easy, more based on practice than theory, the two internships, in addition to the individual and group therapy, forced me to confront every last demon I harbored deep within. The first was in a small town called Watsonville, halfway between Carmel and Santa Cruz, and there, thanks in part to my fluency in Spanish, I counseled in a family center for Mexican migrants, teaching them parenting skills (which I found more than a bit ironic), and working with their abused children. Despite my own Latin background I knew nothing about these people, but I could relate to their experiences with alienation, physical punishment and inappropriate sexual contact; I was able to help the parents to build boundaries, and the children to emerge from their cocoons. I developed close relationships with these kids, devoid of any inappropriate feelings or urges. I experienced the power of compassion to heal, and through helping others, to heal oneself.

The second internship took place on Ward 57, the first AIDS wing, located at San Francisco General Hospital. There, I encountered the full horrors that this disease had wrought, as I tended to those ravaged by AIDS, mentally and physically, with multiple diagnoses often including dementia and substance abuse. I also led a group for young gay men who had been recently infected, most of whom were already experiencing life-altering symptoms. Meanwhile, I continued to deliver meals to the homes of the sick and dying.

 And then I would go home, walk the dog, take a shower and change, and go out clubbing and cruising. It was hard not to feel like I was living on borrowed time.

After a glorious summer in Mykonos, during which I went from romance to romance and adventure to adventure (the apex of the holiday being the night I found myself half-naked on a roof, going at it with a gorgeous Sicilian guy, only to look up and find an irate Greek man in his underwear with a revolver in his hand shouting at us. Apparently, he had woken to find two half-naked guys fucking outside his window. As I had taken some ecstasy a few hours earlier, at first I thought that I was tripping. But reality quickly set in, and we found ourselves running from roof to roof, being chased by the Greek man and his two sons, until we finally jumped and landed in a batch of plants on the balcony below. From there we leapt to the street. By the next morning, the story had made the rounds at the beach, and the Sicilian and I reveled in our momentary flash of notoriety.), I finally ended things with Duke and decided it was time to leave, again. I wasn't sure where I wanted to end up, but Paris sounded like an appealing place to start. Nan threw a farewell cruise for me, and as we sailed around the beautiful San Francisco Bay, surrounded by all my gay friends as well as Nan, Anton and Dad—who had decided to surprise me (no doubt to embarrass me)—I felt excited and optimistic about the adventure that lay ahead. Like I had felt as a child thirty years earlier, on that plane to Switzerland.

A few days later, I found myself on board Air France for the eleven hour flight, with two dogs and seven bags in tow. To keep the anxiety at bay, I decided to take a Xanax. But when I searched through my bag, all I could find were the tranquilizers that the vet had given me for the dogs. Reasoning that they weighed less than me, and that therefore the effect of the pill would be fairly harmless, I decided to take one. The next thing I knew, I was being awoken by the flight attendant. We had landed in Paris and the entire airplane had disembarked. I somehow managed to retrieve the dogs and the bags and get through customs and find my way to the apartment on Rue de Varennes, where I passed out for the next eighteen hours. When I finally emerged, I remembered the move to Switzerland all those years ago, when Dollsie had drugged us up and we had woken up in much the same state upon landing. I was truly my mother's son.

SEVENTEEN

POST-OP

"Wake up, Dude!"

Dimitri is standing over me, and behind him is Baby, the Filipino nurse.

"Your mother is awake," says Baby, "she wants to see you."

"Hurry up! It's past nine. We should have been there a long time ago."

I jump out of Dollsie's hospital bed, surprised to find myself there. We take the elevator down to the main floor, then make our way to the intensive care unit.

"I don't know if I can handle this," says Dimitri as we approach the doors leading to the recovery room where we had left Dollsie the night before.

We can hear her as soon as the doors open. She is making a sound that I have never heard her make before. A deep moan, somewhere between a wail and a whimper, like a dog that has just been hit by a car, helpless, pleading, her pain and fear rising above all the other agony in that room.

"Oh my god," mutters Dimitri, as we approach her bed. She's lying there, all crumpled up, a stunned look in her eyes, panic and desperation and disbelief all rolled into one.

"Where have you been?" she sobs. "I have been asking for you for hours. How could you leave me in this place? All alone. You left me here all alone, all night."

Dimitri and I exchange glances. We should have stayed with her. We abandoned her. We let her down. Dropped the ball. Dimitri leans over to caress her and kiss her and comfort her, while I just stand there, staring at her pain and anguish. I have trouble getting my mind around it. How could it hurt so much? Why is she not knocked out on meds? Why didn't they call us sooner? I go off in search of whoever is in charge, seeking refuge in the medical establishment, staying away from Dollsie's pain. I have been around a lot of suffering in my life, but like Dimitri, I don't know if I can handle this. It's a lot.

Later that day, she is taken back to her room and then spends the next two weeks in her suite recovering, mostly asleep or in a deep drug-induced fog, coming awake at times to greet a visitor, answer a call, attempt to apply her makeup, or go through the motions of lighting an imaginary cigarette. The agony remains constant, and the groan that we heard that first morning becomes a regular thing; a low, rumbling sound that often gives way to what sounds like an exclamation, as if she has been surprised by a fresh wave of agony just as she is recovering from the previous one. Like her pain, which never really goes away over the next ten months, this sound becomes omnipresent.

Greasy arrives with Nan, who has flown from San Francisco to Miami to pick her up and accompany her to New York. Even though Dollsie did not want her mother to see her in this condition, Greasy insisted. She is strong. We exchange hugs. Nan, tall and beautiful and fair in a vague way, like a faded version of both Dollsie and Dad, looks weary, attempting to hide her anxiety and fear beneath a veneer of professional calm. Like me, she has never felt safe in this family. She has dealt with her own struggles to emerge from the shadows and following in my footsteps, she has kept Dollsie at a safe distance and entirely avoided Anton for years. She feels like a long lost twin. Although we are no longer as close as we once were, we have weathered so many storms together, witnessed so much, that our bond remains solid, even if there is distance.

Greasy is looking as spry as ever, despite the long trip. She has been through a lot in her life, including the loss of her country, her husband, and her son, Michael, who died two years ago at the age of fifty-five—like his father—after suffering a massive heart attack while mowing the lawn on a hot summer day, beer and cigarette in hand. She returned to her job at the parish the day after the funeral, and subsequently suffered two heart attacks, the battle scars of a life's accumulation of unacknowledged grief. She is a survivor. Having reached the age of ninety, she knows that the price of growing old is losing the people you love, even your children. She gets by on faith, good deeds, and denial, as Latin women of her generation had been taught to do. She never complains, never feels sorry for herself, and never despairs.

Mother and daughter have never been close; Greasy has never understood or been able to relate to this child who is so much her opposite in every way. But although she had never been able to show it—at least according to Dollsie— Greasy loves her daughter fiercely, and has come to be by her side and do her duty. She putters around the hospital suite all day, answering the telephone and taking down messages, getting into long conversations with whoever is calling, and generally driving Dollsie bonkers.

A few days after the surgery, I catch her trying to feed Dollsie some holy water through a straw and shoving some strange crushed up leaves into her mouth.

"Greasy, what are you doing?" I ask, incredulous. We are under strict orders not to feed her anything until her digestive system has had a chance to reconstitute itself.

"Oh, don't worry, it's not food, it's just some crushed up leaves from Santiago de Compostella that have been blessed by Father Pio. They have been known to heal many people," replies Greasy, who only takes her orders from above.

The nights are rough, the days a bit less so. Visitors constantly appear and a steady stream of plants and flower arrangements arrive on a daily basis. Dollsie and Greasy, who both love flowers, especially orchids, keep tabs on who sent what and distribute the overflow to other patients and staff. Dollsie likes showing off her spoils to the nurses, dropping names along the way, and if the nurses don't recognize them Dollsie doesn't notice; she takes it for granted that everyone knows who so-and-so is. "You'd have to be hiding in a cave in Siberia not to."

My job is to field the visitors. She does not want anyone to see her "in this condition", and she knows that I have no problem keeping people out. But exceptions are made for anyone she considers VIP—and it's up to me to know who's VIP and who isn't. I feel like a combination of *majeur d'homme*, social secretary and bouncer, turning away visitors when she is in no shape to see them, getting scolded for letting in the wrong ones—"why the hell did you let *them* in?"—or for turning away the right ones.

"How could you turn away Juan Pedro and Milagro, Sergei? Do you not realize that he's one of the top decorators in the world right now, and that he's just come straight from Canada to tell me about that fabulous house he did for those people, who built it from scratch to look like Versailles? I can't remember their names. Thirty million dollars they spent. And since I couldn't attend the fabulous housewarming party that they just threw—surely the party of the season—I was invited, of course—the first thing he does after landing in New York is to come see me to show me pictures. Isn't that touching? So loyal. He never forgets that I'm the one who launched him when he arrived here from Chile twenty years ago, totally unknown. How could you?"

We meet with the doctors. The news is not good. In addition to the tumor they removed, which turns out to be malignant, they've also found cancerous lesions on the lymph nodes. No one dares to use the word, but that means that the cancer has metastasized. According to them, the liver looks okay, though. We decide not to inform Dollsie until she is in better shape, telling her instead, whenever she asks, that the results have not come in yet. Anton arrives and we hold a conference in the lounge. I can't remember the last time that we were all together. We haven't wanted to be.

"So, what next?" asks Anton, getting down to business once he has been filled in.

"Things don't look too good," I answer. "Now that we know that it's pancreatic cancer and that it has spread, things look pretty bad, in fact."

"What do you mean?" asked Nan.

"Well it means that she's probably going to die within a year," I answer, matter-of-factly. "According to Ashley, there's nothing that will change that. There are no more operations to be done, and the only thing the chemo and radiation will do is make her feel miserable and maybe prolong the agony for a little while."

"Dude, don't think like that!" says Dimitri, dismayed. "How can you even say that?"

"Just voicing the reality of the situation," I answer, trying to use my professional experience to provide a sense of calm, "Doing my best to keep it real. It's important to keep hope, but there's no sense in living in denial. She's most likely not going to make it, that's just the way it is."

Nan explodes. "Stop trying to bury our mother!" she yells at me, loud enough for everyone to hear, bursting into tears. "We know you've always hated her!"

The other families in the lounge turn around, aghast.

"Thanks for that, Nan. Fuck off," I say, as I get up to leave. So much for the family meeting.

The next day, Dr. Gonzalez breaks the bad news to Dollsie. The Mexican doctor—as she still refers to him—explains to her that the cancer has spread to her lymph nodes, and that the odds are not in her favor. They mention a few new chemo protocols that look promising. And if that doesn't work, they will try radiation. Or a combination of both.

Dollsie has trouble absorbing the news. "But you told me everything was fine!" she pleads.

"Yes, everything looked fine during the surgery," answers Dr. Gonzalez, "but we also told you that we wouldn't know if the cancer had spread until we had done a biopsy of the lymph nodes."

"What about the liver?" asks Dollsie, looking desperately for a silver lining. The liver is the last refuge of hope for her; if the cancer hadn't crossed over, she still has a chance.

"The liver looks okay, so far. We will keep monitoring it."

"How much time do I have left?" she asks, "Give it to me straight, Doc."

"We don't like to speculate about that," he answers, "It all depends on how the chemo goes."

Great. More denial. I resolve at that moment that I will not go out of my way to share any unwanted info with Dollsie, but that if she asks me, I will not hide anything from her. Being a planner, sooner or later she will want to know.

Dollsie insists on staying at MSK through Labor Day weekend; a week longer than necessary according to the doctors. The pain is too much for her or any of us to handle and she has become dependent on Baby and the other private nurses who rotate shifts, caring for her, putting up with her demands and whims and impatience. They are trained to deal with the fear and sense of helplessness of the pampered patients on the nineteenth floor; people who have always done as they pleased and now find themselves completely powerless and at the mercy of others, facing mortality like everyone else.

After Labor Day, we move Dollsie into her two-room suite at the Carlton House, on 61st and Madison. Although we are all glad to finally get her out of there, the transition is difficult. I find a place to rent for six months on West 23rd Street—in the heart of Chelsea and three blocks from my last apartment in this city, fifteen years earlier—a loft that occupies the entire fifth floor of an old building. After moving in I quickly realize that I've probably made a big mistake but it's far away from Dollsie's quarters and in the epicenter of the city's gay life, which I suppose is why I've chosen it.

The elevator is one of those old, scary, cage-like contraptions operated by a lever, and it is usually blocked on someone else's floor, which means a lot of walking up and down. On the first floor of the building is a sushi restaurant, and the whole building smells like a fish market. On the second floor is a comedy school, with people coming in and out at all hours. At night, the wind rattles the large, ancient windows. On two occasions, the panes blow out in the middle of the night, sending shards of glass crashing onto the street five floors below, making a terrifying sound as they land, a vivid reflection of my inner turmoil. Very little works in the apartment, and the landlord, a Frenchman, who acts as if he is doing me a favor by letting me occupy his fabulous Manhattan loft for a mere five thousand dollars a month, can't be bothered to fix anything.

Once Dollsie has settled into Carlton House, Anton and Nan and Greasy leave to go back to their respective homes in California and Florida, and Dimitri and I take over Dollsie's care, mapping out a schedule that ensures that one of us is always with her to take her to medical appointments, and to keep her company in the evenings. Rosario, her loyal Mexican maid, takes over the rest.

I fly back to Paris to settle my affairs and to retrieve the three dogs, Walt and Dollsie's two miniature greyhounds, Sharif and Czarina. I call clients, pay bills, avoid making love with Giovanni, and say goodbye to my friends, and to my life in Paris. I know that between the cancer and the adoption, I will be gone for a long time, and I wonder if it will still feel like home the next time I return, or if I'm already beyond that. I've moved so many times in my life, once a year on average since college, so by now, nothing fazes me. Places, like people, seem to come and go, and if I feel any attachment to them, it's not something I realize until much later, after it's too late to go back.

EIGHTEEN

CITY OF ILLUSIONS

Raphael and I had been friends for almost a decade, and during that time, we had traveled the world—with Peter in tow—hitting the hot spots and acting decadent and glamorous, much like our parents had, or at least mine. He reminded me of Dollsie: exuberant, commanding the attention of a room when he made his entrance, providing entertainment for all. Like Dad with Dollsie, I was content to bask in his glory and enjoy the ride while disclaiming the superficiality of it all, the parties and clothes and trips and sex and drugs. He lived with a wealthy old man and I was a trustafarian, so we were able to do it right.

Moving to Paris was partially an attempt to reclaim some of the unbridled hedonism and freedom of those first few glorious European summers spent together in places like Capri and Saint Tropez and Mykonos and Ibiza, discovering, in our late twenties, a whole new world where we could party and dance every night until dawn; falling in love with beautiful strangers and recovering on crowded beaches; plunging into the limpid waters of the Mediterranean to cleanse ourselves of the previous night's excesses and awakening to the prospects that lay in store for us. Then evening would come, and the ritual would begin again.

After finally getting his green card by convincing Peter to adopt him, which allowed him to leave and enter the country at will, Raphael had persuaded Peter to rent an apartment in Saint Germain. I soon followed suit, subletting a friend's apartment nearby on rue de Varennes for six months.

Dad had followed up my move with a letter begging the question: Why?

"You take after your mother and me," he wrote, "a new locale always brings a renewal of hope, an expectation that things will be different, that you'll find happiness, until that too, wears off, and you are left much in the same place as you were before. I suppose it's normal, after the example we set. But remember, once you're settled in and unpacked, once the novelty of a new place wears off, you wake up and find that along with all the things you've brought with you— your books and clothes and furniture and art—along with all of that, is all the stuff you thought were leaving behind, the stuff that made you want to move in the first place. It's all still there."

True, but it didn't stop me from moving, moving, always moving. During those first few years, Raphael and I were on a high, literally and metaphorically. We experienced Paris more as a state of mind than as an actual city. After six months I moved from Saint Germain to the Ile Saint Louis, a magical island in the middle of Paris, where I lived on the top floor of a small building on Rue Le Regrattier, right by the Seine. Every day, I would walk my dogs around the island, and on hot days they would venture into the river. A few times, I almost lost them when the strong currents started to carry them off, with me racing down the quais alongside them frantically calling them to shore.

In the evenings, we would often host or be invited to elegant dinner parties, mostly composed of foreigners who, like Raphael and me, had no reason to be in Paris, beyond the desire to escape and the thirst for beauty and culture and glamour and decadence which this city of illusions promised. Afterwards, we would go out clubbing—to Le Palace or Le Queen or my favorite—Le Banana—a hole in the wall in Les Halles with strippers on the main floor and a cabaret with live music below. Perpetually enthralled by the music, the boys, the possibilities, and not wanting the night to end, we would either leave with someone we had just met or, failing that, we would head to a seedier place; a sex club where furtive encounters took place in dark rooms and cabins. I would get home at five or six or seven in the morning—often with some random guy I had picked up along the way. I'd walk the dogs around Notre Dame as the sun came up, then go back to bed and sleep until noon, or later. Sometimes I would wake up to find that my guest had departed, much to my relief. Other times, he would still be there, and then the effort—the effort to remember his name and the details of the evening, the effort of waking him and making him coffee and doing everything to send him on his way as rapidly as possible—often felt like it was all too much to manage, and not worth whatever fleeting sexual thrill had occurred a few hours earlier. At times, it made me feel so depressed—the emptiness, the repetitiveness—that I would take to bed again as soon as the stranger had gone, and stay there for the rest of the day.

Meanwhile, looking for something to do, I began to seek out therapists and others working in the field of AIDS. Incredibly, I found out that there were no therapists in Paris who openly identified themselves as gay, and none who specialized in gay patients or HIV/AIDS. The fact that I was open about my sexuality and had experience working with this population—something that would have been commonplace in San Francisco—suddenly made me unique as a professional here in Paris. People suggested that I rent a space and hang my shingle.

I was certain that if I were able to get a practice up and running, I would be good at it, better than most. While literature and writing had always been my first love, in San Francisco I realized that I had found my calling. I had been through a lot in my life, and now—thanks to my experiences in California—I felt I could give back to others. This gave me the impetus to at least try to make a life for myself beyond the endless round of glamorous sorties and meaningless encounters. This was my answer to my father's question.

I rented my first office in the Marais and began receiving clients almost right away. Within six months, I had a decent practice going, at first consisting mostly of young gay men dealing with relationships and sexuality; familiar territory. I learned about identity and desire, inexorably linked for most gay men. I listened, and tried to offer something in return, something indefinable, a smile, an insight, an acknowledgment, an absence of judgment. Sometimes I felt like I had nothing to offer but genuine empathy and humility, but they kept coming back and many of them were able to truly transform their lives. I was a witness to their journeys and paradoxically, I helped them go places that I hadn't succeeded in reaching myself. It was confusing and exhilarating and sometimes mind-numbingly boring, but overall, the process filled me with wonder. For the first time in my life I felt like I was doing something that mattered, that gave me worth.

We were at the dawn of a new century, having just survived two decades of tremendous loss and fear and self-doubt, coupled with unbridled freedom and excess. That was our commonality, our bond. I listened to their stories about searching for love, for security, for understanding, for intimacy and union, often in all the wrong places. I could relate. Having "been there" was part of what made me good at what I did. After all, just like many of them, from the time I began having sex, I had lived with the fear that I might not be alive by the time I was thirty.

Having been trained in California, where I was drawn to the work of Carl Rogers and the   nascent theories of narrative therapy, I broke sacred taboos in the rigid Freudian/Lacanian world of Paris psychoanalysis—referring to the people who came to see me as "clients" rather than "patients" and treating them as equals, rather than as disciples. Instead of focussing on pathologies and labels, I helped my clients rewrite the script, reframe the tale they had been telling themselves for their entire lives, and recast the roles they had been assigned since birth. I viewed them as people from whom I could learn as much as they did from me. In addition to my private practice, I joined the American Cathedral Counseling Center, where Franco-American families went for help.

I felt like I was riding the wave of a new trend. Life is all about timing, and for once in my life, the timing was very good. As a "specialist" in the field of HIV/AIDS, I was invited to appear on television, to speak at seminars, and I headed a volunteer organization for Anglophones in Paris living with AIDS.

Those first three years were glorious; I felt as Dollsie must have felt when she arrived in Switzerland, as if I were living the fairy tale, as if I could have it all.

Then one day, on his way back from Morocco, Raphael phoned to tell me that he wasn't feeling well and asked me to take him to my doctor. After examining him, she ushered me into her office while he was putting on his clothes, and told me that he was in critical condition; that if he did not get back to New York soon, he would have to be hospitalized in Paris, where he did not have insurance. She left it to me to relay the message to Raphael, whose French had not improved much in the three years we had been there.

I explained the situation to him, and asked him how long he had been HIV-positive and why he had hidden it from me for all that time. The doctor hadn't mentioned the disease but I had been in the field long enough to read between the lines. Raphael told me that it had been a while and that he didn't want to go into it. He had always been both private and very proud, and like many Latin men, he felt shame about being gay. He left for New York the next day with Peter, who, as usual, seemed oblivious to whatever was happening.

I went to visit him in New York a few weeks later. He had survived his first hospitalization, he was not going to die, he was home. To thank me, he bought me a Bulgari watch, took me downtown to Soho for lunch, then to the Carlyle for tea. Just like the old days. He tried to put on a good show, as if everything was fine, but I knew better. I was one of the few who could see beyond the facade and I knew that Raphael was trying to maintain some semblance of normalcy, a masquerade of hope. But I decided to put it out there before it was too late.

"Rafi, I don't know what's going on, how you are feeling, because you won't open yourself up to anybody, but I want you to know that you are my best friend. That I miss you and that I'm very grateful for everything. I know this is tough for you, but you gotta keep fighting. You can't give up. Not yet."

"Listen, Sergei, I've had a great life. I couldn't have asked for more. I got everything I wanted. And I don't want to live like this. There are only three people in the world that I love and you're one of them, and I'll give it a while for you guys, but it's only for you. I don't want this. I'm not a strong person."

"Give it six months," I answered. "Just six. After that, if things aren't better, I'll understand if you want to give up. I'll even help you check out. But you owe us six months."

He hung on for six months, hoping they would be his last unless there was some miracle, which he did not expect. He did not want any of us around to witness his decline, but since we were there, with our childish need to see him live no matter what, he felt that he had to accommodate us for a while. A question of etiquette. But it made him angry, impatient, this reminder that there was love in his life and thus responsibility and attachment. He resented us for it.

I returned from Paris two more times during the next few months, and although I felt him slipping away, mentally and physically, I thought he would last a while.

Two weeks after my last visit in May I received a call one night as I was returning home from dinner with Carmen, Raphael's mother, who was visiting Paris and was totally unaware of his condition. It was Peter.

"You better come soon," he said, his voice breaking. "Things aren't looking too good."

I called Carmen to explain that her son was in the hospital and that we needed to get to New York as soon as possible. We boarded a plane the next day, Carmen still trying to grasp why everything was so urgent all of a sudden. I tried to prepare her, but Raphael had made me promise that I would never reveal the cause of his illness, that I would never mention the word AIDS, so I did my best to keep it vague.

We landed in the morning and took a cab straight to the hospital. Once we were on his floor—the VIP wing—we walked down the hall, looking for his room. We had been told it was the last room on the right, the corner room with the beautiful view, but when we reached it, at first I thought we were in the wrong place. The person in the bed with the bloated face and all the tubes could not be Raphael. But as we stared at him, it slowly dawned on us that it was.

For three days and nights, Carmen and I took turns tending to him and fielding visitors. At night, she would sleep in his room and I would sleep on the floor in the visitors' lounge, waking up every few hours to check on him and go smoke a cigarette. I would sneak down to the basement of the hospital, which was under renovation, finding myself in a dark, cavernous space, while my best friend lay dying fourteen floors above. It reminded me of the many nights we had spent in other dark, strange places, doing things we weren't supposed to be doing, reveling in the excitement of the unfamiliar, the danger, hoping that we wouldn't get "caught" by the bug. All the while knowing that inevitably, we would.

Raphael had been caught, and it had all become so familiar, these hospitals full of dying boys, and I was tired. Give me a sign, Raphael, say when. Tell me what you want me to do. Push things along?

The third night, after waking up for the fourth or fifth time, I walked into his room as the sun was coming up over Manhattan. We had made it through another night. Raphael was still alive, making mysterious sounds as the strange machines hummed along. I went home to Dollsie's, hoping she would still be asleep so I wouldn't have to talk to her, and after sneaking into my room, I smoked a big joint and fell into a deep, deep sleep. As deep, I imagined, as Raphael's. I revisited the familiar dreamscape of the recurring nightmare that had permeated my sleep ever since I had first begun sleeping with men:

I find myself at a glamorous AIDS benefit hosted by President Reagan and Elizabeth Taylor. All my friends are here. From my seat at the table, I survey the exhilarating landscape of gorgeous men with smiling faces in black tie. The beautiful couples dance closely to the tunes of Peter Duchin.

All of a sudden, the doors burst open and a swarm of tall and menacing, yet enticing men enter the ballroom, with machine guns jutting out in front of them, like erect penises. I notice the red bands on their arms, and although I can't make out the insignias at such a distance, I know that they are swastikas.

No one speaks. We are caught up in our own impending deaths. Some friends and I are able to slip out into the ornate French gardens surrounding the palace. Inexplicably, we are all dressed in white. We see an open gate at the end of the long garden and start running toward it. Actually, it's more like a romp; for some reason, the whole thing has suddenly become terribly funny. We run along gaily, aware of the necessity of reaching the gate, but not too concerned about whether we will succeed. It feels pastoral, with flowers in the garden and cows in the field and my friends and I all dressed in Sunday-picnic-in-the-country white.

And then we're lost. The gate has disappeared. A group of Indians suddenly shows up and motions us to come toward the tall, thick, manicured hedges. They lead us through the bushes toward a canoe, which takes us down a narrow river. All over the countryside are large billboards that read: "RONALD REAGAN - 15% INFANT MORTALITY."

The next thing I know, we are back at the party, once again in black tie. One by one, guests are being led out of the ballroom. I stand at the entrance, not knowing where to sit. There are so many empty seats - more and more as the night wears on. I approach one of my friends.

"Who are they killing?" I ask.

"Gay people," he says.

"How do they know?"

"They just do."

I watch the tall blond soldiers approaching men—many of them people I know or recognize —throughout the vast, elegant ballroom. They smile a smile of seduction and sit down to converse with their prey. They are all extraordinarily beautiful; the guests are charmed, seduced. Even though we know what the soldiers have come for, the powerful suggestion of sex drowns out the unseen executions. After a few minutes, the soldiers escort their guests out of the room.

I notice one of the soldiers approaching me, beautiful and menacing like an Israeli Mossad agent. His deep blue eyes are like laser beams, piercing me from across the room.   The stride is majestic, determined, animalistic.   His smile proffers untold pleasure and unfulfilled fantasies.   He sits beside me, without saying a word.   His large, muscular body seems to dominate everything: the table, the room, me.   (I recognize him: it's the sadistic chef from Glorious Foods, the catering company I work for, the one who likes to pick up innocent boys and initiate them into the pleasures of bondage.)   The conversation is simple, filled with platitudes.   But the voice... the voice is deep, electrifying, like the roar of a train rushing by.   It is as if I am lying on the tracks, watching it approach, but unable to move.   Paralyzed.

The soldier smiles and gestures toward the exit.   He rises and I follow him.   The light from the chandeliers is brilliant and blinding, the music loud and intoxicating, the other guests invisible.   I know that I am going to die.   Strangely, it does not matter.   The soldier matters; everything else seems utterly irrelevant.

The walk across the room is endless.   I am behind the soldier, watching his long strides, the powerful thighs flexing and bulging like the legs of a horse climbing a steep, rocky mountain.   The soldier doesn't look at me.   He just leads me on and on, across the endless ballroom.   At last, we reach the door.   The soldier turns to me, smiles slowly and invitingly, and gives me a penetrating look that contains both the question and the answer.   Do you want?... Yes, I do..   I confirm my answer with a brief, nervous nod.

The soldier puts his hand on the doorknob and starts to turn it.

I woke up feeling the sheets soaked with sweat cold against my skin, strangely refreshing, as confused thoughts of the gardens of my childhood and Dollsie's parties and gay bars and World War II and Peter Duchin and his band playing "New York, New York" swirled in my head.

I returned to the hospital later that morning. After days of watching Raphael in a drug-induced never-never land and trying to prepare Carmen, the time had come to disconnect the machines. She had held out hoping he would come out of his coma long enough to say goodbye to her, but the doctor had explained that this was not advisable, that he would be in too much pain.

We stood around the bed for an hour—me, Carmen, and several other friends—holding his hands and other parts of his body, waiting for him to take his last breath as we gazed out at the East River and the radiant Manhattan skyline. I was next to his other best friend Isabella, a member of New York's euro-trash set who claimed to be a Spanish duchess, and we struggled ever so subtly over who got to hold his hand; something Raphael would have appreciated. He enjoyed holding court, causing rivalries amongst his courtiers.

After an hour of waiting, with nothing happening, his doctor finally arrived. I had never liked Dr. Nicky Rizzolo, the way he had ingratiated himself into Raphael's life. I had spent a vacation with him and Raphael in Ibiza, and he struck me as a sex-obsessed social climber, not a good thing for your HIV doctor to be. As we perched over Raphael, waiting for him to stop breathing, the doctor whispered in my ear:

"I was just at a charity lunch attended by Elizabeth Taylor, and I met your ex-sister-in-law! Wow, what a gorgeous woman! Loved her!"

"Nick, I don't think this is the moment," I responded, "and by the way, she is a raving bitch. Now can you tell me why nothing has happened? The machines were supposedly disconnected an hour ago."

Dr. Nick went over and checked the life-support machine. "Oops!" he said nonchalantly, right in front of Raphael's mother and the rest of us, "Looks like someone forgot to turn it off! I'm so sorry. I'll look into it. Ready, guys?" he asked, almost cheerfully, as if he were about to cut the ribbon at the opening of some new Manhattan boutique. He turned some dial on the machine, and the whirring, pumping sound came to a stop. Then Raphael's lungs stopped moving, and within seconds, he was gone.

After the service at Saint Ignatius Loyola, we all made our way to Peter and Raphael's penthouse on Fifth Avenue, dressed to the nines, nervously negotiating the hordes of noisy, raucous revelers celebrating Puerto Rican Day, the parade in full swing as we approached the canopy. I laughed, thinking how much Raphael would have appreciated the spectacle. Following the rooftop reception, I smoked a joint in Central Park with a friend and then headed straight for the bathhouse.

I have no memory of that night. All I know was that once again, as I had so often my life, I was turning to sex to escape the loneliness and sadness. Unconsciously, I sought to banish death by affirming my "life force", going from partner to partner with reckless abandon, dancing on the edge of the precipice. Sex had long since ceased to be about pleasure and intimacy. Like Dollsie and her drinking, it had become increasingly desperate and self-destructive, as if I felt the need to punish myself for still being alive, all the while wondering when my turn would come. But even so, these sexual binges kept me in a state deep denial, allowing me to forget, if only momentarily, all the devastation that I had witnessed, the loss upon loss and the terror which had lurked beneath the surface of my psyche for as long as I could remember, since that day in the hospital with Dollsie's cadaverous French hairdresser. After the thrill of the conquest and the intense rush of the anonymous encounter (often enhanced by recreational substances) were over, the loneliness and depression quickly returned. But at least I felt numb, at least for a while, until the next fix.

Six months later, during a cruise through the icebergs of Patagonia in southern Chile with Dad, his wife and Greasy, I came down with something the second day and spent most of the week locked up in my cabin, sick with nausea and migraines. After consulting with a doctor in Santiago who diagnosed a severe case of Hepatitis A, I flew back to Paris the next day, and a few days later, following more tests, Dr. Goujon announced to me that I was HIV-positive. At long last it had happened.

NINETEEN

CHELSEA NIGHTS

I return from Paris a few weeks later with the dogs, just in time for chemo to begin. Dollsie has spent this time bedridden and in agony, and I have my doubts about whether she is ready for all this, but she is undeterred; time is of the essence. Before the sessions begin, she has the hairdresser at Carlton House cut her hair short, and then she asks me to take her shopping for wigs. It's a tough moment for her; for a woman who has been obsessed with beauty all her life, the prospect of losing her hair must be devastating. But she pulls it off with panache and humor.

The chemo sessions begin soon after, and Dollsie seems to sail through them. The worst part is always the arrival. The wait can be long. But by the time she's done with the treatment, she seems fine. Determined to get on with her day. She has no time to lose.

In the evenings, Dimitri and I usually have an early dinner in her suite, and then I head back downtown to the loft and go online to look for a hook-up. Although Paris has its own busy internet cruising scene, which had kept me up many a night, it is nothing like what I encounter when I go online in New York. I feel like I've entered a world with absolutely no limits; the viral version of the gay bathhouses in the seventies. While Dollsie lies in bed at night wondering what happened to her life, where it has all gone, I sit at the computer in the drafty, cavernous loft obsessing about what I have missed during my years in

Paris, afraid to fall asleep and miss a message. I feel like the lonely Buckley boy all over again, desperate to make friends, to belong.

I feel as if I have come full circle, finding myself only a few blocks from the Hotel Chelsea where Mapplethorpe had set up residence for many years, and from my own first Chelsea pad, where it had all begun—the moment when sex had gone from being a pleasure to being something else: a deep need, an addiction, a never ending hunt for someone, something, to fill that insatiable void, physical and metaphorical, which could never be filled.

On weekends, when I am not on duty, I find myself falling into old patterns. Even though I have helped dozens of gay men work through their sex addictions and the identity and intimacy issues that go along with them; and even though I know all too well that most of the time, these outings will only leave me feeling lonelier, hungrier, emptier, "it" is all I think about, the only way I know how to escape.

But I am good at compartmentalizing; I've had a lot of practice. The rest of the time, I am back in Dollsie's world—cancer and chemo and doctors and taxis and appointments and keeping up with her as she runs around doing everything she possibly can to cling to life, to reverse the curse. Then I go back to my other life, where I, too, am fighting mortality the only way I know how: through the kindness of strangers, who come bearing gifts that become like my own personal chemo, poisonous substances which inject me with life, or the illusion of it.

But beyond the drugs and the sex and the ever-spiraling frantic intensity of my nocturnal wanderings, what I want most of all is to be loved, and in my own twisted way, I'm trying to make up for the loss of a mother's love, which only now I'm coming to realize I've missed out on all these years.

TWENTY

CONCEIVING AT THE COSTES & A VISIT TO THE ADOPTION AGENCY

As I drive to Harrisburg, Pennsylvania for my official interview with the adoption agency, which has been postponed twice because of Dollsie's illness, I think of my first misbegotten attempt to procreate with Lilly, a lesbian friend of mine from California who, a few weeks after the death of her lover, had called me out of the blue and asked me if I wanted to make a baby with her. Raphael had recently passed away, and I had always wanted children, so the time seemed opportune.

The next day, she had flown from San Francisco to Paris, and had checked into the Hotel Costes, our favorite hotel in Paris, on Rue Saint Honore close to the Place Vendome. It was decorated in the style of a plush, old-school bordello. I had checked into another room down the hall, and after a lazy summer dinner in the tuscan courtyard, we headed up to our respective rooms to prepare. Lilly gave me the syringe into which I was to ejaculate, which reminded me of a turkey baster, and after returning to my room and putting on some porn, I managed to jerk off into it without spilling a drop. Time being of the essence, I threw on my bathrobe and rushed down to her room, carefully holding the syringe of sperm in my pocket. We repeated the process the following night, and then set off to Capri and Positano for ten glorious days.

Lilly returned to Healdsburg and informed me that our attempts hadn't worked. A few months later, I was diagnosed HIV-positive, and terror ensued. Had I already been contaminated at the time? I had taken a test right before she came to Paris, but had something happened in the meantime? Had they missed something? I called her and broke the news to her, and in a panic, she rushed off to see her doctor and get tested. In the end, everything had turned out fine. Although I couldn't pinpoint when IT had happened to me, it had apparently been after our attempt to procreate. Or we had just been incredibly lucky. But the notion that I had unwittingly put her life in danger through my own carelessness was something that neither of us could get past, and it ultimately severed the friendship.

As I pull into the agency's parking lot, I'm hoping this story won't come up.

I've cleared all the security and background checks—one set of paperwork for the state of Pennsylvania and one for New York—and I've tracked down all the people from my past from whom I need letters of reference: therapists, previous employers, colleagues and friends. My doctor in Paris has signed off on the health forms. A home visit to the loft in Chelsea has taken place, and another one is scheduled in the spring for my home in Paris. I've set up a profile on the agency's website for prospective birth mothers to view, with a bio and pictures of me from different periods of my life and in various settings, including several with children and dogs to show my domestic side. All that's left is the interview, which is to take place over the next two days. I wonder what I'll be asked. I tell myself that I have nothing to hide. Still, I'm pretty nervous.

I'm greeted by the friendly receptionist and made to feel welcome as I await Dr. Berger (ironically, the same name as Dollsie's doctor at MSK, with a different spelling). After a few minutes, he appears, a pale, gaunt man who looks like he hasn't seen a meal for a while. After reviewing the paperwork with me, making sure he has everything he needs, he says, matter-of-factly:

"So I guess my main question for you is this: you seem to lead a terrific life. You live in Paris, you have your own practice, you travel all over, and thanks to your trust funds, you have no financial worries. So why would you want to mess all that up with a kid?"

I pause before answering. I've been asked the question many times, and I have prepared myself for him to ask it as well, but no matter how many times I've attempted to answer it, I still have trouble. I'm afraid of being too honest, of saying too much, or not enough. Also, on some level, the question bothers me. As if being a man—a gay man—I have to justify my desire to have children. After all, does anyone ever ask heterosexual people why they want children?

"Because I love children and I've always hoped I would have some of my own one day, and after working with them for the past ten years or so, I feel like I have a lot to offer. And I'm at a stage in my life where I feel like I've "done it all"—in terms of the gay lifestyle and the money and the traveling and all that—and I want something more meaningful, something less ephemeral."

"And I think I'd be a good father!" I add, almost as an afterthought. I decide not to mention the intense need to love someone and be loved in a way that I hadn't experienced as a child and that has so far eluded me in relationships. I don't want to sound needy.

"Good answer!" he says, grinning, as if I have just passed a crucial test. "By the way, you can relax. This process over the next two days is not about us deciding whether you are fit to be an adoptive parent. You've already proven that with all the material you've provided us. It's really a chance for you to interview us; to let us know what kind of child you are looking for, and for us to put together a profile of the ideal child for you in terms of age and race and other factors. Because once we both agree on that profile, there's no turning back. You are 68th in line at the moment, but a kid could come along any minute, and if that happens, you have to be ready and you have to accept the child no matter what, if it meets the criteria we've established together. You don't get to see pictures of the child or meet the parents first, unless they request it. If you turn down the child for whatever reason, you lose your place in line and start the process all over. There are no exceptions; you must understand that. You must be ready even if your mother is on her deathbed."

"Yes, I understand." I say, amazed and immensely relieved. I had thought I was in for two days of soul searching interviews about my past—drugs, sex, relationships, health—and instead I'm informed that this is a mere formality. Apparently, the fact that I'm financially independent and that I've worked as a therapist with children and families makes me qualified to be a parent. It's that simple. It's a welcome relief after all the paperwork and bureaucracy, not to mention Dollsie's travails. The notion that I can just sit back and relax and let the process unfold itself makes me smile.

"Why are you smiling?" Dr. Berger asks me.

"Because I didn't think it would be this easy. I thought I was here for an interrogation."

He laughs. "Now let's get to the hard part. The profile. This may feel a little awkward, but it's important. You have to know what your limits are in terms of what kind of child you are comfortable with, because if you're not, you may find yourself face to face with a child you aren't prepared to raise."

We spend the rest of the afternoon going through all their criteria: age, race, special needs, etc. I feel uncomfortable talking about race, as if I'm engaging in some sort of profiling, but because I'm not allowed to see pictures of the child or family beforehand, I understand why it's important.

"If you want to hold out for a healthy Caucasian child, the waiting time is roughly two years. If you are willing to adopt an African-American child or a child with special needs, you can have one within three months." The difference is startling, and sad. "White gay parents are traditionally more open to ethnic adoptions than heterosexual parents, and also to kids with special needs," he adds. "They understand what it's like to be different."

I assume he's trying to influence my thinking in this regard, to expand the scope of what kind of child I'm willing to adopt. I'd like to be the type of person who could say yes to anything, but I know myself; for all the mental problems I've dealt with throughout my years as a therapist, I've had very little exposure to children with physical and developmental issues, and I know I can't handle a child who is physically handicapped or deformed. Having grown up in a family that placed such an emphasis on appearance, on looking perfect at all times, it's beyond me.

And when it comes to race, although I'm open to anything, the fact that I can't see pictures of the family beforehand gives me pause for thought. I tell Dr. Berger that being raised by a single gay parent, my child will have enough to cope with, without throwing in the whole racial thing, so after much back and forth, we agree to a combination of Caucasian, African-American, Latin, Arab, Asian and/or "other." My goal is to increase the odds of the child bearing some resemblance to me by coming up with some crazy ethnic mix that might somehow be genetically akin to mine.

We move on to the age of the child, and I tell him that I'm willing to go up to three years old, but would prefer a child under one. The earlier you get the child, the greater the chance of establishing a strong bond, and the less chance of the child being psychologically damaged through abuse or abandonment.

"Okay! Well, looks like we're done for today! I'm going to have Debbie, your caseworker, type up the profile you agreed to and I want you to sleep on it, because tomorrow we'll have you sign a copy before you leave. It's not set in stone, you can always change your mind later on, but as far as we are concerned these are now the official criteria for the type of child you'd be willing to accept, and if we find you one, you must go through with it or lose your place. You understand? I know I'm repeating myself, but it's important that you know what you are getting into."

All of this is going very fast. I can't believe we've already reached the end of the first day of interviews and that I'm already on the list, waiting my turn. It was only three months ago that I had decided to take the plunge and had conducted the agency search online. So much had happened since. Now I was on my way to becoming a father.

I check into a motel, and spend the evening thinking about the enormity of what I am taking on. So often in my life, I have done things impulsively, scrambling to pick up the pieces later and make sense of some momentous decision I have made. Do I really feel up to becoming a father on my own? To dedicating the second half of my life to raising a child? Will my health hold out? To my surprise, Dr. Berger hasn't asked about my HIV status, nor was it mentioned on the health forms. The four doctors who have seen me over the years—in Paris, in Boston where I go for annual checkups, and now in New York—have assured me that my prognosis is excellent, that I am in great health, with no history of any HIV-related complications and no anticipation of any in the future. But while I've been blessed so far, I can't predict what will happen in the future, and I can't help but wonder if I am playing with fate, embarking upon some kind of metaphysical roulette by choosing to adopt a child as a single parent with HIV. There is nothing to suggest that I won't be able to raise the child to maturity, but are the doctors right? Or am I making a colossal mistake?

And have I done enough work on myself to not fuck up a child of my own? Have all the years of therapy paid off? Professionally, I have learned a lot about children and the proper role of parents, but will I be able to apply that to my own situation, or am I damaged goods, too dysfunctional to raise a child given my own history? The last thing I want to do is to raise my child as I have been raised by my parents, and as they had been raised by theirs. Benign neglect is the best way I can put it.

The next morning I return to the agency to conclude the interview. Dr. Berger tells me it won't take long—another hour or two. He reminds me that after I've been on the waiting list for a year, all the paperwork will have to be done over again: the background checks, the financial report, the health forms... Given the criteria I've come up with for the type of child I am hoping for, the wait should be eighteen to twenty-four months.

As we near the end of our interview he asks me what fears, if any, I have about becoming a parent. The superficial gay man in me wants to say: "I'm terrified of having an ugly child, of everyone saying, 'Poor Sergei, look what he got stuck with'." I'm truly Dollsie's son. Instead I say, "Well I guess I'm worried about what my child's going to eat, because I don't cook."

Dr. Berger breaks into laughter. "That's the best line I've heard in twenty-eight years of doing this!" he says. "Classic."

"One more question, and then I'll let you go. I ask this because it's often the first thing birthparents ask me, believe it or not: how important is education to you? What are your goals in that regard for your child?"

"You know, Dr. Berger, I have two Masters degrees and neither one has done much for me in life, beyond the learning itself. I mean, one did enable me to become a psychotherapist, and help many people, and the other allowed me the space to write my first novel, but in the long run, I think education is overrated. There are other paths to happiness and self-fulfillment in life. So while I believe that education is important, I think I would leave it up to my child. There are more important things in life."

"Like what?" he asks.

"Like knowing who you are and being at peace with yourself and living your life with integrity. And as Wayne Dyer says, waking up every morning and asking yourself, 'How may I serve?'"

"Wow," Dr. Berger says, "that's the first time I've ever heard that as well. You certainly are a most unusual young man. Full of surprises. And I think you'll make a wonderful father. This interview is now concluded. I wish you all the best during the next few months with your mother, but just remember to be prepared, no matter what happens. You never know when that child might come."

"Yes, I know. Every day I ask myself, which will come first? My mother's death or my child's birth?"

"How is that for you?"

"Well, it's strange going through the cycles of life and death at the same time. But it's also as if—how can I put it? As if it were meant to be. I don't know how to explain it."

"As if your mother had to leave to make room for someone else in your life?"

Wow.

With that, I get in my rented car and drive back to Manhattan, in a daze most of the way. The last hurdle to my becoming a parent has been cleared. Now, it's back to the waiting game. Waiting for Dollsie to die, and for my baby to be born, and wondering which will come first.

TWENTY-ONE

FAREWELL MANHATTAN

October comes and goes. The chemo isn't working. Not the first cycle, nor the second, which makes her lose the rest her hair. The markers have not improved. The cancer is progressing. It is time to try radiation. Dollsie is not giving up.

Dad comes to visit, all the way from Santiago, Chile. He has been married to his second wife longer than he was to Dollsie, and has lived a pleasant, undisturbed life far away from us all. But they have remained friends, and the bond is still strong.

Watching them together now is strange. Dad has trouble acknowledging or expressing emotion, but his look of lost bewilderment—like the little boy looking for his mother at the train station—says it all. And Dollsie is so moved by his presence that at times she can barely speak. For the most part, she manages to keep up her usual entertaining banter, but at times she lapses into silence, overwhelmed. Are they wondering, like I am, what might have been? How life might have been different had they chosen to stick it out, to ride out the seventies and settle into happy domesticity?

He stays a week. He's always good at showing up when he's needed, but I haven't been able to connect with him. We are in different places. We had been close for a while, especially during the summers I would spend with him in Switzerland during his wife-free years, but after his second marriage, he had changed (as surely had I), and over time, he had slowly retreated back into his repressed, pre-Esalen shell. After he leaves, Dollsie talks about him for days on end, like a schoolgirl raving about her gentleman caller. How kind he is, what a calming presence, what a gentleman, how beautiful and regal and distinguished he looks, "despite being so poorly dressed."

"That woman definitely hasn't done wonders for his wardrobe," she can't help but add. "Where does he shop now? At the Chilean J.C. Penney? What a pity. He used to be such an elegant man." I have to laugh, because Mina often tells me the same thing. They are both incurable snobs, and it has definitely rubbed off on me.

Jacques also comes to visit, often on his way home from work. At eighty nine, he is still active, still obsessed with health, still running from doctor to doctor, mixing his strange elixirs and taking his pills, with bottles covering every surface of every bathroom in his apartment and at his country house in South Hampton. He is terrified of death, and although he and Dollsie had gone through a hellish divorce that had taken up six out of their seven years of marriage, still he comes almost every day to see the love of his life. It is touching to watch both of them nodding off: her in bed, he in the chaise longue. They look like a little old couple.

"Mother, I've always wondered: who was the love of your life? Dad or Jacques?" I ask her one day.

"It depends on how you define love. If it's respect and affection and friendship and shared values and background, it was your father. If you're talking about passion, it was Jacques. Or maybe Georgie," she answers. "You rarely get both. I found it in my grandfather and I spent the rest of my life looking for it in every man I met, and I never found it again. What saddens me is that you seem to have taken after me, changing men like I change outfits."

I laugh. "Yes, I definitely take after you in that department. I get bored easily."

"What about Giovanni?" she asks. "Is it serious? Is that boy going to stick around to raise a child?"

"No, I doubt it. I'm not sure I want him to. I feel like I need to go through the adoption thing on my own."

"Yes, that's probably wise, given your track record. You want the child to know who her real father is."

"Why do you say her?" I ask.

"Because I know. I'm psychic, remember? And so are you, even if you don't like to admit it. You think you are too intellectual for that. They can't possibly give you a boy. When he's sixteen, everyone will think that you are some old pervert out with his boy toy. Besides, a boy needs his mother. A girl doesn't. Most of the women I know, myself included, would have adored to have had our fathers all to ourselves. She's going to be a lucky girl. But you need to settle down. What is it exactly you are looking for? Lord knows I've tried to introduce you to eligible men over the years!"

"Mother, I'm not interested in famous plastic surgeons or french counts or other society types. I never have been. And lately, to be honest, I've been mostly attracted to dark men. And getting through all the racial stuff in this country isn't easy..."

"Dark as in... black?" she interrupts me, then pauses dramatically. "Sergei, if that's the case, please wait until I've gone. I've been through enough. It won't be long now."

I burst out laughing. "Well you're the one who introduced me to all that with the Mapplethorpe exhibit, remember? And you know what they say: once you go black . . ." I say.

"I have no idea what you are referring to. Inventing, as usual."

I have often wondered what she was thinking by bringing her son along to see this outrageous pornographic exhibit, which consisted for the most part of large black and white portraits of naked black men with huge anaconda-like penises spilling forth out of suits and other uniforms, and other images of whips and other objects protruding from beautiful, perfect asses. It marked the beginning of my search for identity: racial, sexual and spiritual. Yes, I thought to myself, trying to retain my composure as I stood there next to Dollsie, transfixed, blushing, yes, that is what I want.

"Just remember," she says, changing the topic, "go where the love is. That was my big mistake. If someone loves you, truly loves you, stick with them. It's rarer than you think.

"And one more thing: in life it's not what you do that matters, it's how you do it. So long as you don't hurt people or rub it in their face, you can get away with just about anything."

The first appointment with the radiologist takes place toward the beginning of November. Having been up to no good the night before, I make my way to Dollsie's apartment in zombie mode. It has been a hectic week, nocturnally speaking. I cannot remember most of it. By the time I arrive, Dollsie is more agitated than usual, and scolds me for being a few minutes late.

"Maybe it won't be so bad," she says in the taxi with all the optimism and enthusiasm she can muster, after she has gotten through interrogating me and making me feel guilty for not being on time. Time has become even more precious to her, and like Mina, she panics every time someone makes her wait. It is all she has to hang on to at this point: the clock is ticking and there is no time to be wasted. People need to be where they are supposed to be.

"Maybe it will be okay and I'll finally lick this thing and we'll all have a nice Christmas in my beautiful new apartment."

"Yes, Mother."

A few years ago, Dollsie had decided it was time to wind down her life in New York and relocate to Miami where most Cubans of her background ended up, whether they liked it or not. They felt the gravitational pull of Cuba, which by now had become the Land of Myths. Dollsie had never cared for Miami, finding her fellow Cubans to be tacky and ignorant, and no matter what, she would always love New York with a passion, but at least she could be a big fish in a small pond again, reigning over the art world and impressing the locals with her hosting skills and fancy friends.

Her new apartment is in a huge behemoth of a development by the sea that looks like a Carnival Cruise ship on land, with a lovely pool area and way too many residential towers crowded around it. She has spent much of the fall on the phone with her decorator, going over every last detail. Now that she can no longer drink, this project has become her big escape. Finishing that apartment and moving into it by Christmas—probably her last one—has become almost as important to her as staying alive. In Dollsie's mind, they amount to the same thing: if she can only get to Key Biscayne, to her perfect new apartment by the sea, away from this nightmare, then everything will be okay. That's how we've always felt about the next move, the next home to be decorated and inhabited: a new beginning. Hope.

The wind nearly knocks Dollsie off her feet as she exits the cab, so frail has she become, and after we find the radiation wing, she is taken off to be examined as I settle into the waiting room. I know that this is going to be a rough day, but I take it in stride. Dollsie will hang tough. She is brave and indomitable. My lifelong scorn has morphed into a grudging respect and admiration for her tenacity and her determination to forge ahead, against all odds. She will get through it. And then I can go home and take a long nap. I don't think that the radiation will make a difference or affect the outcome, but I admire her for trying. I envy her love of life.

After a few minutes, one of the nurses comes out into the reception area to ask me to join Dollsie in the doctor's office. I am surprised; I didn't expect to be beckoned until the session was over and Dollsie was ready to go home. But one look at Dollsie as I walk into the room, and I know that the game is over. Something has happened—more bad news—and for once, she has gotten the information before Dimitri or I can intercept it.

"Oh, Sergei," she says, collapsing into my arms, sobbing, "Oh my poor baby."

I'm surprised to hear her call me that. I look at the doctor for an explanation.

"I'm afraid we can't go ahead with the radiation," says the doctor, managing to convey some empathy while not mincing her words. "We just received the latest scans, taken a few days ago. We found lesions on the liver, too many to remove. Radiation won't be effective, or even possible. I am so sorry."

"So what are my options? What do we do?" asks Dollsie, pleading with the woman to come up with something.

"I am afraid that there is nothing that I can do for you here, Ma'am. I've called your doctors and they will meet with you later on today to discuss possible further options." After a brief, decent interval, she gets up to escort us to the door. It is clear that she is done with this case.

"I think I'll go home now and order some champagne, some caviar, and a shotgun," says Dollsie as we exit. We stumble out of the office, down the elevator, and into a cab. She cries all the way home, feeling the inevitability of it all for the first time.

"How am I going to tell Dimitri?" she asks. "You're tough. You can handle this. You've never needed me. I suppose that was the hardest thing, for me as a mother. You'll be fine. And the others, too. But not Dimitri. He needs me."

"Mother," I say, after a long pause, as I search for the right words, "You've put up quite a fight. I admire you so much."

It is the wrong thing to say, clearly.

"Are you saying that it's over? That I'm going to die?" she asks incredulously, as if the concept were dawning on her for the first time. "How much time do I have left? Are you hiding something from me?" she cries, clutching my arm, terror in her voice. Once again, I marvel at her power of denial. She has been told over and over that her chances are not good, that her options are limited. And she has basically just been handed a death sentence by the radiologist. But despite all the lists and preparations in case "something should happen" she has never conceded that she might not pull through, that she might actually lose the battle.

"I'm not hiding anything, Mother. There's still hope, there always is. It ain't over till the fat lady sings," I say, feeling lamer by the minute. I have spent ten years counseling people with HIV and AIDS and I have confronted and learned to live with my own life and death issues for the past five years, and this is the best line I can come up with? "It ain't over till the fat lady sings"? Jesus.

"Sergei, talk to me straight. Is it over? What do I do? Just give up and go to Florida and wait to croak? Talk to me! You've always been straight with me. Since the age of ten. The only one who never hesitated to speak your mind, regardless of the consequences." Having mistrusted her intentions all my life, I'm still not used to genuine praise from her, and I want badly to rise to the occasion. To not let her down this time.

"You do what you need to do, Mother. None of us knows how much time we have left. So you've got to do it your way. You either keep fighting, or you decide you've fought enough and you take it easy and get what you can out of whatever time you have remaining. You're the only one who can make that choice. Either way, you know we are behind you all the way."

"Thank you, *hijo*. I can't believe this is happening. Three months ago I was so healthy, going to the gym every day, out to parties every night, so happy, so full of life. And now this. I just can't believe it."

"I just admire you so much, Mother. What's so great about life that makes you put yourself through all of this, day after day? That's the part I don't get. I would have given up long ago."

"No, you wouldn't. Otherwise you would have, and you haven't. You're still here. And when you have a child of your own, you'll understand. There's nothing I wouldn't do for just one more day with my kids, for even the smallest chance to be here to witness you and your sister become parents. That's worth any amount of agony."

We spend the rest of the ride in silence.

When we arrive back at Carlton House, Rosario helps her undress and she heads straight to bed, in pain and defeat, with a pack of cigarettes, the phone, the black phonebook, and the remote control by her side. She spends the rest of day making calls, spreading the news far and wide, as I stand by, my exhaustion and sleep deprivation giving way to a feeling of displacement; as if I am outside, peering through the window, watching this sad scene between a dying mother and her fucked-up son.

More consultations follow in the days and weeks to come, including one with another "famous expert" at Columbia Presbyterian named Dr. Fine, who is at the forefront of experimental research for pancreatic cancer. He gives her back some hope; there is a new chemo treatment he is trying out with promising results. How many times have we heard that phrase in the past few months, and exactly what does it mean, I wonder? She can start the treatment here in Manhattan, he informs her, then go to Miami for the winter to "wrap it up" (an unfortunate choice of words, I think to myself).

He is a kind, friendly man who seems to be in awe of Dollsie. She soaks up the admiration, and signs on to the treatment, fervently wanting to believe in this last miracle cure.

But once the sessions start, she feels much, much worse. She spends a lot of time updating her lists and preparing to go to Miami. She gets out when she can, knowing that she probably doesn't have much time left in her beloved city. She takes walks in the park, and when she feels up for it, which is less and less often, she receives friends. They talk about the old days and without uttering the words, they say goodbye. I'm miserable in my drafty loft, feeling the cold and the dampness seeping through my tired bones, and hearing the winds howling angrily, reflecting my inner turmoil. I feel the way I have always felt in this city: as if everything is spinning out of control, as if I'm becoming unmoored.

When she's feeling well enough, which isn't often, we go out to dinner or to a Broadway show, my greatest pleasure in the world. She had started taking us to the theater when we moved back to New York after the divorce, and the Great White Way had become my salvation. Those shows had gotten me through all the messy years, had given me something to dream about. Now we rarely make it through the intermission. I escort her back uptown and head back to my lonely loft and pray that tonight I will cede to the fatigue and find sleep.

"Oh the promise of the night! What does it not hold for the weary." (Theodore Dreiser)

A few weeks later, in early December, as winter settles in, we leave for Miami, Rosario and the two dogs and the seven bags in tow. We both look forward to the gentler, warmer climate. Between all the chemicals running through our bodies, we have a hard time handling the cold.

"I wonder if it's the last time that I will see New York," she says to me in the car on the way to the airport. "What a life. What a city."

Yeah, what a city. The city where I was born; where I had spent my most miserable years following the divorce, friendless and alone and always wanting to run away, disappear; the city I had returned to after college and grad school, only to leave two years later, worn out and defeated by loneliness and sleep deprivation and desire, the temptations too abundant and potent to resist; the city where I had watched my best friend die at the age of thirty-three, and where I now found myself, five years later, engaging in another existential fandango, another bout between life and death.

It was a city that promised much and left many destroyed in the pursuit of that promise. A city of unfulfillment and disillusion and hubris and loneliness and loss. At least for me.

But for Dollsie New York had been something else altogether. She had arrived in 1960 after being exiled from Cuba, with Dad and baby Anton. Secretly thrilled to have escaped the confines of Havana society, she had reveled in the city's pleasures and her newfound independence.

They were a glamorous lot, the young, privileged group of Cuban expats who had dared to venture further than Miami, and to hear their stories, it was a wonderful time to be in New York. They went through most of the sixties without a care, enjoying the parties and evenings spent dancing at El Morocco and listening to Bobby Short at the Carlyle, traveling to exotic locales, experimenting with drugs (something Dollsie always denied), doing their "good deeds" with underprivileged kids in Spanish Harlem and the Bronx while entrusting their own kids to Latin nannies. Weekends and summers were spent on Long Island, going to the beach and drinking and reminiscing about the good old days. If by the end of the decade, most of the couples were in the midst of messy affairs or divorced or headed in that direction, no one could deny that the decade had been a fun one. Dollsie still missed those days and talked about them often. Act One.

Act Two in the City: her seven-year marriage to Jacques, post-Switzerland. The marriage had turned out to be a mistake from day one, a huge one, and she increasingly turned to drink to drown out the guilt and disillusionment. Dollsie found herself trying harder and harder to "make it", socially and personally. She took on too much, wanting to conquer the city and make up for her own life which was in shambles. She had lost many friends along the way: some from the old days who had witnessed her efforts to ascend New York's social stratosphere with scorn and derision; others who had been discarded or simply forgotten in her quest to find whatever she was looking for, and still had not found.

Act Three: life as a twice-divorced woman, still beautiful but on the verge of middle age, trying to make it in Manhattan. She had dated several prominent men, including Jack Warnecke (a Californian architect who had been involved with Jackie Kennedy) and she had almost remarried several times, but her drinking (along with their underwhelming financial résumés) had gotten in the way. I saw little of her during those years, and it seemed like every time I did, she had moved again. It became more and more of a burden to maintain the right address, and the apartments got smaller and darker. For the first time in her life, she worried about not having enough money. She was terrified that she would end up broke, a fear she shared with most of the expats who had left lives of great wealth and luxury behind them in Cuba. And the poorer she felt, the more she would spend on others—entertaining them and spoiling them with extravagant gifts—just to prove to herself and others that she could. To keep up appearances. It was part habit and part compensation, the only way my parents knew how to express affection, the only way they could feel appreciated: by being generous, always ready to write a check to the needy and the deserving. It is what made them—and by consequence us—feel like decent human beings, deserving of all the outrageous privilege that had been bestowed upon us.

After all those years in New York and Switzerland, moving to Key Biscayne, where her saintly distant mother and the rest of her family lived, had felt like a defeat, a definite step down, and even after she had sold her last apartment in the city, she would return to New York for several weeks each fall and spring, taking up residence at the Carlton House for "the season".

We remain quiet for the rest of the ride to the airport, lost in our respective New York memories, struggling to make sense of it all, and bid farewell to the city that we had both called home, for better or worse, and trying to ignore

Rosario, who sobs quietly all the way for her beloved señora. "How wonderful!" says Dollsie, without a trace of irony, as we pull up to the terminal. "Christmas in my new apartment with all my loving children. Just like I wanted. Count your blessings."

PART THREE

IN THE LAND
OF MYTHS

TWENTY-TWO

MRS. DALLOWAY'S LAST PARTY

Dollsie settles into her new apartment at the Ocean Club, which has been finished just in time for her arrival. She is happy with the way it has turned out and she knows that she might only have a few months to enjoy it, which makes it all the more precious to her. The master bedroom and living room give out onto terraces facing the sea. The decor is typical Dollsie: elegant silk fabrics with an oriental twist, perhaps more adapted to New York or Paris than Miami, but which signal to the visitor that this is the home of a grand hostess. As with all the other homes she has decorated and occupied—except for the chalet— there is nothing cozy about the place, nowhere to just hang out. The layout is all about the entertaining: walls have been knocked down to enlarge the foyer and living room, and the furniture is arranged to allow a good "flow" for large numbers of guests navigating the relatively small space. Dollsie has mastered the art of adapting the grand salons of her past to contemporary dimensions.

She had hoped that I would move into the guest room, but as usual, I opt instead for Greasy's home, a few blocks from the Ocean Club, which has stood unchanged for fifty years, a temple to the past: post-Cuba and pre-divorce. From the age of fifteen, I had always chosen to stay there instead of at Dollsie's, which had been the cause of many an explosion. She couldn't stand the fact that I felt more at home at Gulf Road than at Casa del Mar, her chic condominium on the beach purchased with the proceeds of her two divorces.

I can still remember, at the age of five, standing in the doorway as I watched the ambulance taking my grandfather away, never to return. Greasy had lived in this house ever since, patiently biding her time until the day came when she would be able to return to her homeland.

Everything in the small, ranch-style house is old and comfortable, furnished with the retro fifties living and dining room sets that Greasy had somehow managed to smuggle out of Cuba, weathered by decades of kids, animals, and post-hurricane flooding. The main house is cluttered with everything Greasy has ever owned. She does not believe in throwing anything out, especially anything that had come from her home in Havana. I sleep in the pool house, where I've always slept, which is separate from the main house. It affords me privacy and easy access without going through the main house when I go out late at night and come home in the early hours, which I've been doing for as long as I can remember.

After all the places I've lived, the grand homes and New York pads and elegant Paris abodes, this simple one-story house on Gulf Road is still my refuge and I am relieved to be there again after the tumultuous months in New York. This is as close to home as anywhere has ever felt, except for the chalet, which now feels more like a dream. Like Greasy herself, this house has stood fast through it all, including several hurricanes.

After spending a few days in bed recovering from the trip, Dollsie resumes her routine: doctors' appointments and rounds of chemo and whatever social life she can handle. After chemo, we often go out to lunch and shop. She has many visitors, so I have more time to myself. Like New York, Miami is a place where I feel perpetually alone, where I have spent too much time chasing guys and not enough time making friends, and I have little to show for it after all these years. No one to just hang with. By default, I resort to the company of strangers.

In the evenings, after Dollsie has finished receiving visitors, we have dinner on trays in her room and watch CNN. One night, as she's drifting off to sleep, a report comes on about gay weddings in San Francisco. Long lines of same-sex couples are forming at City Hall, hoping to tie the knot before California's Supreme Court overturns the mayor's decision.

"Look, Mother, there's Nan and her girlfriend!" I exclaim.

She bolts straight up, momentarily forgetting the pain in her abdomen. "What? Where? Please tell me you're joking. God, if I have to watch my daughter march up to City Hall to marry that woman—who by the way, looks so much like a boy that one wonders why Nan wouldn't just choose the real thing—then please strike me dead now!"

After reassuring her that it was just a joke, I collapse with laughter.

"It's not funny, Sergei. It's really not. Lord knows I've tried, but I don't think I ever recovered from the bartender/truck driver. The one who looked like Roseanne Barr's little sister. You know what it is to discover your daughter prefers women? And under those circumstances? It's one thing to have a gay son; I don't know many people in my set who don't have one. But a gay daughter? It's simply incomprehensible. And revolting. I can't help it—Lord knows I've tried to overcome my feelings and accept it—but I just can't."

"What did you think she was doing at Madeira all those years? Sewing?" Dollsie had made Nan go to an all-girls boarding school rather than to a co-ed one like St. Paul's or Taft or Deerfield, and she had regretted it ever since.

She sighs, her way of signaling that this conversation is over.

"Maybe she'll meet a nice man one day. I still believe it's a phase. I must have scared her off from men, with my success. Maybe she just wasn't up to competing with me."

"Or maybe it was those hormones they gave her at the age of fifteen to stunt her growth," I say, provoking her.

"Now let's not get into that again, Sergei. I did it for her own good. The doctor told me that at the rate she was going, she would be well over six feet. Very hard to dress and to feel desirable as a woman when you hover over most men. So when they mentioned that experimental treatment, I thought it was a good idea. Little did I know it would retard her period by several years. Maybe that's what caused it."

"That must be it, Mother."

Christmas is coming up, and Dollsie begins to prepare for her last big party, her farewell bash. The day has always been much more—and less—than a family affair; the guest list vacillates between fifty and a hundred, consisting of both her society friends and the family members that she studiously avoids the rest of the year but always invites to Christmas lunch out of a sense of noblesse oblige. She feels that she is doing a good deed by mixing her fat, loud, poorly dressed and tacky Cuban kin with her sophisticated European and Latin friends, many of whom hail from the art world. Over the past few decades, she had become prominent in Miami's emerging art scene, as a collector and patron of Latin American artists, and she had parlayed this into a lucrative gig as a "consultant" to Christie's Auction House and Barclay's Bank, essentially paid to throw parties for her prominent friends, while also receiving a cut from any new business they generated.

Dollsie considers herself to be the matriarch of the family, even if her mother is still alive, for the simple reason that she is the only one who had, according to her, "made something of herself" following the Cuban exodus, the only one who had maintained, more or less, the same standard of living, the same taste and elegance and manners and wardrobe as her grandparents. The rest of the family had slipped into what she considered to be mediocrity, indistinguishable from the masses of other Cubans who had come to these shores unwillingly, slipping comfortably into the new middle class of Miami, with its aspirational American values, while perpetuating the myth of their exalted origins and inculcating in their children a sense of grandeur and glory about the past, and a deep, unrelenting hatred for Fidel Castro, the man who had taken it all away.

.

From the beginning, Dollsie and her mother had both ventured beyond this nobility-in-exile mentality; Dollsie by marrying well—both times—to ensure the continuance of the lifestyle to which she had become accustomed and felt entitled, and Greasy by joining the workforce; first as a secretary at McGraw-Hill in Manhattan, then following her husband's illness and their subsequent move to Miami, working as a secretary for Bacardi, which belonged to close family friends from Cuba. Upon reaching retirement age, she had refused to quit working, becoming the parish secretary for St. Agnes Church in Key Biscayne, where she had remained until she was gently eased out at the age of ninety, following her son's death.

One would be hard-pressed to notice that they are related at all, much less mother and daughter. Dollsie and Greasy, while close on a visceral level, have never been able to bridge the vast emotional gulf between them. Dollsie has always been jealous of her mother's saintly image, her irreproachability, which stands in marked contrast to her own flawed, slightly scandalous reputation as a twice-divorced woman—the second time to a Jew!—who has not always placed her children above all else (as Latin women are expected to do) and who has two gay children to show for it. But despite their differences and conflicts, they have always been there for each other; Greasy acting as her daughter's personal assistant, and Dollsie reciprocating by making sure that all of her material needs are met, including the clothes and grooming befitting a woman of her station.

And yet, I have never seen the two hug each other, nor express any kind of warmth or appreciation for each other, be it physical or emotional. I cannot ever recall seeing them go out for a meal together, just the two of them. Having been raised by German governesses, and thus not used to physical affection, Greasy had not known how to express her love for Dollsie who, from the beginning, had been too much to handle. Willful and temperamental, like her father. Over the years, Greasy had learned how to stay out of their way and ignore both of their frequent outbursts. But despite her inability to show affection, Greasy has always loved Dollsie with great ferocity, even if Dollsie claims to have never felt it.

According to Dollsie, she had never felt loved by her father either. The man she so much resembled, the mythical Princeton football player/World War II veteran that I knew so little about. During those last months, I ask her to tell me about my grandfather John; about the vague stories I have heard throughout my life about his drinking and his dark days in Cuba living alone at the sugar mill, forever in the shadow of his powerful father-in-law, Fico. John's brother had committed suicide while at Princeton, for reasons having to do with his sexuality, it was rumored, and the loss had cast a long shadow over John's life. As he aged, he must have found himself increasingly tormented by demons from the past, and although we were never told much about him—Greasy always maintaining that he had been the ideal husband and Dollsie refusing to utter his name—I could trace a direct line between him and Dollsie and myself: sensitive, troubled souls with self-destructive streaks who had fought inner demons all our lives, and had succumbed to compulsions and addictions along the way, to dull the pain and erase the loneliness.

"Sergei," she tells me, "I've never spoken about my father to anyone. Except once in therapy, after eight years. I told him, 'Dr. Feder, I'll tell you about my father today, and then I'll never speak of it again.' And that was the last time—the only time—I ever discussed him."

"And the shrink let you get away with that?" I ask. "Seems to me like you wasted eight years of therapy."

"Some things should never be discussed. It's a matter of loyalty. Neither Mother nor I have ever talked about your grandfather. Ever. He was a wonderful man, and he did the best he could. Whatever problems he had and whatever he did or didn't do to me is of no consequence. It's a question of loyalty. End of subject."

That is one of the few things mother and daughter have in common: a great capacity for denial in the name of loyalty. It was pretty much how my family reacted to any scandal which threatened to rear its ugly head and shatter appearances. There were some things you just didn't talk about. Like the coke-addicted cousin who had hung himself in his tawdry studio in a distant part of Miami. Or his older brother, who was doing fifteen years in a federal penitentiary for ripping off the government in a public housing scheme.

Even now, with Dollsie approaching the end of her life, mother and daughter are caught in the same dance of denial; since neither one can reach out to the other, when they are around each other they both slip into their usual mode of discourse, *everything is fine, what pretty flowers.* Dollsie claims that it's because she does not want to upset her mother with bad news, and Greasy deflects what bad news she does hear by doing what she has always done: not talking about it and going on with the business of life. She runs errands for Dollsie, makes sure that I am well taken care of at Gulf Road while I tend to Dollsie, and fills her days with so many good intentions and trivia that she inevitably falls into a sound sleep at night. I have never seen the woman lose a night's sleep over anything in her life. I envy her for that.

Just before Christmas, Dollsie asks me to take her to see her *santera*, her "godmother". She has been a follower of Santeria—an Afro-Cuban religious tradition that originated with the West African Yoruba tribe—for many years, seeing no contradiction between this and her Catholic faith. She believes in both. Her santera, an ancient, shriveled up little black woman called Olga, greets us in her small, run-down house in a shabby neighborhood near Little Havana. The small bungalow is filled with pictures of the many African and Catholic Saints of Santeria—Ochum, Chango, Elegua— and the tools necessary to carry out its voodoo-like rituals: altars with candles, rocks, sand, vials of herbs and potions, and outside, chickens waiting to be executed, their blood to be used for sacrificial rites. I recognize many of these strange objects. Dollsie had used them to try to get rid of Jacques during their marriage, going through the rituals every night; spitting on the rocks and blowing smoke at them, chanting incantations to the saints so that the gods might hear her prayers and some calamity might befall him.

Dollsie is dressed all in white, the color of Santeria, as is Olga.

"What have you come for, mi hija?" Olga asks.

"I have come to say goodbye, Madrina. They say I am not well. That I am running out of time. I want to know what the saints say. Is there any hope?"

The old lady throws some shells, studies the results for a long time, goes over to the altar, spits on her pet rock, lights a candle, and does some incantation as she rocks back and forth, waving her hands above the candle. "You may go now," she tells Dollsie, gazing deep into her eyes. "The saints will protect you."

Dollsie cries all the way home. The visit hasn't gone as she expected. She came looking for salvation, and instead, she feels like she's gotten another death sentence. Yet another one.

Christmas Day arrives, the last of a lifetime of Christmases with Dollsie. Memories of waking up in Gstaad to a big tree with tons of presents piled up around it, which multiplied as the years went by, exponentially linked to the guilt she felt for having made such a mess of her life, and ours. We would tear through the wrapping, keeping a watchful eye on whose pile was bigger and who had received the most expensive gifts, a foolproof way of measuring where we stood in Dollsie's eyes. For there was always a favorite, a less favorite, and an outcast. The outcast usually received a couple of Brooks Brothers boxes filled with boring clothes for school, while the favorite opened his presents with confidence, certain that he had gotten everything he had asked for, and then some. We had all taken turns being the favorite, only to find ourselves cast aside after some unforgivable transgression.

After being up most of the night—again—I stumble into Dollsie's new pad around ten, thinking I am late for the opening of the presents. I have always been a reluctant participant in the day's frenzied activities, turned off by the excess of gifts and random people and drinking, the pointlessness and waste unwanted reminders of my own life. But this time it is different. I'll do whatever it takes to make it a good one for her.

The maids are running around the apartment getting everything ready for the party, and Dollsie is in a state, upset over her latest blow-out with Anton, which had taken place the night before. The two had been on the outs since his visit to New York in September, when she had inadvertently screamed at his daughter one day to shut up while she was on the phone.   It was more out of habit than any intentional malice toward her granddaughter whom she adored, but Anton and his wife had cut the visit short, and had not spoken to Dollsie since.   And although they have come to Miami to spend Christmas with her, they seem determined to sabotage the day in any way they can: by skipping Mass and showing up late for the unwrapping of presents, dressing down for the family pictures which Dollsie has brought in a photographer to capture, and acting as if they don't give a fuck that this is almost certainly her last Christmas.

As we start opening gifts, we are painfully aware of the pile of unopened presents that Dollsie has gone to great lengths to assemble for her granddaughter. Just as Dollsie and Dad had shown the measure of their love by how much they gave us, so, too, had we mastered the art of showing our own love by how we accepted the gifts—or chose not to.   Generosity was their weapon, gratitude, ours.

After the gifts have been opened with as much enthusiasm as we can muster, we head to Mass.   Dollsie keeps looking around, hoping that Anton and Anna will show up.   They don't.   I sit beside her, overwhelmed with grief.   Ever since that Sunday in August when Dollsie and I had attended mass at MSK with the other cancer patients in various stages of dying, I have not been able to walk into a church without breaking into tears.   Watching Dollsie pray like that, trying with all her might to believe in the words, to believe that she can be saved, forgiven—that her life can be extended—makes me feel closer to her than I have ever felt in my life.   And while my prayers are vague, less fervent and more detached from the outcome than hers, I share the same desire for deliverance from guilt and regret, for absolution, the same sense of having fucked up my life, the same desire for release from the quest, the lifelong search for that something that will make me feel at peace, whole again.   Something real.   Something to erase the grandiosity and narcissism that have always made Dollsie and me feel like something was missing; that something better lay in store for us.

Dollsie prays and prays.   During the handful of times that we attend Mass together, between Labor Day and Easter, I have found my mother again—or perhaps for the first time—and at last I understand what it means to be Catholic. Ultimately, it doesn't matter where you stand with the Church, or even whether you believe in God.   Being Catholic means finding repentance and deliverance in the idea of God; it means learning to forgive by example.   It means being able to sit next to a mother that you have spent a lifetime hating and castigating and judging, and to finally be able to let go of all that. To replace the hatred and judgment with compassion and grace. After all, who am I to judge? After being awake all night seeking another kind of salvation and redemption through chemicals and the arms and naked body of a stranger, I am overcome with a great feeling of peace and relief. At last.

Dollsie has had her own twisted relationship with the Church—going so far as to request—and receive—annulments for both of her marriages (thus making bastards of all her children) so that she might feel welcome to receive communion again. She used to say that the best thing about being Catholic was that one could sin on Saturday, confess on Sunday, and start all over again on Monday. But I don't have to go to confession to feel the power of self-forgiveness. I can sit in my pew and acknowledge how misguided and lost I have been for most of my life, how much I have felt wronged by others and wronged them in turn, and how I have dishonored my own body and soul by always giving into the impulses to cope with the loneliness and pain of being alive. This is a place that can handle whatever I put out there. Whatever it is, it is okay. All of it. No need for analysis. It doesn't matter what you've done, or why. All that matters is the power of redemption: acknowledging one's sins—against oneself and others—and seeking grace and salvation through forgiveness and expiation.

As we emerge, we both feel drained, yet relieved, as if a burden has been lifted. We return to the apartment, where Dollsie and Nan begin to dress for the party, wearing the matching antique ceremonial gowns that Dollsie had brought back from our trip to China thirty years ago. She has worn this Imperial robe, fashioned from a rich, red brocade, along with a few others she had collected during her exotic trips, for every Thanksgiving and Christmas celebration since. Nan, who usually refused to join her mother in playing dress-up, not wanting to betray her lesbo-feminist convictions by transforming herself into some eighteenth century geisha or imperial princess at court, gives in this time. Hell, I would have worn the robe if Dollsie had asked. It's her last Christmas and her eldest son hasn't bothered to show up with her only grandchild to open presents or attend Mass. Dollsie is devastated, and already in severe pain before the party has even started.

As the guests begin to arrive, Anton and his wife and daughter and Anna finally appear, dressed as if they were going to a picnic on the beach instead of

Christmas lunch; it's one more way of giving Dollsie the finger on this sacred day. I realize that they are in deep denial; a refusal to believe that she is dying, coupled with the notion that even if she is, it's not the end of the world. Happens all the time. It doesn't take a therapist to realize that there is a little misplaced anger going on. Anton's rage isn't about whatever happened between Dollsie and Anna back in September; it's about whatever had or hadn't happened between mother and son throughout their lives. As the eldest, he had taken the lion's share of abuse and expectations, and all his life he had tried to live up to them, whereas I had been content to rebel. Since Anton can't verbalize this, all that's left for him to do is sabotage her last Christmas. It strikes me as both ludicrous and pathetic; I am grateful that, for all the discord between me and Dollsie, for all the distance and recrimination, I am now well beyond that. Rather than causing me rage, her illness and impending death have taken the edge off, have softened me. She can no longer do me any harm, and I no longer wish to inflict any on her.

I feel sorry for Anton; he's almost fifty and still looking to her for approval, seeking his own redemption in the eyes of the mother who had made him suffer so. Like her, he has made a mess of things with his marriages and his unbridled ego and deep sense of entitlement. And like her, he has gone through life devoting much of his energy to suppressing the tremendous rage that always threatened to explode at any moment—the kind of rage that would lead to being pinched or slapped or screamed at—or being whipped with a belt before he even knew what he had done wrong. When you've grown up with that kind of unpredictability, that erratic craziness, it's hard to contain your own anger. We had all found our own strategies for coping with those feelings, for rising above them and staying cool, but it erupted when you least expected it.

The party itself is like every other party that Dollsie has ever given, except of course this time she is dying. The same guests, the same food—caviar, shrimp with pink sauce, Cuban lechon, black beans and rice, salads and key lime pies. The same bartender and caterers and maids. I don't remember a single conversation I have that day. I do remember sneaking out on her bedroom balcony to smoke a joint once or twice. How cheerful everyone is, even though they have come to bid her farewell and that in their powerlessness to change the course of things, this is the one thing that they can do for Dollsie: be cheerful. Make her party a success. Dollsie has always lived for her parties and her image as a perfect hostess, finding joy in the planning, in the details: the flowers, the food, in the ritualistic preparation, the perfect presentation, the *mise-en-scéne*, and we are all as determined as she is to play our role, to make this last Dollsie party a big hit, as she is fond of saying.

I am one of the first ones to leave; way too early, as usual. I walk home along the beach, joint in hand, dehydrated and already feeling the effects of too much food and drink and smoke. I long for bed. I have lost track of how many nights I've been up since we arrived in Miami. I live in a semi-permanent state of sleep deprivation, awake all night and longing for sleep all day, and I know that like Greasy with all her fussing over papers and accumulated junk, this is my way of keeping busy—by being too exhausted to process what is happening.

As I slip into a coma-like nap, which knocks me out for several blissful hours, I picture Dollsie still at the party, with all her drunken friends, putting on a good show for them even though she can no longer drink and is in a great deal of pain, secretly praying that they will leave soon so that she can regain her bed, but not wanting the party to ever end.

TWENTY-THREE

ABSENT ALMOST ALWAYS

We survive Christmas, and move on to New Year's Eve, another last in a series of lasts. Dollsie insists that we dress up and go through the motions: champagne and caviar in her new satin covered living room, followed by the gala in the dining room of the Ocean Club. I watch her dance with Dimitri, envying the love they share, the closeness, and I wonder if I, too, will rise to the occasion and ask her to dance. Dancing with her has always made me cringe—too close for comfort—and I have gone out of my way to avoid it when the occasion called for it, perhaps out of embarrassment or spite, to punish her for being drunk. I have been punishing her for most of my life.

A few weeks later, Greasy has a heart attack. I'm in the living room, watching TV and smoking a joint; I have long since convinced myself that either she can't smell anything or that even if she does, she won't know what it is. And even if she does know, I know that she won't say anything to me about it. She's had a lot of practice not seeing what she doesn't want to see: first with her father, then her husband, then her children, then her grandchildren. We, in turn, have always encouraged her denial and done exactly as we pleased.

"Sergei," I hear her calling from the bedroom, in a faint voice, "I'm not feeling well," she says, adding, "I'm sorry to bother you." I go to her room and help her get up, figuring that if she walks a little it might pass. She has suffered from stomach trouble ever since her son Michael died two years earlier, and as a therapist, I assume that her symptoms are due to her bottled up grief and her inability to emote. She pads to the kitchen to select pills from the medication tray, and drinks a glass of water. I figure that Dollsie's illness is really starting to affect her, so I offer her a Xanax to calm her down, and surprisingly, she accepts.

She lies back down, and about half an hour later, she calls my name again. "I'm sorry to bother you again," she says, when I get to her bedroom, "but I think we need to call the paramedics." She looks pale and frightened. I call 911, then attempt to spray down the living room so it won't smell so much like weed when they get here, and run to the pool room to change out of my bathrobe. By the time I return, the paramedics have arrived. I glance over and notice the ashtray full of joints. I wonder if I will be arrested. The medics ask me what happened and what medications she has taken. When I tell them about the Xanax, they look at me, incredulous.

"You gave her a what?" one of them asks.

"Yes, I figured she was just having an anxiety attack, so I thought it might help."

"Hasn't anyone ever told you that you are NEVER supposed to give somebody medication that hasn't been prescribed for them? Especially an elderly person with a heart condition? Surely you know better!"

"My bad," I mutter, stupidly.

They go into action, attaching monitors to her and giving her shots and getting the stretcher ready to take her to the hospital. I call one of my cousins, also a paramedic, to let him know. I prepare a bag with some of the things that she will need; her medications and her toiletries and her rosary.

Greasy withstands the assault of interventions, smiling weakly, embarrassed to be causing such a fuss. They keep asking me questions about her medication schedule and her general condition, and I answer as best I can, feeling guilty about my ignorance. I have accompanied her to many doctors' appointments, I know about the stomach trouble and about a previous close call a few months earlier when they had torn one of her veins while attempting to insert a stent, but in the last few months, it has been all about Dollsie. Even though she is in her nineties, Greasy has taken a back seat to the rest of the family, as usual. Like a good Latin martyr, no matter what she is going through, she has a way of making you feel like she is always okay. I have been so immersed in Dollsie's world and in my own drama that I haven't taken the trouble to ask her how she is doing, to check in with her. I have been there without really being there. Absent almost always.

I follow the ambulance in my car, praying that she's going to make it, and wondering if they will write up a report about the pill and the weed. After parking, I enter the emergency room and find her settled into one of the beds in the patient area, waiting to see a doctor. She seems tired, but better. She attempts to carry on a conversation with me and those attending to her, asking them politely where they are from and apologizing every few minutes for all the bother. She encourages me to go home and get some rest, but I'm in full mea culpa mode and not going anywhere until I know she's alright.

The attending doctor is a black woman, which I know will make Greasy cringe. She asks me about what happened, and I tell her about the chest pains and the pill I gave her.

"You gave her a what?" she says, echoing the paramedic, and smiling with disbelief.

"A Xanax," I repeat, relieved that for some reason, she finds this amusing.

"Do you realize that you could have killed her?" she says, trying to be stern. Clearly she thinks that I am slightly demented and she is enjoying the story. "I shouldn't laugh, because you really could have killed her, but actually it turns out that you might have saved her life with that pill."

"How did I save her life?" I ask, disbelieving.

"I said you *might* have saved her. Your grandmother has had a heart attack, and although no one would ever recommend giving someone a Xanax for that, you might actually have helped to calm her down before the fact, thus making it less severe."

"So I didn't cause the heart attack with the pill?"

"That's most unlikely." she says, in her Haitian accent, "but please don't ever give your granny any creative medication again."

I spend most of the night by her bedside. She asks repeatedly for coffee, which they refuse to bring her. It's a sign that she is feeling better. She is out of danger, but because of her age she will stay in the hospital for a few days for observation. I head home at dawn as my cousin arrives to relieve me.

That afternoon, I take Dollsie to her appointment at another hospital. She wants to stop at Mercy Hospital on the way to see her mother, but I talk her out of it. It will just cause more agitation for everybody, starting with me. Dollsie is in a lot of pain, more than usual, and we need to get that checked out ASAP.

Her doctor examines her and decides to admit her to the hospital for a few days for further tests. Dollsie protests, explaining that her mother has just had a heart attack and is also in the hospital, but the doctor insists. "We need to figure out where we are at this point." So off we go to the admitting room, and after going through all the paperwork, we get Dollsie settled in a private room. She gives me a list of things to bring back to her later. I stop by Mercy to see Greasy, head home, rest for a while, and return to Baptist Hospital with Dollsie's things. At least the two hospitals are more or less on the same route.

Dimitri and the others have gone back to their respective lives after the holidays, so I spend the next week shuffling back and forth between hospitals, visiting Greasy who, as always, is the perfect patient, then visiting Dollsie, who is miserable. She hates the hospital and is terrified that she will end up there permanently. The nurses have a hard time dealing with her imperiousness and impatience, and she feels that no one is treating her with the proper deference due a VIP. And no matter whom she complains to—the head of nursing, the social worker, the chief resident, her own doctor—she is repeatedly put back in her place. This is not the nineteenth floor of MSK. She is just another slightly hysterical cancer patient to them; one amongst many, something she cannot accept.

After the weekend, they are both released. Greasy has fared well, Dollsie has not. The news is not good. The tumors have continued to expand, despite the latest round of experimental chemo. The cancer just keeps growing. Nothing seems to be able stop it, or even slow it down.

I come down with shingles. A searing pain around my waist and down my back, like two big intercepting loops of nerves on fire. I lie in bed for several days, in agony, taking anti-virals and smoking pot and wondering when the pain will stop. I have been in overdrive for months and now I am paying the price. Eventually, the pain starts to recede, just in time for my birthday in February. Anton has come back to see Dollsie. Following a long talk on the phone after his disastrous Christmas visit, he finally gets it: she isn't going to make it. It has finally registered.

For my birthday they take me out to Casa Tua, Dollsie's favorite restaurant in Miami. It feels more like a Florentine villa than a hot spot on South Beach, and reminds me of our childhood trips to Italy. I wonder aloud when the three of us had last dined together, if ever. It will probably never happen again, and I marvel at the three us sitting there having a lovely, civilized dinner. We, who have caused such chaos with our narcissism and our volatility, our unmet needs, and our unbridled, raging egos forever unsatisfied.

From the beginning, it had always been about Dollsie and the boys. Dad had always kept to the sidelines, and Nan, the pretty wallflower, had felt pretty much ignored by everyone for most of her childhood. Dollsie had focused all of her energies on her two eldest sons, and we were the ones who had bathed in her terrifying glory and attention at the expense of her daughter and husbands, enduring the recriminations, the whippings, the high expectations, the constant yelling, the ever present guilt and shame, the incestuous affection. She had wanted and expected us to be perfect; testaments to her womanhood and motherhood, and she had pushed us in every way she knew how. She had raged at our failures, and we had learned how to rage back at her for hers.

And here we are, at the end of her life, making polite conversation, the two of them trying to build me up and make me feel good on my birthday. And actually managing to have a good time. For we have always been a family that thrives on chaos and crisis. That's when the best comes out in each one of us, making us feel like knights in shining armor coming to the rescue, like the heroes we have always imagined ourselves to be.

Three days later, the night before Valentine's Day, I go out on an all-night bender. Giovanni is due to fly in from Paris the next day and I'm not sure how I feel about his arrival; about having to deal with him and his needs on top of everything else. I arrive home at seven in the morning. Walt lies panting by the bed, his breathing heavy and labored, making an ominous, rasping sound. I resolve to take him to the vet later, but first I desperately need to rest. I put on the Judy Collins CD that I listen to every night, my jangled nerves and troubled, sleep-deprived soul comforted by her beautiful, soothing voice and her sad melodies, and I drift off into a restless sleep.

When I wake up around noon, I find Walt lying completely still at the foot of the bed. Lately, he has not been able to climb up onto the bed and join me. The room seems weirdly quiet, except for the hum of the air conditioner, and in my drug-induced haze, I slowly realize that he is dead. He had waited by my bed all night for me to come home, and only then had he let go. I cry uncontrollably all afternoon. For Walt and our fifteen years together, and for everything I have put him through, and by extension, myself, in the last few months: the flights, the long hours of absence, the lack of walks and love and attention. I cry for Dollsie and all that is yet to come, but mostly I cry for my own loss. I have lost my best friend, again. I am inconsolable.

Giovanni arrives in the evening. I pick him up at the airport in tears and take him straight home. I decide that we need to bury Walt in the backyard, and that it can't wait until morning. So we grab a couple of shovels and start digging in the dark, neither one of us knowing what we are doing, going as far as we can until we hit some kind of pipe. The hole is not as deep as I would like but it seems deep enough, so we lay Walt on top of the pipe, and shovel the dirt back into the hole again. For days, I worry that raccoons will dig up the body, or that the rain will wash away the dirt and bring it to the surface. We decorate the grave with stones and Mexican votive candles and other stuff found around the house and yard. That night I dream about my rabbit that Tata had bludgeoned to death long ago. I have not dreamt of those pets in years.

Giovanni returns to Paris a few days later, and although he has been a help to me, providing me solace and enveloping me with his warm, familiar body, I feel like things are over between us. Our six months of being apart have shown me how little I miss him, how little I need him, and how little he brings to my life despite his best intentions. He is a sweet kid, well-meaning and loving. But like a kid, he depends on me for everything and I feel like I have to let that go. I can't handle anyone else needing me right now. I can barely keep myself going enough to be there for Dollsie. And even though he wants to be there for me, to take care of me and help me through all this, I won't let him. Like my parents and grandmothers, I have spent a lifetime convincing myself that I don't need anybody. It is easier to believe that one can do it all on one's own, and having money fosters that illusion.

March comes, and the doctors make it clear to Dollsie that she is running out of time. "How much time?" she asks, over and over. Perhaps a few months, the doctor tells her. So she decides to spend her last Easter in Gstaad, to bid farewell to the place where she had been happiest since leaving Cuba forty-five years ago. The doctor warns her that the trip will do her in; she is in no shape to travel, and if she does, things will progress more rapidly. But she won't be stopped. So arrangements are made to fly her back to Switzerland for one last visit, eight months after we had left for New York to try to save her life.

TWENTY-FOUR

GSTAAD, MY LOVE

Before joining Dollsie and the others in Gstaad, I stop over in Paris for a week to check up on things and prepare for Dr. Berger's visit, who is flying over from Pennsylvania to conduct a home inspection. I am almost certain that I won't be returning to Paris to live with the baby, but he says we need to "cover all of our bases, just in case." Eddie, my houseboy, has managed to keep the place in decent shape, despite the perpetual mess created by Giovanni and two other friends who are squatting there in my absence.

That first night, Giovanni tells me that he wants to break up. My initial reaction is surprise that he thinks we are still together. I realize that I've let the relationship drift over the past six months, without giving it a moment's thought. So of course it's not surprising that he wants to end things. I'm relieved—I realize that I would not have had the strength to leave him. But the relief gives way to intense anger, provoked by long dormant feelings of abandonment: how dare he leave me when my mother is dying? After everything I've done for him? Couldn't he have waited a few months? I spend a sleepless night, restless with rage, and in the morning, I ask him to pack his bags and get out.

Dr. Berger arrives the next day. The home inspection itself takes about an hour. I invite him out to lunch, figuring he should at least enjoy a few good meals after flying all this way, but he tells me he's not into food. From his gaunt appearance, I suspect that he, too, is dealing with his own health issues, but I don't pry.

He asks me how things are going.

"Okay, I guess. Actually, they're not going well at all; Dollsie is getting sicker by the day. It feels like we're in the home stretch. And my dog just died, and yesterday Giovanni and I broke up, so it looks like I'll be doing this as a single parent."

"I'm sorry to hear that," he says. "Do you feel ready to go through with the adoption without a partner?"

"Well it's not like I expected him to help much in the parenting department. He's not there yet in his head, and I knew that when I signed on for this. Still, I hadn't expected to do it entirely on my own. I'm definitely ready, I'm just not used to the idea yet, if that makes sense. And the timing is terrible. Just when I could most use some support."

"Sergei, I know you are going through a lot, and unfortunately, that's just the way it goes sometimes. We can't always count on good timing when it comes to the big stuff like life and death and relationships. But I have to know that you are prepared. You've moved up on the list, and even though you've got a ways to go, you never know when a birth mother could look through all the profiles and say to me, 'I want him to be the parent of my child.' It could happen tomorrow, and you'd have to leave your mother's bedside to go get that baby. And you would have to be ready, mentally and otherwise. Are you?"

"Yes," I say without hesitation. "I'm ready."

"Then that's good enough for me." With that he takes off. I've cleared the last hurdle.

I drive to Gstaad the following day. I arrive mid-afternoon, just in time for the massages that Dollsie has lined up for herself, Nan and me with Hans, her trainer/masseur, at the Bellevue Spa. Dollsie takes the first one, so that she can go home and rest after a long day of making her rounds to bid farewell to her friends. She's only been there for a few days, but the visit has already taken a great toll on her.

I'm next, and as I'm introduced to Hans, I think to myself: "So this is the Austrian stud that Dollsie is always going on about? He's okay, but nothing to write home about." I'm relieved. I won't have to worry about getting distracted during the massage. He tells me to disrobe and lie on my back so that he can massage the front first, and then he leaves the room. I take everything off and slide under the towel, looking forward to it after the long drive. There's nothing I love more than a good massage. After the divorce, when we returned to Switzerland in the summers, Nan and Dad and I would have backgammon tournaments every night, and translate our winnings into massage minutes. For Dad, I think that it was the only way he could get in touch with his body and allow physical contact. Like Dollsie, he hadn't been held much as a child, so that when he discovered massage at Esalen many years later, as an adult in his thirties, it had changed his life.

For a while, after Dollsie left, Dad had fantasized about abandoning everything—his career, his mother, the big house that Dollsie had found and decorated before leaving him and which now felt unbearably empty—and moving to Big Sur to become a massage therapist. But he had not gone through with it; such a breach of duty was beyond the realm of the possible. Instead, he had begun to host massage groups in Genthod, seeking to recreate what he had found in Esalen, and when we came to visit during summers and Christmases, he would teach us new techniques. Every night, in the bed he had shared with Dollsie, we would take turns giving each other massages while watching television. It never felt weird or incestuous, which kind of surprised me, because I would have been incapable of doing the same thing with Dollsie.

Hans comes back into the room and starts with my legs, working his way up. His hands are big, strong, and sensual, and as he approaches my thighs, I begin to feel the stirrings of an erection. No big deal, I tell myself, just ignore it and he will, too. I'm sure he's seen it before, many times, and the towel is covering me, so just lay back and enjoy. But before I know it, his hand is on my dick, stroking it gently, bringing it to full arousal, and then, as I feel his mouth start to go down on me, I practically jump off the table. But I don't, paralyzed with shock and excitement. What the fuck is happening? Is this dude—Dollsie's masseur—really sucking my dick, right after he's worked on my dying mother? Really? I keep my eyes closed the whole time, and make no attempt to stop him, more out of amazement than anything else. After I cum, he wipes me off with a warm, wet towel. He then resumes his massage until the hour is up. On my way out, he hands me his telephone number. Flustered, I leave the room, and find Nan, who is up next, and Dollsie, who has just finished dressing after using the steam room and the sauna.

"How was it?" Dollsie asks. "Isn't he wonderful? Those hands are absolute magic."

"Oh yes, thank you so much. Just magical," I mumble, as I head for the locker room, trying to avoid their gaze. I haven't been this embarrassed since the summer after college when Dollsie had walked in on me astride my boyfriend. "Oh sorry, I thought I heard the cat crying," she muttered as she opened the door on us, only adding to my humiliation.

After I finish dressing, I join Dollsie again in the reception area. Nan has already gone in for her turn.

"Would you like me to book another one for tomorrow or the day after?" Dollsie asks me.

"Uh, no thank you, I'm good."

"Well that's strange. I've never known you to turn down a massage before."

"I've come to spend time with you," I answer, "not to get massages."

That evening, after dinner at the chalet—Dollsie no longer takes pleasure in going to restaurants, the effort of eating has become too great—I tell her that I'm heading out to go have a drink with some friends. I drive over to Hans' apartment, which is in the basement of a chalet not too far from ours. We have a drink and talk for a while, and then have sex on his futon, which turns out to be less exciting than when I was on the massage table with Dollsie and Nan right outside. I return to the chalet late. The next morning, as I come down for breakfast, I find Dollsie and Nan glaring at me.

"You slept with him, didn't you?" says Dollsie, in her *Mommie Dearest* voice. "Right there on the massage table. With your sister and me right outside in the waiting room." I'm completely taken aback and at a loss for words.

"What are you talking about?" I stammer, trying to figure out how the hell they could have found out about what happened.

"It doesn't take a genius to figure it out, Sergei. You were acting most strange when you came out of that massage room. And then I offered to book you another massage, which you turned down. Now when in your life have you ever turned down a massage? And then last night, you say you are heading out to see 'a friend'. What friend? You haven't had friends here since you were ten years old!"

"And to think I went right after!" chimes in Nan. "That's just gross! I hope he washed his hands at least!"

With that I burst out laughing, more out of nerves than anything else. I don't want to admit to anything, not because I have anything to hide, but because I know that Dollsie is capable of getting Hans fired. And I see no reason to feel guilty about what happened, but Dollsie obviously does.

"What is this obsession you have with screwing everything in a uniform? This isn't the Castro. How do you think it looks to have my son having sex with my masseur?"

I realize that she's genuinely upset. I can't figure out why. It's not like anyone found out or anything. But she stays upset with me for the rest of the stay. And she has obviously told the others as well, because they all pretty much ignore me for the rest of the week. I feel bad. I've taken something away from her—I'm not sure what—and I've ruined an important moment. I've let her down, yet again.

She continues with her visits, back-to-back, determined to bid her farewells to every last person in the village who has meant something to her over the past thirty years. I don't know how she does it. I see very little of her. She also goes to see the cows—her "girls"—every day, accompanied by Nan. I feel left out. She is punishing me. Just like she always has.

But now that she is dying, I marvel at her tenacity and strength. I understand how miserable and confused she must have felt all those years, because I've been there myself. I now see how it was all but inevitable that she would become an alcoholic—like her father before her and her brother—to cope with her disillusionment, with the guilt and shame and grandiosity that had kept her from embracing her authentic self all of her life. To keep the depression at bay. During the past few months, I have seen glimpses of the other Dollsie, the loving mother whom I had forgotten even existed. I also see how inevitable it was that her children would head down the same path, following in her footsteps, struggling with our own impulses and cravings and addictions, always trying to escape the pain and emptiness. Always seeking to reclaim the fairy tale, heading toward another distant shore where we might at last find ourselves on terra firma.

Easter is over, and it is time to go back to Miami. She bids farewell to the mountains and to her beloved cows and makes all the arrangements for her very last event: her funeral and the reception to follow at the Palace. For she has decided that Gstaad is where she wants to be laid to rest, and she is determined to go out with a bang. And no one can put on a party like Dollsie. She has even gotten the mayor to agree to let her be buried in the local cemetery, something unheard of for a foreigner. Part of me wonders why she doesn't just stay here, since this is where she wants to end up. Perhaps she wants to die in Miami for her mother's sake, or perhaps in her mind there is still a glimmer of hope.

By now the tumor is visibly protruding from her upper abdomen, and no amount of pain medication and make-up can mask the agony. She has put on a good show, without complaint or self-pity, and with tremendous dignity and will. She knows that last impressions are as important as first ones. It is her last hurrah, and she plans on making a grand exit. A private plane has been arranged through friends to fly her from Geneva back to Miami. On our way to the airport, she has one more stop to make, one more farewell to get through, the most difficult one of all: saying goodbye to Mina.

We arrive at 12:30 on the dot, and make our way to the same table which Mina and I had occupied eight months earlier; the day this journey began. They are both so physically depleted and filled with sorrow and I don't know how any of us will get through the meal, but a lifetime of practice provides them both with the resources they need to pull it off with perfect poise and composure, each making a colossal effort not to fall apart. They've both gone to great efforts to look presentable—for each other and for me—and they manage, for the most part, to keep things "peppy", as Mina would say. I just sit there, a silent observer, witnessing these two forces of nature, these two women who—along with Tata—had ruled my world and tended my emotional landscape, for better or worse. Now Dollsie is on her way out, with Mina and Tata not far behind, and already I feel like an orphan. But along with the overwhelming sadness of the occasion, I also feel great admiration for them. And deep gratitude, along with a sense of completion. I feel whole again.

TWENTY-FIVE

GRAND EXIT

Once back in Miami, Dollsie takes to her bed, and spends her days getting ready for what she now knows is inevitable and imminent. As the doctor predicted, the trip to Gstaad has finished her off. She asks him, for the last time, how long she has left, and finally, she gets a simple, unambiguous answer: not long. Maybe a few weeks, maybe a few months.

She also requests if he can keep her alive until June 15th when some new tax laws go into effect. It is the last thing that she feels she can do for us; hang around long enough to save us a chunk of money on death taxes. The doctor laughs, not realizing that she is being serious, and says he will do his best.

Dad, who has driven me nuts all year by maintaining stubbornly that everything is going to be just fine, like an ostrich with his head in the sand, finally begins to realize that she is not going to make it and asks me what he can do to help. I tell him to write her, like he had during their courtship. He's always been much better at expressing his thoughts on paper, where he feels safe, rather than in person. He writes to her every day. Long letters where he revisits the old days in Cuba and New York, and their families, and "the children", and all the good times they had together. Like the young girl she had once been anxiously awaiting a letter from her handsome Swiss suitor, every morning she eagerly anticipates the arrival of the mail.

The letters touch her deeply, and she carries them around in her purse, like prized possessions. In one, he writes: "You have packed more into a lifetime than most of us could fit into multiple lives. You have lived your life to the full-est, on your own terms, and you've given your children a great example of what it means to really live, to embrace life no matter what it puts in your way." She reads that passage over and over to anyone who will listen during those last few months, and each time, she is brought to tears.

For Mother's Day, my friend Larry flies down from New York with a surprise for Dollsie. He and I had dated when I lived in San Francisco, but it hadn't last-ed. He reminded me too much of Dad. I pick him up at the airport with two huge duffle bags. He and his partner collect teddy bears, which, like Dollsie's cows in Gstaad, cover every surface of their home in the city. For me, this was a never-ending source of hilarity—these two grown men with their collection of teddy bears that they actually named and took turns sleeping with and travel-ing with—but when Dollsie had visited their apartment one day after chemo a few months earlier, she had been enthralled. Thrilled beyond belief. So since Dollsie can't have her "girls" with her, Larry has decided to bring "the guys", as he calls them, to Miami for a visit.

We invent some pretext to get Dollsie out of the house for a moment—no easy feat in her condition—and while she is gone, Larry and I unpack the bears, placing them on every surface, in every room. When she returns half an hour later, she finds her entire apartment covered in teddy bears of every size and hue, in every imaginable outfit. She yells out in delight, just like in the old days when she would spot a herd of cows and make Dad stop the car so she could go pet them. "How magnificent!" she exclaims, taking it all in, her eyes lit up with wonder, experiencing a moment of pure joy, one last time. She is beaming.

Rosario and I help her dress for lunch at the Ritz Carlton next door, which turns out to be her last outing. By then it's clear that the end is near and no one is in the mood to celebrate. It's the only time I can ever remember a quiet family gathering with everyone lost in their own depressing thoughts, focused on putting up a brave front.

After lunch, we take her home to rest. As Rosario helps her into her night-gown and eases her into bed, with the greyhounds faithfully by her, one on each side of the warm, protruding tumor, she says to me:

"Sergei, since it's Mother's Day, I have something for you. In the second drawer of my desk."

I walk over to the faux Louis XIV *écritoire* which, like Dollsie, is on its last legs after a lifetime of many moves.

"What am I looking for?" I ask.

"My diaries. A black one and a red one. Please bring them to me."

I retrieve the diaries. One is a faded black school girl's diary, the other, a shiny red leather bound book with the words "All I Know About Parties" inscribed on the cover.

"These are for you, my darling. I want you to have them so you can finally write your version of *Mommie Dearest*. Thank god your two first novels didn't get published!"

"Thank you, Mother," I say, as I struggle to hold back the tears. "But what makes you think I'm going to write about you?"

"Of course you will. What else could you possibly write about?" she exclaims. We both burst out laughing. Only Dollsie.

"Just be kind," she says. "There's also a letter in there. Promise me you won't open it until after I'm gone.'

"I promise, Mummy."

"Mummy? You haven't called me that since you were a little boy. Music to my ears," she says, fighting back the tears.

"And there's one last thing." She pauses dramatically.

"Yes?"

"In my closet, at the back, under my hat boxes, you'll find two boxes of letters. I probably should have destroyed them a long time ago. Or at least one of them. But now I want to entrust them to you, since you will probably be the one going through my closet anyway! You're just like your mother, too curious for your own good. Anyway, I don't know if I'm doing the right thing, but I thought you should read them. It might help you understand me better, and yourself. Because although you've never been able to accept it, you and I are very much alike in so many ways."

"I don't know what to say. Who are the letters from? What do I do with them?"

"You'll find out. And you will know what to do with them. Just make sure you get to them first. Your siblings would never understand."

The next morning, I am awoken by a call from Paris. Thierry, one of my closest friends, has hung himself. He had attempted suicide several times in the past, always after being dumped by a boyfriend. Thierry and I had been very close during my first few years in Paris—many people had thought we were a couple—but we had grown apart during the last few years, as I moved away from the party scene and he became increasingly engulfed by it. I had tried to warn him that he was not someone who should be doing recreational drugs, that he was too fragile to handle the highs and lows, to no avail. I had succeeded in getting him into therapy, but that hadn't helped either. He had continued to party, to seek oblivion from the pain of living.

His last half-assed attempt had been a few weeks earlier, following my visit to Paris. When I heard about it, I sent him an angry e-mail telling him that I had spent the past year watching my mother fight for her life, someone who wanted so desperately to live that she was willing to try anything to gain just one more day, and that if he found life to be so worthless, he should make sure to succeed the next time he made an attempt.

And now he's dead, this beautiful Eurasian boy, and the guilt is more than I can handle. Instead of feeling sad, I just feel angry at the waste of it all.

A week or so later, Dollsie's pain escalates further, and she goes into a tailspin. Dimitri and I take her back to Baptist Hospital, against her will. By the time we get her admitted and into a room and sedated, we are both total wrecks and decide to take the evening off, calling in her friends for reinforcement. We go home and drink and eat and smoke until we are comatose.

The next morning, feeling somewhat refreshed after a rare full night's sleep, I head to the hospital, wondering what state I will find her in. I stop by the nurse's station to ask how the night went. Very rough, they tell me. She has been out of control, completely unhinged, driving the staff crazy all night. Sounds like Dollsie, I think to myself. Maybe she's rallying her energies for one last fight. I walk down the hall to her room, and knock before going in.

"*Oui?*" she answers, "*Entrez.*"

I wonder why she is speaking French, and when I open the door, she looks at me with puzzlement and says, in a little girl's voice, "*Bonjour mademoiselle*, are you my new nurse?"

"Very funny, Mother," I say, attempting to laugh.

"*Pardon?*" she says, "I am looking for my son. Have you seen him?"

It takes me a long minute to realize that she has no idea who I am. Something has snapped. I wonder if they've given her too much morphine and if that's why her gay son who lives in Paris has morphed into mademoiselle in her mind.

"*Pardonnez-moi, madame,*" I say, playing along, and go back to the nurses' station to ask them to page the doctor. I then return to her room, trying to act as normal as I can while I attempt to figure out what the hell is going on. I send Dimitri a text message: "Get the fuck over here. Something is very wrong."

While waiting for the doctor to show—it feels like one of the longest hours of my life—I listen to Dollsie tell me about her life in great detail. About her gay son in Paris and her "pride and joy" Dimitri and her other two children in California—"that godforsaken place"—her homes and her childhood in Cuba; her grandfather Fico and her horses and the ranches and the sugar mill... As if I were a total stranger.

Finally the doctor enters, with Dimitri right behind him, and we head out into the hall to talk.

"Your mother seems to have taken a turn for the worse," he explains, stating the obvious. "Things are going to move fairly rapidly from here on in. There's not much more we can do for her, so we suggest you take her home and make her as comfortable as possible. Let hospice take over so that she can be in the comfort of her own home, surrounded by her loved ones, when it happens."

Just like that. Dollsie is dying and the doctor is discharging her. His job is done.

"But what happened?" I ask. "Did they give her too much morphine or something?"

"It's hard to tell if it's the increased medication they had to give her to sedate her, or if the cancer has progressed to her brain. Probably a combination of both. The only way we can know is to lower the medication but I strongly advise you against that. She will be in unbearable pain if you do."

"So she won't be regaining awareness?" asks Dimitri, with a pleading look in his eyes, "We won't be able to say goodbye to her?"

"It's hard to tell," he repeats. "Doubtful. Unless you reduce the morphine, but as I said, I don't recommend it. I'll be available by phone any time you need me. I'm going to go sign the discharge papers so you can take her home. The medics will take her by ambulance, and you can follow. Don't worry, she'll be fine." And with that, he walks away, to continue his rounds.

We are too stunned to take it all in, but they don't waste any time. Before we know it, Dollsie is being lifted onto the stretcher and wheeled out of the hospital by two medics, with Dimitri and me following.

"Where are we going?" she yells out, panicked. "Where they are they taking me?"

As we pass through the waiting area of the emergency room, she screams: "NO ME DEJEN MORIR AQUI CON TODOS ESTOS NEGROS!" ("Don't let me die here with all these blacks!")

Although she had never been able to entirely overcome the racism that had been ingrained in her in Cuba—a sort of genteel Caribbean mentality which had more to do with birthright and class than with skin color—she had gone out of her way to expose us to aspects of black life (as she perceived it to be), frequently taking us with her to Harlem, where she would pay the crack dealer on the corner ten bucks to watch her Jaguar while she performed her good deeds, retaining her composure even in the most dire, tragic situations, so we would see how fortunate we were.

She had also embraced other aspects of black culture as it was manifesting itself in the seventies and eighties, joining the board of the Dance Theater of Harlem and frequently hosting its director, Arthur Mitchell, and members of the troupe. The year I graduated from Taft, we traveled to Russia with the company, who had been asked to perform in honor of Ronald Reagan's historic first visit to the former Soviet Union and the new spirit of Glasnost. We followed the President wherever he went, like a merry band of exotic troubadours. It was the first time that most Russians had ever seen black people "in the flesh", dancing half nude. It was a powerful moment to witness; their introduction to the United States of America.

After the President left Moscow, Dollsie and Nan and I—along with the dance troupe—had boarded the overnight train to Leningrad, and everyone had gotten incredibly drunk on vodka, starting with Dollsie, who had bought several large tins of caviar on the black market for the occasion. While she and her pals spent the evening entertaining the troupe by making fun of the bull dyke escort who had been assigned to accompany us during the voyage, flirting with her and getting her drunk as well, I wandered the halls of our compartment, trying to pick up one of the dancers. But they seemed far more intrigued by glamorous Dollsie than by her horny eighteen-year-old son.

So after being exposed to black culture throughout my life, I'm as shocked as the people in the waiting room—most of whom are either black or Latin or both—by this desperate *cri de coeur.*   Where had it come from?

"Faster," I mutter to the medics, who are also black. I hope they won't hold her outburst against me. With much difficulty, they load her into the ambulance and Dimitri and I follow it to Key Biscayne. When we arrive at the Ocean Club, the medics jump out and come toward me, looking very frazzled.

"Guys, your mom freaked out on the way. No one could restrain her. She kept saying that we were kidnapping her and that she had to get back to her horses. She tried to open the door of the ambulance several times and jump out. We thought we might have to pull over to restrain and sedate her."

"Oh wow, I'm so sorry," says Dimitri, ever the polite one.

They open the doors to the ambulance and Dollsie emerges in a state of hysteria the likes of which I have never witnessed, ranting and raving like the Madwoman of Chaillot.

"Get me out of here! Where are you people taking me? Who the hell are you anyway? Let me go, let me go!" she screams at us. Dimitri and I stare, aghast, wondering what is happening and how we are going to cope with this. I want to tell the ambulance drivers to turn around and drive her right back to the hospital. No one has prepared us for this. I have accepted the inevitability of her demise from the start, and I have been around so much death in my life that I no longer fear it. But this? I can't wrap my mind around it. How is it possible to totally lose one's mind, from one day to the next?

We get her up to the apartment, which she does not recognize. The hospice nurse has been warned and is waiting with more morphine, which she somehow gets Dollsie to swallow. The medics leave, and between the four of us—the nurse, Rosario, Dimitri and me—we manage to get her washed and changed into a nightgown and into bed. She resists us with all her might. I'm amazed by the strength and ferocity that she still possesses, even though her body has by now wasted away to nearly nothing. She is not going gently into the night.

Once in bed, it is not long before she tries to climb back out, furious at us, these strangers who are detaining her.

"Get me dressed, you idiots! Can't you see that I'm late for my party? Bring me my horses! Where are my horses?" she laments, over and over, completely inconsolable and beyond any capacity for comprehension. Then she bursts into tears, crying helplessly and clutching her stomach in agony, and then finally, she falls asleep. After a while she wakes up, and it starts all over. She tries to get out of bed so she can get to the bathroom, determined to do so without our assistance, then forgetting what she is getting up for, and becoming angry at us all over again, before collapsing in bed.

This goes on for thirteen days and nights. We take turns keeping her company while fielding all the visitors, an endless stream of friends and associates from all stages of her life coming to say goodbye. We fight over how much medication she should be given, and how much food and water. The doctor has not given us any instructions so we rely on the nurses and hospice people to get us through this. Nan and Anton arrive from California and want to lower the doses of morphine, on the theory that she is being over-medicated, and that if they give her less morphine, she will regain her lucidity and we will have her with us for a while longer. Dimitri and I are adamantly against this, repeating what the doctor told us. At this point, our only goal is to keep her out of pain as much as possible, and whatever has sent her over the edge—the cancer or the morphine—I am grateful for it, because she is being spared the horror of it all. She is in too much pain to eat; the tumor is so large that it is evident how excruciating it must be for Dollsie to digest anything. But Greasy and the others keep trying anyway. To them, not feeding her is tantamount to starving her to death, and that is not something they can live with. All I care about is making sure she has as much pain medication as she needs, and keeping her hydrated.

The days go by in a blur. Her two miniature greyhounds rarely leave her side, nestling up against her tummy, on either side of her tumor. I cannot tell if they sense her pain, or if they are just feeding off of the heat generated by the throbbing mass. Visitors come with platters of Cuban food, and hold vigil by her bed nervously groping their prayer beads, reciting their incantations with feverish intensity. I smoke, read, and try to spend time with Greasy, in order to prepare her for her daughter's imminent death, while the siblings run around in a frenzy of activity and errands, trying to avoid the unavoidable. Since Thierry's suicide, I am pretty much numb to it all.

Every night, the nurse asks me if we should increase the medication, to make her more "comfortable and speed things up". And every night, I respond, "not yet". The others are not ready to let her go, and I don't feel comfortable making that call, not just yet.

Time loses all meaning. Dollsie recedes further and further away from the present, back to a time and place when she had been happy, in Cuba with her horses. I find out that an old beau of hers, her first, had come to visit her the day before she had gone into the hospital and lost her mind, and that they had reminisced about riding together on the beach in Varadero at the age of fifteen. This is the image that stays with her during her last days. The only one of us that she recognizes is her mother, and she calls out for her incessantly, like a two-year old.

"*Mama, Mama,*" she says over and over, moaning in pain. The rest of us are invisible to her. When she looks out the window to the beach and ocean, it is not Key Biscayne she sees, but the landscapes of her childhood: the sugar mill, the ranches, Varadero beach. She looks surprisingly beautiful during those last days; ethereal, translucent, almost radiant, as if she is almost free of the pain that has consumed her, unceasingly, for months and months.

On June 5th, Ronald Reagan dies. The timing seems so fitting. I know that Dollsie can still hear me, so I tell her about the news, recalling the time that she had finally been invited to the White House, after years of campaigning through her friend Jerry Zipkin, a "social walker" who was close to Nancy. The invitation had taken much longer to arrive than she would ever have anticipated, and it galled her that so many of her friends in New York had made the trek to Pennsylvania Avenue before her.

For the occasion, she had chosen an outrageous dress by Bernard Perris—a tight fitting black bodice attached to some crazy black and red mini-skirt with many layers of organza, which she had opted to accessorize with fishnet stockings and very high heels. Already a tall woman, well into her forties, the dress made her look ridiculous, like Spiderman in drag or something. I couldn't believe that this was what she was choosing to wear to a White House dinner, after all those years of trying so hard to wrangle an invitation. Neither could Jerry. We begged her to reconsider, but determined to make her mark, she had gone ahead with the outfit.

I recount to her the details of the evening as she had described them to me and others so many times: being seated at the President's table and flirting shamelessly with him, and then hitting the dance floor with him as Nancy glared and everyone else stared at the tall beautiful Cuban lady in the crazy dress. It had been, according to her, a wonderful evening, one of the pinnacles of her life. After that, I had nicknamed her RuPaul; a name which had stuck.

At one point, I feel her slipping away. Her breathing is more labored, and I go to get the nurse. She tells me that this might be it. Apart from the nurse, I'm alone in the house with Dollsie. The nurse leaves the room, closing the door behind her. I let go, crying like a baby, thanking her for all the good times, for all the wonderful adventures, the trips, the generosity, the misplaced love. Most of all, I thank her for the example she has given me over the past ten months; the courage and dignity and grace, the fierce determination to live one more day, for us, her children. We had been loved all along. We just hadn't realized it. Life had gotten in the way.

"I love you," I say to her, meaning it for the first time since I was a little boy. "Thank you for showing me the way, for setting the example, for helping me to choose life, once and for all, after all that tortured ambivalence."

She does not die. The nurse seems surprised.

I have made my peace with her, at last.

The following night—June 6th, the anniversary of Raphael's death—her breathing becomes even more labored. The nurse lets us know that the end is approaching, and suggests that we give her a little extra medication to "help her get through it." We know that the time has come, and we give our assent. An extra dose of morphine is administered, and we settle in for the evening. Nan heads out to get a bite to eat, Anton falls asleep on the couch, and I roll a joint and run a bath. Dimitri stays alone with Dollsie for a long time, saying good-bye, reviewing their lives, expressing his gratitude and sorrow and deep love for her, accompanying her on this last part of her journey, easing the pain and the fear with his voice and his caresses.

The nurse knocks on my bathroom door. "I think it's time," she says, "You better gather your other siblings."

I jump out of the bath, throw on some clothes, go to wake up Anton and find Nan. We gather around the bed, all four of her children present for the moment of her passing, fulfilling her last wish. We are together again, a family. Although her breathing becomes more and more painful to witness, her spirit has already left this world. She seems at peace. At long last, Dollsie has found peace.

At 1:30 a.m., her breathing stops. It is over. We stay with her for a few more minutes—Anton, Nan and Dimitri on one side of her, me on the other—and then the nurse takes over. We hug each other, and the others go off to call their loved ones. I can't think of anyone to call.

I head out to the balcony, light a cigarette and watch the moonlit waves dancing on the sea and crashing against the shore. And in the distance, I see Dollsie astride her beloved Noy, a young fearless girl galloping through the water on her mighty steed, fierce, ready to conquer the world, confident and happy, knowing that all of it is hers just for the grabbing. Dollsie has found her horse at last, after a lifetime of searching, and they ride off into the distance, back to her mythical island after a strange and wondrous voyage.

TWENTY-SIX

GOING HOME

The funeral takes place at St. Agnes in Key Biscayne, where the services for Dollsie's grandmother and father and brother had also taken place—along with my friend Claudia—and where Greasy had served as parish secretary for most of the past three decades. All of Key Biscayne is there, for Dollsie and for Greasy. As my brothers and I walk in with the casket, I am blinded by the tears, which seem to ambush me, almost ferociously. I can feel my face transfigured by the grief. People are staring at me. I try to regain my composure. Both of Dollsie's ex-husbands are there, looking utterly bereft, as if they were still married to her. Dad's relatives from Buffalo are also there. They had given her the nickname Dollsie when they had met her as an eighteen-year-old bride-to-be. It sounded less, well, less Hispanic than Dolores. The name had stuck.

The place is standing room only, with most of Miami's high society present, as well as representatives from all of the charities and companies she had been involved with over the years: the International Rescue Committee, the Dance Theater of Harlem, Christie's, Sotheby's, Barclay's Bank, various museums, and several Cuban organizations dedicated to overthrowing Castro and reclaiming their homeland.

Once again, as I have often in the past, I marvel at how easy it was for so many to love this extraordinary woman, yet how difficult for those of us who had to live with her. The great paradox of Dollsie's life.

Only two or three friends from New York have flown down for the service;

253

old friends with whom she had long ago lost touch as she sought more rarified circles. None of her social friends are there—the hundreds of "devoted friends" who had attended her functions and parties over the years. Not one; they expect us to hold a memorial service in New York. These are the same people who will fly to Paris or London for a fashion show or a party, but they can't be bothered to come down to Miami for a funeral. Part of me can't blame them because Dollsie had let it be known that she wanted three services: one in Miami, one in New York and one in Gstaad. But the four of us have already decided, more or less unanimously, that two funerals are enough. Even for someone as larger than life as Dollsie. We don't have the heart for a third. "After all," I say, by way of expiation for the guilt we all feel, "even Princess Diana and Jackie only had one funeral!"

After the service, while the others gather for one last party at Dollsie's place, Anton and I follow the hearse to the crematorium. We watch silently as they slide the casket into the giant oven. Neither of us wants to stand there and visualize her ravaged body and her still beautiful face being reduced to ashes, so we leave and return to the apartment where the gathering is already dying down. Apparently the place had been packed, standing room only, and people had left. It makes sense. She was always the life of the party. Without her, what's the point of lingering?

Once the guests have departed, I go to Dollsie's closet to retrieve the boxes, and leave the apartment surreptitiously, not wanting anyone to notice. I rush back to Greasy's and after undressing and taking a plunge into the pool and rolling a joint, I lock myself in the pool room and open my precious cargo, eager to discover what lies within.

One box contains all of her correspondence with Jacques, the other with Prince Georgie—the two Russian men who had captured her heart and fought to wrest her away from my father for years. It is as if, along with her journals, she has given me the keys to her entire life. I decide to save the journals for the journey back to Gstaad with Dollsie's ashes, which will be buried in the local cemetery, after one last party in her honor at the Palace.

I start reading. The letters from Jacques are poetic and inspired; romantic and ardent, full of rich, passionate quotations from Baudelaire, Rimbaud, Pasternak, and other French and Russian poets and philosophers, taking her on a splendid voyage with his brilliant mind. They are filled with beautiful declarations of love and extravagant promises, appealing to the young girl who had sat in her grandfather's lap, hungry for love and attention, surveying his dominion and learning the ways of the world, basking in his power and daring herself to be like him, to expect so damn much out of life. I am transported; at last I understand why she had fallen for him, to the detriment of everything else in her life.

The letters span almost a decade—from the mid-sixties, shortly after I was born, until my parents' divorce nine years later—revealing Jacques' determination to conquer her, and her frantic attempts over the years to resist; to remain with Dad and be a good wife and a good mother to her children. Her letters to him are moving and touching, expressing her pain and confusion and desperation, and Jacques', patient, resolved, unwavering.

The second box of letters, from Prince Georgie, the "White Russian", come as a shock. They are passionate in a different way; perverted, graphic, sadistic, revealing a side of my mother that I never dreamed existed. A tortured, twisted side. I feel dirty reading them, but I can't put them down. Like a cross between the diaries of Anaïs Nin and Last Tango in Paris. They remind me so much of my own sexual journey, of all the crazy things that I have done with random men in random places, the pushing of limits, the desire for degradation and submission. They are deeply disturbing but also profoundly cathartic, relieving me of the shame and guilt about my own dark side that I've carried around for as long as I can remember. How had she come to the conclusion that I needed to read this? How did you know, Mummy? When I reach the end, I wonder why she has kept them all these years, in her closet, for anyone to see. But I know what I must do: destroy the evidence. It's the least I can do for Dollsie. I go out back and burn them in the yard, one by one, near Walt's grave.

The next day, I head to the airport for the long flight to Geneva, the last leg of a voyage that had begun ten months ago. At the time, I had thought I was leaving for a few days, but now it feels like I've been gone a lifetime. I find myself alone with Dollsie again, for one more trip together, the last of so many throughout our lives—happy and sad, adventurous and perilous.

After takeoff, I place the box containing the urn with her ashes on the seat next to me by the window, and I pick up the black book. As I open it, the letter falls out, surprising me. I had forgotten about it. Sipping a Bloody Mary and wishing I had a cigarette, I begin to read:

My Darling Sergei, my beautiful boy,

By the time you read this, I will be elsewhere, at peace, free of pain, watching over you all with so much love and gratitude. You will never understand what you did for me this year, by leaving everything—your man, your job, your home, your life—to be by my side. To have my son back after so many years made everything that happened to me this year worth it. Everything. I am so deeply grateful to you. And so very proud. You were my rock.

Sergei, I hope I've been able to convey everything you have meant to me, everything I feel for you. I have tried this year, even though I know it can never make up for the past. But just in case I haven't, there are two things I want to repeat so that you can finally know them and forever keep them in your heart.

The first is that I have always loved you so very much. I didn't know how to show you that love, for I was never shown it myself, and I didn't realize how hard on you I was, but please believe that I have always loved all of you beyond measure. My greatest failure and regret is that you in particular never felt that love. And because of that, you've gone through life being so very hard on yourself and others. I bear the blame for that. I hope you can forgive me.

Which leads me to the second thing. I wish you could see yourself the way I see you—the way others see you: as a beautiful, gentle, brave soul full of love and humor and compassion. I have watched you this year with so much admiration, such awe. I am so proud to be able to call you my son. What a man you have become. What dignity. I guess I must have done something right.

But until you believe this yourself, you won't love life the way I have. Even though we are so much alike, that is the great difference between us. I have loved my life with a passion that was sometimes too much to bear. You must love yours too. For your sake, and for your child's. You must let your depression go, once and for all.

The hardest part about saying goodbye to you is realizing that I will not have the great joy of meeting your child and watching you with her. For I know the universe will send you a daughter. A beautiful little girl of your very own.

And I know, beyond a shadow of a doubt, that you will be a wonderful father and that your child will be the happiest girl in the world.

Don't make the same mistakes I did. Tough love is the only thing that I knew growing up, and I thought that was the way I must raise you also. Be gentle and kind, as you have been with me this year. But most of all, love yourself enough so that she grows to love and admire you as much as I have. Let her see the Sergei that

I saw this year and always knew was there. Not the one you've so often seen when you look in the mirror.

Finally, I hope more than anything that you allow love into your life. Not just your daughter's love, but the love of a partner, a man who will cherish you and be by your side and help you raise your beautiful child. Don't follow my example, always pushing others away, out of boredom or fear or because I thought there was something better out there. Find the one that loves YOU, and stick with him. Allow him to love you on his own terms, not according to your expectations or demands, because no one ever will ever be able to meet them. In the end, that's all that matters. I realized that far too late.

That's all, mi amor. Please enjoy life. It is so precious. And so very short. I will always be watching over you, and I look forward to the arrival of your child. What a lucky little girl she will be. And you will never be alone again.

With eternal love and gratitude, God Bless,

Mummy.

As the flight attendants go about their routines, setting up trays and serving drinks to the pampered passengers in business class, I lose all sense of time and place. The tears come again, like a tsunami, overflowing, spilling on to the pages, seemingly without end. People are undoubtedly staring at me—after all this is Swissair, they're not accustomed to such overt displays of emotion—but if they are, I'm unaware. I put the letter away, and wait for the tears to stop so that I can move on to the journals.

With Dollsie by my side, I revisit her life, in Cuba and beyond. I read about her days at the sugar mill, astride her beloved black horse Noy (who would later be killed by Castro's guerrillas), riding through the fields of green cane rippling in the breeze, with her grandfather Fico by her side, in his white guayabera and Panama hat, her heart beating with joyous anticipation as they approached "America"—the mill that his father had built for him— thrilled by the pound and grind of the machines as they mashed up the cane, the erotic smell of the raw, unrefined sugar. During these walks, Fico would survey his lands and tell her with quiet pride about the early days, and how he had turned forests into productive land, building an empire whose sugar would be sold throughout the Americas.

How she had loved this place called Cuba, this land of myths where everything seemed possible, and which had then suddenly vanished.

I read about her early flirtations, her teasing and cajoling and first attempts at
seduction, her longing and desire, her budding narcissism, the cruel games she
played in the name of love. I read about her summers in Europe with Fico and
Nani, those glorious summers she had often told us about, which always began
with a long stay at the Crillon in Paris, where she would spend her days studying
languages and visiting museums with her Russian governess; making the rounds
of friends and couturiers with her grandmother; or going to the jewelers on the
Place Vendome with Fico to help him pick something out for Nani and for his
"lady friend" and—if Dollsie had been especially good—for herself as well. After Paris, they would take off in the motorcar—along with their chauffeur and
maid—for destinations like Biarritz and Venice and Salzburg. She was the only
grandchild invited on these trips. By putting her on a pedestal, Fico had instilled
in Dollsie, at a young age, the conviction that a special destiny lay in store for
her, and this had led to a lifetime of searching and frustration and disillusion.

At fifteen, her parents, fearing that she was becoming too spoiled, too entitled, had sent her back to the States to attend Dobbs, a boarding school outside
of New York. She had hated every minute of it. She had no friends, detested
sports, and was at a loss when it came to the chores that the were required,
which she would pay her roommate half of her allowance to carry out for her.
Each summer, she would return to Cuba, to Havana and the sugar mill and
the ranch and her beloved Fico. By then, he had become an important man in
Cuba; an influential senator with aspirations to the presidency. She basked in
his glory, following him wherever he went, whether to inspect his properties, or
to his office in the majestic senate building, or even to deliver gifts to the mysterious lady who was his mistress.

I read about the last crazy summer before her engagement, when Dad had
chased her around Paris and across Europe, courting her assiduously, outfoxing
the three other suitors who were also in hot pursuit that summer: Carlos, the
brazen Cuban playboy who had been tracking her for years; and the Princes
de La Tours D'Auvergne, two brothers who would show up in every European
city and resort that Dollsie and her grandmother stopped at, charming her with
their gallant French ways, attempting to outdo each other with grand schemes
of seduction, determined to take home the big prize. I read about her attending

the famous Bal de Brissac, and leaving with one of the princes only to have Dad appear at her hotel at eight a.m. with a bandaged ankle which he had twisted while jumping over a fence in an attempt to follow them. The image makes me smile; I hardly recognize the man who would become my father.

After Paris, she and Nani had sought refuge at La Bourboule, a spa in Auvergne, where the princes had appeared, along with Dad. And then had come Venice, where they had been joined by Carlos, who would follow Dollsie by gondola wherever she went, even showing up at the Danieli one night at four in the morning, wasted and insistent, causing much excitement with Nani and the hotel staff.

Following that heady summer, the best one of her life according to Dollsie, Dad had proposed, and they had married the following year in Cuba, only to leave eighteen months later.

Even though I am reading her journals for the first time, it is as if I know the passages by heart. These are the stories she had recited to us over and over, with embellishments added each time.

And then I get to the red book—*All I Know About Parties*—begun right around the time of my birth and covering the early years of her marriage and her years in New York. On the inside cover, she has inscribed two quotes:

"Il est plus facile de rêver sa vie que de la construire" (It is easier to dream one's life than to build it).

"I believe in being faithful to a man - for at least six years."

I'm taken aback. The two quotes contain the entirety of her life like book ends.

The first mention of me takes my breath away: *"Sergei was born two months ago—he is fat, and white, with blue eyes and a most peculiar hunger, which is constant. Finally, after going through miscarriage after miscarriage and another operation, he was conceived during our second honeymoon in Greece, where I spent my days praying to the gods and making delicious love with my Suiso.*

"I pray we can make him a man equipped to face life and love it. I pray he will be proud enough to build and not destroy. I pray he will always have a twinkle in his eye and lightness in his step."

I stare at those words for a long time, transfixed.

I read about how deeply in love with Dad she had been at first, placing him on a pedestal, a little in awe of him and fearful of the intensity and seriousness of his love for her. I read about their "hectic and stormy" three-month honeymoon through Europe, and their subsequent move to Mina's country house in Grez-sur-Loin, a "small fortress" consisting of three little houses connected by bridges, ivy and an antique well, with a large stone crucifix in the middle of the garden. She had burst into tears the first time she had seen it and had cried for a week. She had tried to adjust to village life, ordering elaborate menus to be prepared by Anna, their chef who had trained at the Cordon Bleu, and setting out every morning with her straw hat and gardening gloves and basket to cut roses and arrange them into bouquets. To occupy herself in the afternoons, she went to Fontainebleau and painted nudes and walked her miniature pinscher Borzoi in the Bois. And while JJ wrote his novels, she played the same make believe games she had played as a child.

And then winter came, and with it, the end of her rose cutting and art classes. She started to feel the walls closing in on her. She began to cough and cry and fight with Dad all the time. After the incident in the fountain, they left and returned to Cuba, where their marriage blossomed.

I read about her early years in New York, the thrill of living in such a fabulous, exciting city with such a beautiful man and wonderful husband, knowing freedom for the first time. In meticulous detail, she recounts glamorous nights spent at El Morocco and other fashionable clubs. Her entries are full of superlatives. She is on top of the world. I revisit her trips to Greece and Morocco and Turkey; exotic adventures to distant lands taken with their friends—other young, glamorous couples living the golden life. Untouchable, almost divine. At the apex of their youth and beauty.

And then slowly, the tone changes. She reveals doubts about her marriage, her ability to make Dad happy, the growing dissatisfaction she begins to feel, the wanderlust. She writes about summers spent on Long Island, in a "provincial, boring place" called Lawrence, where they rented an ugly, rambling house, with the jets taking off from nearby Kennedy Airport, making conversation impossible. Bored, she spent her days on the beach, watching her babies and listening to the other wives and mothers discuss children and babysitters.

She tries to bridge the great divide between the perfect husband and the fabulous apartment and the marvelous life that everyone is always reminding her how fortunate she is to have, and her growing discontent and restlessness. Her dissatisfaction, her feelings of emptiness and the frantic search for something she cannot identify; the fear that time is passing too quickly, and that she will never find what she is looking for. She feels guilty for having these feelings and struggles to conquer them and appreciate what she has, or at least settle for it. More and more, she finds herself going through the motions, rarely feeling anything.

And then she meets Jacques. The rest of the journal, spanning five years, is full of anguish, sadness, despair, uncertainty, confusion. She is torn between staying with Dad, the husband that her family had picked out for her, handsome, kind, generous, dutiful, distant, and the "little Jewish man"—as her mother and mother-in-law called him. His culture and brilliance, his passion, his self-made fortune and ambition remind her of her grandfather Fico: both powerful men who had set out to conquer the world on their own, and had succeeded. The kind of man she imagined she would have been, had she not been born a woman. Back and forth she goes, one moment deciding that she is leaving Dad to marry Jacques, the next resolving to never see Jacques again, for the sake of the children. Along the way, she becomes more and more despondent, feeling increasingly alone, losing herself in depression, helpless against the violent, unceasing, see-saw of her competing desires: whether to destroy everything she has and begin anew with this man, knowing she will lose much in the process, or whether to stay and endure. To learn to be grateful for what she has, instead of wanting something that she can't have. She contemplates continuing with both of them, since they are both willing to share her rather than give her up, but in the end, feeling torn and tortured, she cannot accept this arrangement, for she "must belong to one man." She must choose. Either way, she knows that she is giving up a lot—too much. And then I come across a passage about her father, the man she had so rarely mentioned, whose absence had loomed large:

I barely knew him. Since childhood, I had lived in adoration of Fico, and John never figured. I never felt he was my father; at times I thought that I must have been adopted. We hardly ever saw him, and when we did, nothing was there. How terribly sad! I only saw his his drinking, his giving up. How could I have not seen more, done more?

Just before he died, because I could control him better than Mother, I brought him from New York to Florida, a sick, young man (he was only fifty five). I tried to prolong his life but it was too late. Could I have done so before?

He spent three months in a house that JJ had bought for him and Mother here in Key Biscayne. He loved the house, the sea, and he dreamed of getting well, fishing, working. Then he spent weeks in the hospital, and I stayed by his side as he slowly died, in agony. He finally died in my arms, little by little, during that long night. As I held his hand and tried to infuse life into it, his breathing recorded by those infernal machines in the intensive care ward, I saw two beautiful, enormous pink clouds drift by, and I felt his spirit leaving that room - John, who had had so much to offer, who must have suffered so.

Oh John! I hope you have found happiness and peace! I, who felt so far away from you here in life, feel so close to you now, so much like you so often, now that you are no longer here.

How inexcusable, how terribly sad this failure on my part. Then, I didn't know that one can never judge -- that life puts you in situations that can break you, or something in you. I was so intent on trying to stop you from making others suffer that I never thought of you, who must have suffered more than any of us. How you must have struggled with yourself, how you must have tried... How blind I was, how misguided and selfish and unfeeling.

I release you, I forgive you for those things you did to me. I shall never speak a word of them to anybody. And I hope you forgive me.

I pause for a long while, overwhelmed with a haunting sense of *déjà vu* and projection: it is as if I had written these words about her. The regret is almost more than I can bear at that moment, but then, I feel a soothing calm come over me, like a little boy being caressed by his mother after a bad dream. I have found the missing puzzle piece. Closure at last.

The journals end with a recounting of her latest operation, this time to remove a cyst, and with these words, familiar in their unresolvedness.

Life once again ebbs out of me... Enough self-pity! Enough complaints! God has given me so much - magnificent children, the world's riches, a devoted husband who is also a great human being. How dare one crave more? And yet one dares... How pretentious and ungrateful.

Onward with a smile... Yesterday is gone... Sleep, eat, go out, dance, laugh, don't stare into space. Doctor, the anesthetic please, at once! Not too much, only enough not to feel... The house looks great, feed the bird, put snapshots in an album, read the Times, how about some iced tea? Think about the trip. Morocco! The bazaars!

Two directions, two men.

"*Préparez vos ceintures pour l'atterrissage,*" the flight attendant announces. I look out the window, startled. In the distance I see those snow-covered Alps, so familiar, ever present, immutable, like the cows that graze along its pastures after the snow has melted. As we approach the airport, we fly over Lake Geneva, shimmering in the morning sunlight. I bask in this glorious landscape of my childhood, where we were happy once upon a time. I turn to the urn beside me and gently caressing the box, I murmur:

"Dollsie, we're home."

POSTSCRIPT

ONE YEAR LATER

TWENTY-SEVEN

ANSWERED PRAYERS

I landed in Paris on a warm summer day in June. The next morning, I would drive to Gstaad to check in on Dollsie. It had been a year since her death, and I hadn't been back to Gstaad since the memorial, which had been held in the gardens of the Palace, on a magnificent day with clear blue skies and a gentle breeze. Everything had been perfect, just as Dollsie would have wanted. All of her friends had shown up to pay their respects, from the summer jet set to the local villagers. The only hitch had been when the manager had told us at the last minute that we could not bring a cow into their gardens, but we had prevailed, insisting that Dollsie would have had it no other way. The black and white cow, accompanied by her owners, a yodeler and his wife, and covered in ceremonial bells and garlands of flowers, had been the hit of the party. It felt as if Dollsie was still there, still running the show, breaking all the rules and providing merriment for all.

After the funeral, I had stopped by La Gottaz to see Mina. For the first time ever, words had failed us; Dollsie's death had caused her to withdraw deep within, to a place I could no longer reach. From there, I had flown to Ibiza one last time, to close on the sale of my apartment and pack up the contents and ship them to my new home in New York. I had bought the pad out of nostalgia, and a desire to hang on to some vestige of my halcyon days. Now it was time to let the mirage go and move on.

A week or so later, I returned to New York, to settle into my new apartment—two floors of an elegant townhouse in Tribeca. I had rented it a few months before Dollsie's death, after moving out of the loft, and it had stood empty since. I had hired a young decorator to fix the place up, hanging the paintings that Dollsie had left me and which I had transported to New York in a U-Haul a few days after the funeral, along with a couch and a statue of Buddha. I set up the nursery, and once everything was in place, the wait began.

I don't remember much about those first few months in New York. As I had following Raphael's death, I went off the deep end for a while. Without Dollsie, my life felt suddenly very empty, unmoored. For the first time in a long time, I had no one to take care of: no patients, no Dollsie, no dog. It was time to learn to take care of myself again.

And then, after dancing on the edge once too often, peering into the abyss, I realized that if I didn't pull back soon, I might put it all in jeopardy. I decided that I needed help and found myself in the able hands of Dr. Ladd Spiegel, a gentle soul with a practice in the heart of Chelsea. Slowly, he led me out of the fog, and helped me to process the grief and prepare for the birth of my child, giving me the space to make mistakes and do what I needed to do as I found my way. He felt that I had always been too hard on myself, that I had internalized Dollsie's voice and then used it to berate myself whenever I did something wrong. Over the years, this had become a vicious cycle where I would go to extremes of pleasure and perversion, and then punish myself with more self-destructive behavior. I remembered Astrid, the girl in the Swiss sanatorium. Miraculously, I had emerged relatively unscathed.

"You're lucky. High functioning (no pun intended)," he told me one day, chuckling. "You get what you want or need out of something—or someone—then when the bad starts to outweigh the good, you get rid of it. That's great; not everyone knows how to protect themselves like that. That's how you have survived. You are stronger than you think."

Gradually, I found myself letting all of it go, the internet and the sex and the drugs, along with all of the losses I had accumulated over the years which had reinforced my pervasive sense of loneliness and propelled my behavior. I no longer felt the desire to implode or obliterate my pain. I could let down my guard, and finally put the demons to rest. Dollsie was at peace; I didn't have to keep fighting.

I grieved for Dollsie and Raphael and Claudia and Thierry and Walt and all the others who had come into my life and departed too soon, leaving a void. I grieved for the HIV which I had pushed aside for all those years, with a frenetic sexuality to affirm my existence; sex as denial of death. I mourned the passing of an easier, more trusting time, and for everything I had lost in the process: the little things that one gives up day by day without realizing, which in the end are tantamount to relinquishing life itself, and that only now, with the imminent arrival of my child, was I healing with a renewed commitment to life. Not just to life itself, but to living it, as Dollsie had.

With Dr. Ladd's encouragement, I gave myself permission to put the past behind me, once and for all, and I welcomed clarity back into my life. I began to feel hope again, even the unfamiliar stirrings of joy: soon, very soon, I would become a father. For the first time I felt truly confident that I was up to the task, and for this small miracle, I would always be grateful to this kind, wise man. When I concluded my sessions with Dr. Ladd shortly before Easter, I felt as if I he had helped me recover from some type of PTSD that had built up over many years, as each loss added layer upon layer. That Sunday, as I attended Easter services at a black pentecostal church in Brooklyn with Sam—a sweet and sexy man that I had been seeing for the past few months as I found my way back to health and sanity—I witnessed all the sinners going forth to be saved, and while I was not brave enough to stand up and join them, I knew that I, too, had found grace through salvation; I had admitted to myself that I was powerless, and in my newfound humility, I had embraced my humanity.

Carlos, the swarthy Portuguese driver that I had known for years, was waiting outside the baggage area at Charles de Gaulle as I emerged with my suitcases. It was Sunday, so instead of his usual dark suit, he was dressed in his soccer sweats. The sight of him cheered me up, as if a friend had come to pick me up instead of a driver, and after collecting my bags, we took off in his sedan, taking the route I was by now so familiar with: the autoroute leading to the périphérique which encircled Paris, and then exiting onto the Boulevard de Clichy, driving down empty streets, past the Marché aux Puces, already buzzing with activity at this early hour. It had always been my favorite time of day in Paris, when most of the city was still asleep, except for those of us just getting in from another *nuit blanche.*

On my way into the city, I turned on my cell phone, and impatiently jabbed at the buttons, waiting for the change of continents to register so that I could check my messages. I was happy to be back. I looked forward to the café au lait and the croissant from the corner bar, and then sleeping for the rest of the day. I longed for my cave-like room at Avenue Frochot, so dark, so quiet, the only light coming from the high bay window which looked out on the garden.

A message popped up on my screen alerting me that I had a missed call from the adoption center in Pennsylvania. My heart skipped a beat. Could this be it? I had been waiting for two long years, going through the bureaucratic hoops and the never-ending paper work, the home visits, the check-ups, the interviews... I figured that my turn had to be coming soon. But as a single gay man, I also knew that it might take me a little longer than the average heterosexual married couple. Better not to get my hopes up.

"Hi Sergei!" said the social worker in her usual peppy voice. "It's Gail from the Adoption Center. Dr. Berger would like to talk to you as soon as possible. Please call when you can! It's important."

Okay, so maybe this was it, I thought to myself. I looked at my watch and figured out what time it was back in the States, and realized that I would have to wait until evening to call back. I didn't know how I would get through the next eight hours.

As I unlocked the rusty gate that led into the lush, enclosed garden which had made me fall in love with the house, I was struck yet again by the other-worldly beauty of the place, and I marveled at how casually I had been able to leave it almost two years ago. I thought about how dreadful the past two years had been, and for a moment, my heart sank. All I wanted was to walk into my empty house, which Eddy had dutifully prepared for my arrival, and to soak in my tub for a while before going to bed. The thought that my life might change yet again in a few hours seemed suddenly too much to bear. Maybe I wouldn't return the phone call until the next day.

I walked down the garden path, passing the wall of tall bamboo stalks and the last of the season's roses, and up the stone steps to the back door. I entered through the kitchen, which led into the dining room, painted lacquer red, and the elegant living room, with its beautifully paneled walls taken from some di-lapidated château in the countryside and tall French windows which opened onto the balcony and garden. Beyond the salon was my bureau, where I received clients, covered in the same paneled wood and separated from the living room by massive sliding doors.

Then I descended the spiral stone staircase which led to my bunker, as I affectionately called it, a former cave which had been converted by the previous owner into the kind of luxurious bedroom suite I had always coveted: a cozy bedroom with vaulted ceilings, an adjoining sitting room which looked out onto the garden, and a large, wood-paneled dressing room/bathroom, with custom-made closets, a marble bathtub/Jacuzzi, two lavish sinks, and a shower/steam room with a scented eucalyptus machine. The fact that it was all underground, carved out of the building's former storage areas, made it all the more decadent. Over the past few years, it had become my haven, my refuge, my den of iniquity, a place to disappear for long stretches of time.

I took a bath then steeled myself to call Mina. Now ninety-three, she was on her way out, having decided, after Dollsie was gone, that she too would die to rectify the terrible injustice that God had wrought by allowing Dollsie, a vibrant woman thirty years her junior, to depart before her. She had spent the last year in bed, willing herself to let go. She had tried everything: not eating, not drinking, sneaking extra Valiums when she could, smoking more. All to no avail. She had been the closest person to me throughout my life; a combination of grandmother, mother, friend and confessor, and to see her deteriorate like this, at a snail's pace, to hear her voice through the mental fog and to try to summon her back from the no man's land where she had sought refuge, was almost more depressing than anything I had gone through with Dollsie. It felt like I had lost them both at the same time. I made the call, half hoping that one of the dames de companie who took care of her around the clock, and who had come to be more important to Mina than her own family, would pick up.

The phone rang many times before one of the ladies answered and told me that Madame was asleep, that she had been sleeping a lot more lately, but that she seemed to be doing "well," an assessment that I was not up to challenging this time. I hung up gratefully and let the exhaustion carry me off into a deep sleep.

I awoke to the insistent ringing of not one but two phones. I felt disoriented and it took me a while to figure out where I was. The bed seemed familiar, and after blinking several times, trying to adjust my eyes to the dark, I realized that I was in Paris, and that I had slept most of the day. I let the phones ring, taking my time to identify the sounds, until I remembered the agency's message from earlier in the day. I jumped out of bed and ran to the phone, feeling totally disoriented.

"Hello?" I mumbled, still half-asleep.

"Sergei? Dr. Berger. We've been trying to reach you for the past twenty-four hours. Congratulations!" exclaimed the voice at the other end, "We have some good news for you!"

"Hello," I muttered again, trying to wake myself up.

"Sergei, are you sitting down?" I had just laid down again, but the question made me bolt right up. "We have a mother who would like to meet you. She's having the child in a month but it might come sooner due to complications. She lives in Virginia. How soon can you get here?"

"I can be there in three days," I said, feeling numb, not realizing what I was saying.

"Great! Do you want to hear more about your future baby?"

"Sure," I answered, on automatic pilot.

"He or she is going to be born in Charlottesville, Virginia. We can't confirm the sex yet. You know the rules; you aren't allowed to know until the baby is born, in case the mother changes her mind. But we can tell you that the baby is half West Indian and half Saudi Arabian. Quite a mix, eh?"

"Yes it is," I said, and then asked, "what exactly does West Indian mean?"

Dr. Berger laughed. "It means that he or she is from the West Indies, in the Caribbean. A mixture of African-American, Native American and Latin. We thought the mix might appeal to you, being part Cuban and all. How does that sound?"

I was too stunned to make sense of it all, but by now I was awake. Wide awake.

"It sounds wonderful," I managed to say, my voice breaking as I felt the tears flooding my eyes. He kept talking and the tears kept coming and as we hung up a few minutes later, I realized that I had seventy two hours to get from Paris to Gstaad, and then back to Paris to catch my flight to New York, and then from New York to Charlottesville. I could have skipped Gstaad, but I felt like I needed to give thanks; show gratitude, something I had so rarely done in my life, especially when it came to Dollsie.

As I left Paris the next morning for the drive to Gstaad, I realized that this time, I was probably leaving Paris for good. I knew that my life would never know that kind of thrill again, the freedom of riding home on my Vespa at dawn after a night of mad, passionate love making with a beautiful stranger, in a city where I could be as invisible as I chose, and where there seemed to be no limits, where everything seemed possible, now and forever. As Hemingway wrote: "If you are lucky enough to have lived in Paris as a young man, then wherever you go for the rest of your life it stays with you, for Paris is a moveable feast."

I bade farewell to the city where so much had happened. As with Dollsie's time in Vincy and Gstaad, those first few years in Paris had been the most exhilarating of my life, heady and exciting, at times vertiginous.

And then, like Dollsie, as I approached the end of my third year in Paris, it had all come tumbling down. Raphael had fallen ill and had died shortly thereafter, and suddenly Paris seemed to lose its magic, and I, my sense of wonder and joy. By the time I found out I was HIV-positive six months later, I was beyond caring, so consumed had I been with his loss.

Upon learning the news, I had burst into tears. Tears of relief, not sorrow: after constantly worrying about It for almost twenty years, the worst had finally happened, and now I could release all of the terror and guilt and apprehension that I had carried around with me everywhere I went like a Sword of Damocles, wondering when I would meet my undoing. I would never have to go through the paralyzing anguish of going to get tested every six months, reliving in my mind every risk I had taken in the intervening period as the needle jabbed into my arm and withdrew the precious pints of blue blood, and then the wait, the endless and agonizing wait, which back then could last as long as a week or two, until the doctor finally announced the good news. Each time, I would emerge from the office in a state of profound gratitude, making a solemn vow to God that I would never, ever take another risk; that I would never allow another penis to penetrate me without a condom, not even for a second. And the following weekend, the same thing would happen all over again: after a night of partying and drinking, I would find myself in bed with a hot man, and then all my resolve fell by the wayside. Whatever he wanted, I did, each time placing my life in the hands of a seductive stranger, like the guests at the white party in my dream, powerless to resist as the handsome soldiers escorted them to their awful fate.

Far from living my seroconversion as the calamity I had imagined, I subconsciously welcomed it; unlike depression and the other demons which had plagued me throughout my life, this was something solid, something tangible. And it freed me from all the constraints and terror I had been living under all those years. The worst that could happen had finally happened. I experienced a kind of paradoxical relief.

And after working in the field for all those years, comforting others, I knew enough about the disease and the progress that had been made in recent years to believe that in all likelihood, I would survive this. I would not die young, at least not from this. I didn't believe that I would die old either, but I figured that with any luck, I would have at least twenty to twenty-five years of good health ahead of me, and would probably make it to my late fifties or early sixties, which at the age of thirty-three, seemed good enough for me. Unlike Dollsie, I had never loved life enough to want it to last forever. But I also knew that on some level, everything had changed. Nothing would ever be the same, especially Paris. The exhilarating, carefree adventure of those years had come to an end.

The drive to Gstaad took about seven hours, and this time, I didn't miss the exit, no longer feeling the need to get lost in order to avoid having to spend more time than was necessary with Dollsie. I went straight to the cemetery in the nearby village of Saanen, with its strategic location, its magnificent views and proximity to all that she had loved most in life. I didn't stay long. There was not much to say except thank you. There was no unfinished business between us. I was grateful for the year we had spent together; it had prepared me to become a father. I had stopped running away from her, had learned how to become a son again. She had shown me what it means to be a parent, to love a child so much that you would go through any type of hell just to be around them for one more day. She had taught me what it is to choose life. She had not died in vain; she had finally taught me how to be a man.

And I had no doubt that she still had a hand in running the show. As I left the cemetery, I thanked her for whatever part she had played in bringing this child to me on the anniversary of her death. Beautiful timing. I spent the night at the chalet, with Dollsie's cows and her unmistakable scent still lingering throughout the house. I hoped that we would keep the chalet in the family so that one day, my child would experience it the way I once had: with innocence and wonder. The next morning, I left the car in the garage, and walked down to town to catch the train to Geneva, from where I would board a flight to New York, ready for the new journey that lay ahead.

EPILOGUE

Yasmina wakes me up, rolling over into my arms and kissing me, as she does every morning by way of greeting.

"Dad! I had a lot of dreams!" she exclaims, and then proceeds to tell me all about the flowers and butterflies and other animals that populate her nocturnal landscape, a vivid narrative which stumbles out of her in her eagerness to fill me in on what I've missed during the night.

We get up and go out to the terrace, which overlooks the port and village, and beyond it the Aegean sea. It is just past nine, and already blazingly hot. Those who don't have to work are either still asleep or taking their first plunge of the day into the sea or staying indoors until it is time to gather at the cafés on the port for the morning social hour.

We spend our summers on a beautiful island in Greece called Hydra. The islanders adore Mina; they've watched her grow up. The old *yiayias*—the grannies—love to rub her nappy sand-filled hair, and the young waiters and shopkeepers ply her with candy and treats, hoping no doubt to plant seeds that will bear fruit down the road. They call her *koukla*, which means "baby doll". When she takes her daily donkey ride through the port, she turns to the day tourists as they snap pictures of her and says, in her diva voice which reminds me so much of Dollsie, "No pictures! I said no more pictures!"

There are no cars or motorcycles on the island, and at this hour, the only sounds one can hear are the dogs barking at each other from one hill to the next, as if they were exchanging the morning gossip like their owners, and the occasional donkey braying in protest as he carries a heavy load up the steep narrow steps to one of the many homes perched atop the port, and the dozens of church bells, which ring all over the island, every hour on the hour, and the infernal cacophony of the cicadas, struggling to breathe as the heat begins to set in.

It has been three years since Mina died, at last, after an endless, miserable decline which lasted, unbelievably, for three more long years after Dollsie. She passed away on a splendid morning in early March, as Yasmina and I were driving down from Gstaad for a visit, gazing upon the beautiful lake and the majestic Alps beyond as we made our way, glad to be alive.

Tata died soon after, in her village in Galicia in the north of Spain, surrounded by the relatives who had cared for her like a queen since her retirement. The three women who had informed my life, who had helped shape me into the man I am, were gone.

A lot has happened since then, and I am grateful to be here, in this place, with this child, fully present. Today is Father's Day, and I think of Dad. I haven't spoken to him much since Mina died. Shit happens, as they say; another story for another day. A lifetime of trying to get close to this complicated man has come to an end for me.

No regrets, no guilt, no sadness. But what about the judgment? Have I let go of that? Has he? Have I accepted that this man, whom everyone thinks of as the most generous, giving man in the world, has never really known how to express love to his own children, beyond his ability to provide for us materially, because he never received any from his parents? I wonder if Mina ever embraced him maternally, or told him she loved him, or if she ever really acknowledged his lifelong efforts do the right thing, be the dutiful son. I wonder how he felt about all the affection that she had showered on me instead, and whether that had in turn affected his ability to love me.

I wonder if I will ever see him again. With the deaths of Dollsie and Mina and the ensuing drama, I found myself cast adrift and on my own, no longer feeling as if I were a part of this family. It is a difficult reality to absorb.

But what would I ask Dad if I were to see him again? I would ask him what it felt like to be dropped off in Buffalo by his mother at such a young age. What he understood of all this, how much English he spoke, where he thought his parents had gone. I would ask him how he spent those years, whether he felt abandoned and lonely, and whether he had ever, just once in his life, been able to shake off these feelings. And I would want to know if it is true that he did not recognize his mother when she came back to pick him up at the end of the war. Or was it she who had not recognized him? Had I gotten the story wrong?

I would ask him what it was like being married to Dollsie—his polar opposite—for seventeen years, and why he had accepted this arranged marriage in the first place. Was her excess of love the mirror image of his inability to experience it, stemming from the same lack of affection they had experienced growing up as children of privilege, rarely seeing their parents and surrounded by nannies and tutors and servants? Did they ever really feel as glamorous and fabulous as the image they projected to the world?

And what about his years in Esalen, where he would escape the confinement and rigidity of his dutiful Swiss banker life and wander along the cliffs of Big Sur, in the nude, being touched and massaged, doing all that gestalt stuff, the primal screaming and the role playing, and coming out of his shell for the first—and last—time in his life? Where had that person gone? Had it disappeared beneath twenty-five years of married bliss to his second wife, a small-minded, conventional woman who undoubtedly gave him the praise and affection and security that he had never known with his mother—or mine? Did he sometimes lie awake at night, longing for those Esalen days?

Does he remember the family ski trip when, at the age of five, I left my Pluto stuffed animal—my security blanket—on the plane, and instead of skiing and socializing with Dollsie and their friends, he spent the entire vacation with me, on a quest to find Pluto—knowing full well that we never would?

Does he remember anything from the decades of correspondence, which he keeps in boxes, refusing to throw anything away? Does he acknowledge that I, too, was a dutiful son, or does he find me terrifically ungrateful? Does he understand the hurt? Probably not. He never understood his own.

We drifted. Who knows why? For the rest of my life I will try to understand this paradoxical man—a man who has led a charmed life, filled with success and worldly goods, free of tragedy, yet a man who has never really expressed any emotion, whether it be joy or pain or anguish or sadness. A man I have only seen angry twice in my life—once when my brother and I were ten minutes late leaving the communal pool in Gstaad, and he stormed into the locker room in a fury and dragged us out half-naked into the snowy winter night—yet one who seems to harbor so much disappointment, so much frustration and unfulfilled expectations, or a lack of expectations altogether. A man whom I have never seen shed a tear, who smiled throughout his mother's funeral—the woman he had spent a lifetime trying to please.

One of the recurrent themes of my life has been how shocked I am at what passes for love in families—my own, and the ones I have worked with. But as I gaze at my fierce, beautiful brown daughter, this extraordinary little creature who has turned my world upside down, who gives me more affection in one day than I ever thought I had the right to expect in a lifetime, I know that I am deeply blessed. She has come into my life to teach me the meaning of love. My indigo child... She found something in me that I never knew was there, or had long ago forgotten.

She has taught me that love is not about how perfect you are as a parent, how much you give your children, what schools and parties and camps and clothes and houses you crowd their lives with. Perhaps loving a child is not so different from loving yourself: you mess up, you forgive and let go, you don't carry the guilt and the shame around like some albatross. You set the ego aside, the needs and wants and desires which crowd your mind. Or at least you try, and when you don't succeed, you come back. You find your way back to your child, to yourself. You don't just go through the motions.

"We're a team," as Yasmina and I often tell each other, when we are attempting to do something new, something challenging and adventurous that takes us out of our comfort zones, like jumping off a rocky ledge into the deep green-blue sea that you only find in Greece.

That's what I would like to ask Dad most of all: after all those years of writing letters and sending checks and buying presents and setting up trust funds and paying for extravagant trips and doing whatever he could to show up at all the right times—to perform his duty—trying as hard to be a good father as he had tried to be a good son—did he ever feel like we were a team?

Yasmina—or Mina, as she goes by these days—is the love of my life, pure and simple, the best thing that has ever happened to me and one of the few things that I have done right. I am raising her to be aware, confident and independent. To be who she wants to be and to not be concerned with what Wayne Dyer calls "the good opinion of others". At the age of six, she has more emotional wisdom than I've acquired over a lifetime, and I know, beyond a shadow of a doubt, that her life will be happier, more carefree, and less lonely than mine has been.

I take my morning dip in the small, deep pool, and as I wash up and collect our beach stuff before heading down to the port for breakfast—fresh orange juice and a café frappé and Greek yoghurt with nuts and honey for me, a grilled ham and cheese sandwich and a chocolate milkshake for Mina—she looks up from her painting to contemplate the view.

"Look, Daddy!" she exclaims in wonder, "I can see the world!"

After a pause, during which we both gaze out and marvel, she adds, "I love you, Daddy. Thank you for my wonderful life."

And at that moment, I know, beyond of a shadow of a doubt, that Dollsie is looking down on us and smiling beatifically, along with Mina and Tata. I raise an imaginary toast to the heavens, thanking the gods for my good fortune.

"*Gracias a la vida*," I whisper, filled with wonder and gratitude.

June, 2011
Hydra, Greece

ACKNOWLEDGMENTS
& SOURCES

I would like to express my deep gratitude to those who helped bring this book to fruition: Max Regan, Charlotte Gusay, Gerald Sindell, and Marti Leimbach. They encouraged me to tell my story, and they sustained me in the telling with their vision, wisdom and humor. I also wish to thank Liz Eldridge and Marlene Eldridge for their attention to detail; Rebecca Hicks for her expertise and design aesthetic and her generous contributions to this endeavor; and Courtney Shore and Lola Disparte, without whom this book would not have reached the finish line. And finally, I owe a big thank you to my daughter Yasmina, for her endless patience. Hopefully, one day she will appreciate this labor of love.

As Gore Vidal once wrote about his memoir Palimpsest, "A memoir is how one remembers one's own life, while an autobiography is history, requiring research, dates, facts double-checked." In composing this narrative of my life, I have attempted to remember events and conversations as they happened and to place them in the proper chronology, drawing upon my mother's diaries, letters and other family correspondence, conversations with family members and friends, and my own writings and journals. I have no doubt that in spite of my best efforts, errors remain, and for that I take responsibility.

While I have sought to avoid factual inaccuracies and intentional misrepresentation, memory has its own tale to tell, with its own truths and distortions colored by dreams and imagination and the passage of time. Throughout this tale, I have privileged these subjective forces, the "remembrance of things past," which is after all, the purpose of writing a memoir, what renders it authentic and provides catharsis.

In order to protect the privacy of those who appear in this book, I have changed some names and other identifying details.

I have no doubt that my siblings would tell a different story. This is mine.

PHOTO CREDITS

Cover design: Rebecca Hicks
Cover photo: Sergei as ring boy at family wedding, Buffalo, NY, 1969. Credit: Family Collection
Back jacket: Portrait of Dollsie in Red for Town & Country, 1971. Credit: Cy Gross
Author photograph: Ray Thibodaux

PART 1
Chapter 1: Baby Sergei in Mimorey, Switzerland, 1965. Credit: Family Collection
Chapter 2: Playing with Mina's necklace, Buffalo, NY, circa 1969. Credit: Family Collection
Chapter 3: With Dollsie, Bal des Fleurs, Chateau de Vincy, Switzerland, 1971. Credit: Family Collection
Chapter 4: Creux-de-Genthod, Switzerland. Credit Family: Author
Chapter 5: With hat, circa 1972. Credit: Family Collection
Chapter 6: Jasmine Schoellkopf Boissier greeting dignitaries, location & date unknown. Credit: Family Collection
Chapter 7: Dollsie & Jean-Jacques on their wedding day, Havana, 1958. Credit: Family Collection
Chapter 8: With Mina, Chalet Albosco, Gstaad, Switzerland, circa 1973. Credit: Family Collection.
Chapter 9: Gstaad. Credit: undetermined
Chapter 10: Young Dollsie, Cuba, 1950's. Credit: Family Collection

PART 2
Chapter 11: Portrait of Dolores with Greyhound by Pedro Menocal, 1969
Chapter 12: With Dollsie, New York, circa 1980. Credit: Family Collection
Chapter 13: Dancing with Dollsie, Buffalo, 1969. Credit: Family Collection

Chapter 14: At the White House with Nancy Reagan, Dollsie, and AIDS victim Celeste and her grandmother, 1988. Reprinted by permission of The White House

Chapter 15: Dollsie in white, Key Biscayne, Florida, circa 1970. Credit: Family Collection

Chapter 16: With Walt and Lucy, Carmel, California, 1993. Credit: Author Collection

Chapter 17: Dollsie astride her horse Noy, who was later killed by Fidel Castro's guerrillas, Cuba, 1950's. Credit: Family Collection

Chapter 18: With Raphael, Princeton, New Jersey, 1989. Credit: Author Collection

Chapter 19: Lying down, Key Biscayne, circa 1969. Credit: Family Collection

Chapter 20: With Dollsie at graduation, Georgetown University, Washington, DC, 1987. Credit: Author Collection

Chapter 21: At United Nations Ball (with sister wearing the Bernard Perris "spider-woman" dress that Dollsie wore to a State dinner at the White House with Ronald & Nancy Reagan), New York, circa 1988. Credit: Author Collection

PART 3

Chapter 22: Dollsie with hat, circa 1980. Credit: Family Collection

Chapter 23: With Dollsie at the lighthouse, Key Biscayne, circa 1970. Credit: Family Collection

Chapter 24: Dollsie with cows during her last visit to Gstaad, 2004. Credit: Author Collection

Chapter 25: Dollsie riding, Cuba, 1950's. Credit: Family Collection

Chapter 26: With Dollsie on the beach, Key Biscayne, circa 1969. Credit: Family Collection

PART 4

Chapter 27: Avenue Frochot, 2004. Credit: Author

Epilogue: Yasmina, Hydra, 2008. Credit: Olivier Rieu

ABOUT THE AUTHOR

Sergei Boissier was born in New York City and raised between New York and Switzerland. Prior to moving back to the States in 2004, he was a psychotherapist in Paris for ten years, in private practice and at The American Cathedral Counseling-Center, specializing in child and family counseling, gay individuals and couples, and HIV and Health-related issues. He served as President of FACTS, an organization devoted to assisting English-speaking people with HIV/AIDS living in Paris. He is the author of "Children with AIDS in the Bronx," published in "BETRAYAL: A Report on Violence Toward Children in Today's World" (edited by Caroline Moorehead, Doubleday, 1990), as well as two unpublished novels.

He and his daughter Yasmina live in New Orleans and Hydra, Greece.